Modernity and the State

Modernity and the State
East, West

Claus Offe

The MIT Press
Cambridge, Massachusetts

First MIT Press edition, 1996
© 1996 Polity Press

This book was printed and bound in the United States of America.

Library of Congress Cataloging-in-Publication Data

Offe, Claus.
Modernity and the state: East, West / Claus Offe.
p.   cm.—(Studies in contemporary German social thought)
Includes index.
ISBN 0-262-15046-8 (hardcover: alk. paper).—ISBN 0-262-65047-9 (pbk.: alk. paper)
1. State, The. 2. Welfare state. 3. Social policy. I. Title. II. Series.
JC11.033   1996
320.1'1'09049—dc20   96-3429
                                                                  CIP

Contents

PREFACE   vii
ACKNOWLEDGMENTS   xi

Part I Modernity and Self-Limitation

1 The Utopia of the Zero Option: Modernity and
  Modernization as Normative Political Criteria   3
2 Bindings, Shackles, Brakes: On Self-Limitation Strategies   31

Part II State Theory: Continuities and Reorientation

3 The Theory of the State in Search of its Subject Matter:
  Observations on Current Debates   61
4 Social-Scientific Aspects of the Regulation–Deregulation
  Debate   72
5 Constitutional Policy in Search of the "Will of the People"   89

Part III The Politics of Social Welfare

6 State Action and Structures of Collective Will Formation:
  Elements of the Social-Scientific Theory of the State   105
7 Beyond the Labor Market: Reflections on a New Definition
  of "Domestic" Welfare Production
  With Rolf G. Heinze   121
8 Democracy Against the Welfare State?   147

vi   *Contents*

 9 The Acceptance and Legitimacy of Strategic Options in
   Social Policy   183
10 A Basic Income Guaranteed by the State: A Need of the
   Moment in Social Policy
   With Ulrich Mückenberger and Ilona Ostner   201

Part IV The New East

11 The Politics of Social Policy in East European Transitions:
   Antecedents, Agents, and Agendas of Reform   225
12 After the Democratic Revolution: New Burdens of Proof   254

INDEX   262

Preface

Actors, in order to be able to act, need to locate themselves within a sometimes immensely complex space of options and constraints. They need to know where they stand, and where other actors stand. Few would probably disagree that one purpose of political analysis is to assist in this task of self-location, at least as it pertains to collectively relevant courses of action and kinds of outcomes. I believe that, compared to that task of self-location, attempts to answer the classical question of "what is to be done?" are of a clearly secondary nature and importance. This is so partly because the authority of academic intellectuals to offer plausible prescriptive answers to that latter question must be doubted. But this is even more so for the reason that political agency, that is, the capacity to make collectively binding choices and to carry them out, has become so problematic. Instead of asking what is to be done, we might more fruitfully explore whether there is anybody capable of doing whatever needs to be done.

The essays collected in this volume are all about charting the landscape of agency. Many of those political agents that were well known to political analysts of earlier times and were taken for granted by them seem to have lost, in the West and in the East alike, much of the evidence of their capacity for action. This applies equally to virtually all of the *dramatis personae* with which political analysts used to populate their stage. To be sure, states and governments, citizens and social movements, social classes and political parties, elites, administrative authorities, interest groups, coalitions, nations, blocs and associations are all well and alive; it is just that neither the spectators nor they themselves seem to have a very clear notion about their distinctive domain of action. As their rules and roles, their identities, missions, and responsibilities are becoming uncertain, so is the very idea of political agency. What turns out to be surprisingly and essentially contested is the answer to the question "who is in charge?" It is tempting to speculate for a moment about the causes of such uncertainty.

At least four of them come to mind. First, the breakdown of the Berlin Wall and the end of the Cold War involve the consequences of the implosion of a powerful center of (economic, ideological, political, military) control and the appearance of new (national as well as would-be national) actors. Further repercussions of these momentous events have made established agency patterns and agendas of the states belonging to the OECD world crumble. To illustrate, is it national armies or NATO or the UN or "rapid reaction" forces assembled by participating states who are in charge of safeguarding borders and people in ex-Yugoslavia and elsewhere? The answer is that any of these answers is as good as any other, and that nobody knows who is in charge of giving an authoritative, effective and legitimate answer.

Second, borders have become penetrable, be it by design (as in EU or NAFTA arrangements) or *de facto* (as through the globalization of capital, goods and labor markets). It has been argued that the rapidly increasing porosity of borders renders the sovereign impotent and democracy pointless. Again, the question is who is in charge to assign responsibilities – that is, to perform the key and constitutive political function of defining political functions, or what German constitutional theorists like to call *Kompetenzkompetenz*.

Third, centers of collective agency are paralyzed by "postmodernist" social and political trends. Membership densities, voter turnout, elite support, and trust in political institutions are all sharply declining according to time series data from many countries, while volatility, fragmentation, localism, fluctuation, and the rapidity of succession of issues and themes are all increasing. A widespread cult of difference leads individual actors to believe that other individual actors are insufficiently "similar" to themselves to make it worth their while to join forces with them in the formation of robust, durable, and large-scale collective actors. Social classes at the point of production do not coincide anymore with "consumption classes," as little as the latter coincide with educational classes or cultural milieux. What remains is informal association on the basis of ascriptive "passport identities" (such as gender, generation, territory, and ethnicity).

Finally, political agents have lost the certainty of their roles and domains because the political economy of postindustrial and global capitalism no longer provides the clear-cut categorization of "places within the system of production" in which forms of collective action (political parties, associations, trade unions) were once anchored. In the European Union of the mid-1990s, there are more university students than apprentices, more unemployed people than farmers, and more old age pensioners than blue collar workers – with the respective former elements of these couples being primarily shaped in their rights and resources not primarily by their control over certain means of production, but by public policies. These groups are constituted as "policy takers," as the places that people occupy within the societal division of labor and consumption are increasingly "policy-determined," often transitory, contingent, and dependent, as opposed to "objective," durable, and creative of the sense of some "commonality of social fate" which would then facilitate the formation of collective actors.

These and other causes may be responsible for the widely shared sense that sovereignties have become nominal, power anonymous, and its locus empty. The cost of cooperation that is necessary to "get things done" is experienced to increase steeply – from international peacemaking to industrial restructuring, from university to health reform. If effectiveness is one of the criteria of good government (or of political agency more generally), there are not many agents these days that can make much of a claim to it. While conservatives (in the conservative sense of the word) idolize "state strength," that is, the capacity of executive agents to make binding choices among relevant alternatives, today's so-called conservatives who are in fact libertarians relinquish the aspiration for strong agency by asserting TINA logic ("there is no alternative"). True, a strong state is not desirable in and of itself, as it can become, unless constrained by effective rule of law and democratic mechanisms, a threat to citizens and their rights. But neither is a "weak" state a desirable alternative, to the extent that political strength (of governments, parties, or other collective actors) is a crucial device for the protection of collective interests and for reformist strategies of social change.

While high levels of effectiveness and control do not necessarily generate trust, support, and legitimacy, low levels of effectiveness will almost certainly undermine favorable orientations of consistencies toward political agents. Apathy and cynicism are natural responses to the failure of agents to get things done and to achieve stated objectives. It is thus the coincidence of the impotence of formal centers of agency with the dwindling of civic commitments that forms, at least implicitly, the reference problem of all the essays in this volume.

The two essays in part I adopt a deeply ambiguous notion of modernization and modernity – one that is seen, following Max Weber and the tradition of Critical Theory, as proclaiming and at the same time undermining liberty. The second essay, originally contributed to a festschrift for Jürgen Habermas, also contains some normative argument about how the associative reappropriation of state functions by an activated civil society might at the same time tap the resources of civic involvement and cut the agenda of formal state agencies to manageable proportions.

Part II applies concepts and categories introduced in the two introductory chapters to policy debates that emerged, in West Germany as elsewhere, in the 1980s. Here, I explore the dilemmas and antinomies of regulation vs deregulation, etatism vs market orthodoxy, and representative vs plebiscitary varieties of the practice of democracy.

The core substance of democratic politics, it is claimed in the essays in part III, is the question to what extent market outcomes must be accepted (in the name of efficiency) or corrected (in the name of equity and justice). What we need to understand is the factors and mechanisms that lead to the tipping of some presumed balance one way or the other – a topic that is explored in chapter 6. Democratic politics in itself, as argued in chapter 8, does not gravitate toward an activist, interventionist, and "welfarist" solution of the basic dilemma, contrary to much of the conventional social democratic creed. Chapter 7, co-authored with Rolf G. Heinze and later developed into a joint book (*Beyond Employment*, Polity, Cambridge, 1992), discusses institutional arrangements that could complement and partially replace the core institution through which production is organized in capitalist societies, the labor market; labor power can be allocated to productive tasks in ways that differ from its sale for money, just as the means of subsistence can be made available to citizens in other ways than as compensation granted in proportion to labor performed under an employment contract. Tax-financed basic income, the latter variant of "de-commodification" (a neologism the author hit upon in 1974 in a discussion with Gösta Esping-Anderson) is explored and justified in chapter 10, co-authored with Ulrich Mückenberger and Ilona Ostner. Chapter 9 analyzes the logic underlying the welfare systems as we know it in continental Europe.

Finally, and in conclusion, some aspects of the new political economies of Central East Europe are discussed. The two essays in this part aim at the demonstration that, after the demise of authoritarian state socialism with its paternalistic welfare egalitarianism, the issue of balancing and correcting market outcomes is as central and contested in these new market economies as it has always been in the West, and that the very success of democratization depends on the extent to which the newly operative "satanic mill" of the labor market (Karl Polanyi) is embedded in appropriate structures of social security.

Acknowledgments

The author and publishers gratefully acknowledge permission to reproduce or translate from previously published material in this book.

Chapter 1 is translated by John Torpey and reprinted from *Praxis International* 7:1 (1987), pp. 1–24, © Blackwell Publishers Ltd; chapter 2 is translated by Barbara Fultner and reprinted from Axel Honneth, Thomas McCarthy, Claus Offe and Albrecht Wellmer (eds), *Cultural-Political Interventions in the Unfinished Project of Enlightenment* (Cambridge, Mass., 1992), pp. 63–94, © MIT Press (original German edition © Suhruamp Verlag 1989); chapter 3 is reprinted from T. Ellwein, J. J. Hesse, R. Mayntz and F. W. Scharpf (eds), *Yearbook on Government and Public Administration* (Baden-Baden, 1987–8), © Nomos Verlagsgesellschaft; chapter 4 is translated by Charles Turner from J. J. Hesse and C. Zopel (eds), *Der Staat der Zukunft*, Forum Zukunft vol. 5 (Baden-Baden, 1990), pp. 107–26, © Nomos Verlagsgesellschaft; chapter 5 is translated by Jeremy Gaines from "Die Verfassungspolitik auf der Suche nach dem 'Volkswillen,' " in G. Hofmann and W. A. Perger (eds), *Die Kontroverse. Weizsäckers Parteienkritik in der Diskussion* (Frankfurt, 1992), pp. 126–42, © Eichborn Verlag; chapter 6 is translated by Charles Turner from "Staatliches Handeln und Strukturen der kollektiven Willensbildung – Aspekte einer sozialwissenschaftlichen Staatstheorie," in T. Ellwein et al. (eds), *Staatswissenschaften: Vergessene Disziplin oder neue Herausforderung?* (Baden-Baden, 1990), © Nomos Verlagsgesellschaft; chapter 7 is translated by Charles Turner from "Am Arbeitsmarkt vorbei," *Leviathan* 14:4 (1986), © Westdeutscher Verlag; chapter 8 is reprinted from *Political Theory* 15:4 (Nov. 1987), pp. 501–37, © Sage Publications, Inc.; chapter 9 is translated by Charles Turner from "Akzeptanz und Legitimität strategischer Optionen in der Sozialpolitik," in C. Sachsse and H. T. Engelhardt (eds), *Sicherheit und*

xii   *Acknowledgments*

Freiheit. Zur Ethik des Wohlfahrtstaates (Frankfurt, 1990), ˉpp. 179–202, © Suhrkamp Verlag; chapter 10 is translated by Charles Turner from "Das staatlich garantierte Grundeinkommen – Ein Sozialpolitisches Gebot der Stunde," in H. L. Krämer and Claus Leggewie (eds), *Wege ins Reich der Freiheit. Festschrift für André Gorz zum 65. Geburtstag* (Berlin, 1991), pp. 247–78, © Rotbuch Verlag; chapter 11 is reprinted from *Social Research* 60:4 (New York, 1993), © *Social Research*; chapter 12 is translated from C. Offe, *Der Tunnel am Ende des Lichts. Erkundungen der politischen Transformation im Neuen Osten* (Frankfurt, 1994), pp. 81–94, © Campus Verlag.

Modernity and the State

PART I
Modernity and Self-Limitation

1

The Utopia of the Zero Option: Modernity and Modernization as Normative Political Criteria

The social sciences have been concerned with the theme of "modernity" during the past 25 years in two different contexts. These contexts are sharply separated from one another but, it appears in retrospect, they are at the same time related in an ironic way. On the one hand, there is the context of historical-sociological *modernization* research. This research concerns itself with general, descriptive and explanatory statements about the conditions and motive forces of modernization. It analyzes the developmental paths which premodern or traditional societies historically have taken to overcome (or with which they could today overcome) the characteristics of rigidity, stagnation, and persistence in order to approach the condition of the democratic-capitalist industrial societies, which modernization theory at least implicitly describes as normatively desirable. Despite all the empirical detail and methodological refinement of the studies carried out in the 1960s with the close cooperation of historians and sociologists, Americans and West Europeans, it would not be unfair to their authors to note a certain perspectival fixation on *one* question, namely, "Wherein lie the conditions of the possibility that 'we' have become what we are today, and that others might follow in this successfully pursued path?" On occasion, as this modernization research was in full bloom during the 1960s, the concepts of "modernization" and "Westernization" were treated quite unabashedly as equivalents. "The achievements of the Western world are being urgently recommended to the developing countries for imitation. Modernization is interpreted as progress."[1] In this regard, in a critical treatment of modernization research, which on the whole evaluates the chances and perspectives of this type of work in positive terms, Hans Ulrich Wehler warns that modernization theory is coupled too closely with certain goal and value assumptions and thus, "by its attachment to the occidental model, exposes itself to the danger of explaining away or even absolutizing given contemporary conditions with a proud, 'it has been attained.' "[2]

The context in which the concept of *modernity* has stood within social-scientific theory construction since the middle of the 1970s, on the other hand, is quite different. Here, the perspective is no longer shaped by the self-confident preoccupation of the Western social sciences with "the others," who are glibly referred to as "latecomers" (or indeed by the attempt to "take them in" ideologically). To the contrary, these debates take place in the skeptical atmosphere of a preoccupation of "modern" societies with *themselves*; that is, a self-scrutiny of the structures and normative premises, of the stability and prospects for the future of already "modern" societies. This shift of perspective in the social sciences is codetermined by a series of contemporary historical and internal, disciplinary circumstances, only a few of which I shall refer to here: the political and economic crisis experiences of the 1970s, the rapid intellectual loss of face of important tenets of classical Marxism, the renewed reception of the "dialectic of enlightenment" as well as of the Weberian theory of "occidental rationalism," and the aesthetic, social-philosophical and sociological symptoms, conjectures, and prognoses concerning the passage into a "postmodern" stage of development of Western culture and society. What seems to me ironic in this change of perspectives and contexts is not so much that the gaze is turned away either from "the others" or from history and toward one's own contemporary cultural and structural conditions, but rather that the situation of "modern" societies appears just as blocked, just as burdened with myths, rigidities, and developmental constraints, as modernization theory had once diagnosed to be the case for "premodern" societies. In any case, "modernity" is no longer exclusively the desirable endpoint of the development of others, but rather the precarious point of departure for the further development of one's own ("Western") society. In this respect, postmodernists and neoconservatives seem bent on outdoing each other in the severity of their respective critiques of the principal concept of modernization, namely reason or rationality.

In what follows I should like to sketch a mediating position between modernization euphoria and modernity skepticism. I would like to examine how and why the political-moral intuitions motivated by modernization processes are at variance with and remain unredeemed by the structures of modernity which have developed in Western societies (section I); why from this experience of disappointment, which now constitutes the background of nearly all relevant debates, no necessary reason may be derived either for the outright erasure of those fundamental intuitions or their termination with appeal to the higher validity of antimodern moral principles (section II); and why, to the contrary, adequate latitude exists for a further modernization of the structures of modernity itself – that is, for an application of the principle of modernization to its own structures. I hope to show in conclusion that the exploration and utilization of these possibilities actually provide the background theme of numerous contemporary political controversies and developments (section III).

I

Like many fundamental concepts in the social sciences, the concept of modernity has a dual, namely an analytic *and* a normative political status. It describes characteristics and, at the same time, establishes a dimension of evaluation in which premodern or antimodern ideas or social relations can be criticized as deficient, retarded, regressive, etc. This simultaneously empirical and normative double application of the term "modernity" is justified by the notion that the structures that develop in modern societies can be decoded as the realization (however limited) of the normative intentions and revolutionary projects nurtured by modernizing elites and ideologies in the past. These founding ideas of modern society were formulated in the Western world in the late eighteenth century and achieved their practical form in British industrialization and classical political economy, in the French Revolution and (one might add with Marx) the philosophy of German Idealism.

It is normally assumed that the propelling normative idea, the dominant philosophical motif of European modernization processes (and of those which stemmed from Europe) was the emancipation of reason and subjectivity. Since the eighteenth century, this developmental process, shaped socially and intellectually by the way-stations of the Renaissance, the Reformation, and the Enlightenment, has taken concrete form in political institutionalizations which can be characterized somewhat schematically by the sequence: national state–constitutional state–democratic state–welfare state. Each of these developmental steps may be unproblematically depicted as a progressive movement in the aforementioned normative dimension. Always at issue is the roll-back of boundaries constraining the freedom of decision and action of social actors, a gradual "transformation in the direction of the expansion of capacities and autonomy."[3] New latitude is cleared for the application of the actors' subjective reason, their options are increased, and the contingency of what can be achieved in action grows. To this corresponds in the technical and economic spheres a freeing-up and an increase of contingency in the spatial dimension (transportation and communications), in the temporal dimension (banking), and in the energy sphere (physical and chemical exploitation of new energy sources and a rapid drop in the proportion of human and animal power in total energy consumption). From a complementary perspective, this may be described as a process of cumulative deinstitutionalization, as the progressive neutralization of physical givens and traditional privileges that have become politically and philosophically untenable, as a virtually methodical discontinuation of the past. In sociological terms, two processes which reinforce one another intersect in modernization. One process consists in the decoupling of actors, organizations, and social subsystems in relation to other systems: a process which is unanimously documented in the theoretical literature by means of such concepts as individuation, emancipation, separation, autonomization, self-governance, "disembeddedness," etc.[4] The other process consists in the decline of traditional commitments, routines, facticities, and expectations. Autonomized action becomes unrestrained and boundless, "insatiable" (as Marx says of capital) in the pursuit and expansion of its own particular values. Just as familiar as this dual process of the expansion of contingency and the destruction of tradition are the fields of action gripped by that liquefaction of the conventional. These include the four spheres of material production, cultural reproduction, political participation, and bureaucratic domination.

Material production With the tremendous increase of options that occurs in this field of action, the penetration or expansion of the *market principle* (at first to commodity markets, then to labor and capital markets), of the principle of rational *organization* and of the principle of rational *technique* allied with scientific research and teaching become interdependent. The establishment of these three principles allows all social actors involved in material production the constant possibility of deciding where something will be bought or sold and what will be produced how. For, over the long term, in none of these questions can one afford simply to adopt the premises of the conventional and customary.

Cultural reproduction The sphere of cultural norms and values as well as of aesthetic criteria of validity are also subject to an equally pervasive proclivity toward transitoriness and innovation. In the modernization process, traditional monopolies of interpretation, claims to absoluteness, and doctrinal compulsions become obsolete, and accordingly the orienting norms of the sciences, of occupation, leisure, art, family, sexuality, religion, education, etc., become variable, subject to choice, and unstable over time.

Politics The totality of "that which can happen," with which one must reckon, and for which past experiences provide no reliable rule of thumb, also grows in the realm of political conflicts. Whosoever takes a position, in whatever form, on whatever issues, and with whatever interests, is in liberal-democratic political systems to a greater degree a matter of choice, and is subject to more rapid variation, than anywhere else.

Public policy Positive law – which is formally defined and cut off from its roots in "custom and habit" – and bureaucratic administration create in modern societies a capability, still hardly imaginable only a century ago, for the state executive to bring authority to bear comprehensively and reliably on highly specific groups, matters, etc., with a multiplicity of prohibitions and commands. The explosive growth of the possible domains of action is here encouraged, as in the previous three cases, through systematic application and selective use of formalized knowledge and information technologies which permit speedy cognitive access from any one point of the system to any other point.

Regardless of how self-evident and commonplace they may sound, all these claims about growing choices over social contexts give not just a crude but a downright misleading and one-sided picture of the realities of a modern social structure. They serve me here merely as a foil against the backdrop of which I would like to consider the exactly opposite claim: namely, that it is precisely modern societies which are characterized by a high degree of *rigidity and inflexibility*.

In order to bring into view this rigidity, which derives from contingency and accumulates with it, it is necessary first to recall the facts of specialization and functional differentiation. *Specialization* here refers to the development of institutions and means of communication that are "responsible for" each of the four above-mentioned spheres and which are in each case particularly adapted to the task of generating options and putting at the disposal of social actors the criteria of selection among the growing options. Consider for purposes of illustration the process of the separation of "household" and "firm" and the corresponding intellectual technique of "rational bookkeeping." Only when this technique is available is it possible for an economic concern to grasp and actively expand the horizon of its available options, and to choose rationally among them in the language of capital accounting. Scientific research, bureaucratic domination, and political, moral, and aesthetic discourses are other examples of specialized processes for the continuous exploitation of new territory. Particular media and institutions are necessary if the focus is to be sharpened for (as yet unperceived) options and if the choice among them is to be steered according to defensible criteria. One could say more generally that the continuous *expansion* of options in the aforementioned spheres of action goes hand in hand with – indeed, is mediated by – a countervailing constriction of the selection filters through which action proceeds. In order to be able to exploit new options, one must not only "make oneself familiar with the matter," but must also always be capable of disregarding criteria of judgments that are "irrelevant." The flip side of this sharper, more precisely refined selectivity is thus those characteristics of action which are often diagnosed as apathy, narrow-mindedness, insensitivity, unscrupulousness, etc. The individual's renunciation of "interpretation" and a narrow-minded, monomaniacal, and "convulsive self-importance" is, according to Max Weber, the Janus face of refined selectivity, to which the individual retorts in desperate pathos: "Specialists without spirit, sensualists without heart: this nullity imagines that it has attained a level of civilization never before achieved."[5] But reproaching social actors for pathological one-sidedness and self-importance is only *one* of two possible critiques of modernization; the other refers to the *consequences* of action and the social *conditions* that issue from such a one-sided type of action. The absence of concern for consequences leads to problems of order and coordination, and generally to consequences that are "anarchic," crisis-inducing, and which undermine the "social tolerance" for modernization processes.

The other important factor is that of *functional* differentiation. This entails (in contrast to the case of "segmental" differentiation) that in principle *all* actors participate or at least can participate in *all* subsystems with their specialized means of communication ("inclusion"). There are then no spheres of socially exclusive functions (of Junkers for officers' careers, of the poor for services of the welfare state, of the tax-paying educated bourgeoisie for political elections and attendance at opera openings), but instead a tendency for each individual to be connected with and to have access to *all* functional spheres, assuming that she or he submits to the appropriate highly selective scheme of institutions, criteria, and special communications.

If one were now to combine the three characteristics of modernity noted above (namely expansion of options, specialization, and functional differentiation), the result is a set of coordination or compatibility problems. When traditional constraints on the horizon of options are relaxed, when specialized institutions and "languages" are developed with which these horizons can be actively expanded, and when the development and evaluation of these options can no longer be made the privilege or exclusive responsibility of sectoral communities of specialists because such sectoral increases of options tendentially involve "all" – then the difference grows between those demands and options which in a "local" perspective are "possible" and those which out of a "global" perspective (of all those who do not participate, but who are nonetheless affected) are "tolerable," assimilable, and acceptable. Not everything that is "possible" is thus also "defensible." One must, for instance, forego the short-term maximum profit or the pristine purity of a moral position dictated by an ethics of conviction because such options become unassimilable for other spheres of action and unacceptable given the foreseeable consequences for the actor herself or himself. The larger the horizon of "actually" possible options becomes, the more difficult grows the problem of establishing reflexive countertendencies which would make reasonably sure that one's own action remains compatible with the "essential" premises of other affected spheres of action.

This is in no way meant to imply that the urgency of such coordination problems is equally great for all strategic actors of all subsystems. On the contrary, social power relations exist precisely in the asymmetry of the degree to which actors in various subsystems are forced to undertake reflection concerning this compatibility and to take others into consideration. It would thus certainly be rather audacious and, given many political-economic factors and developments, contestable to assert that in the liberal-democratic welfare states of the Western industrial societies such an asymmetry between investors or employers on the one hand and state executives on the other did *not* exist; this asymmetry would indeed have to increase to the extent that the political systems in question are in fact welfare states. Regardless of such asymmetries, however, all "modern" societies must be of such a kind that all subsystems are under the same pressure of constantly entering into relation to the other spheres of action, as well as of sacrificing the exploitation of a portion of those options in its own realm of action in order to stabilize this relation. To put it the other way round: in "modern" societies, no subsystem can afford consistently to behave "recklessly" and to claim in principle superior authoritativeness vis-à-vis all other fields of action. The problem here consists precisely in that solutions of such coordination problems are merely (ex post) given as systemic *conditions of continued existence*, not as (ex ante) *motives for action*; that is to say, there is no agency that could produce such motives for coordinative action in both legitimate and reliable fashion or otherwise assume responsibility for solving this task.

A distorted picture thus emerges if one naively insists upon the idea that "modernization" is equivalent solely to "an increase in options," without at the same time considering the contrary idea that, in order to manage the coordination and compatibility problems and thus to secure the further existence of the system, inadequate and incompatible options must be continuously filtered out – and their number grows in step with the number of options themselves. Still more: the coordination problems grow with our knowledge of the distant effects and interferences which particular actions can exert upon the conditions of other, later action. And the more such knowledge is available and the better it is demonstrated that one can acquire missing knowledge through (timely) research activities, the more difficult it becomes for one to make use of the excuse of ignorance. The progressive liquidation of traditional *constraints* on action which takes place in the modernization process potentiates the needs for *limitations* (which however are not afforded by institutions) with the help of which the compatibility of subjectively chosen actions, otherwise increasingly precarious and toppling into "anarchy," can be ensured.

Now the grounding, construction, and observation of such "limitations," which can be expected to perform the synthesizing achievement of making the entire array of options tolerable and mutually assimilable, are the central themes of political philosophy, of constitutional and policy doctrines, as well as of empirical political science. The cross-section of relevant considerations that I will touch upon in what follows is thus correspondingly modest. I want to suggest the following theses. (1) The central problems of modern societies are not their further modernization, that is, the further increase of options, choices, and possibilities of action, but rather the invention and securing of those secondary rules of selection which as a synthetic principle can achieve the *coexistence* and enduring compatibility of variegated horizons of options. (2) Such models of a "modern" synthesis are subject to the twofold criterion of adequacy; on the one hand they must be "modern" in the sense that they must respect the emancipatory possibilities of rational subjectivity, and on the other hand they must be synthetic in the sense that they prove themselves *effective* regulators of coordination and compatibility. The central focus here is on the critique of those conceptions of order that commit the error of violating *both* the first *and* the second of these criteria of adequacy.

A provisional result of these considerations is that the characteristic and decisive criterion of modernity consists not only in the increase of options available in action but, equally and contrariwise, in the existence of regulative mechanisms that steer the actually occurring selection of options in such a way that these options are brought into a relationship of harmony and mutual accommodation, and at least do not wreak havoc upon one another and thus destroy one another *as* options. Social systems would in this sense be "modern" to the extent that they bring the disintegrative consequences of specialized expansions of capacities under control in a manner that itself is not regressive and antimodern, that is, directed against the principle of the expansion of capacities itself. It is this difficult problem which is often more obscured than revealed by such vague formulas as that of a "liberal order" of society.

There are three classical solutions to this problem of order, which are associated with the keywords "state," "market," and "community" (or, alternatively, with the political philosophies of Hobbes, Locke, and Rousseau). These positions are "classical" not just in the sense that they represent particularly pure and consistent elaborations of their respective fundamental ideas, but also in the sense that they can no longer play a practicable role in the present but rather are merely relevant as illuminating examples of why this is *not* the case. The notion that the need for regulation and compatibility-ensuring mechanisms conjured up by modernization – that is, for "order" – can be dealt with by the conferral upon one social agency of unlimited power to make binding decisions and to keep domestic peace lives on in all *statist* approaches, to be sure, but it proves obsolete if for no other reason than simply because the order to be produced by the state must already be presupposed in circular fashion as being at hand prior to the state; for upon what else besides such a presupposition is the peacekeeping potential of the state power to be grounded? It is true that the notion that the problem can be handled by way of a strict separation of spheres between state and civil society, between economy and polity, continues to inspire *liberal* thought; but its power to persuade suffers from the blinders with which this cast of thought shutters itself against both the constitutive function of political domination in economic processes and against the phenomena of social power, social classes, and political conflict which emerge from economic processes. The idea that order can be achieved via the separation of the spheres of economy and politics (or through the spontaneous self-coordination within and between these spheres that is expected from this separation) is today, in both normative and (above all) in descriptive terms, to be banished to the realm of utopian or ideological delusions. For the recipe "simplification through separation," insofar as the division is to be made between "economic" and "political" spheres of action (as economic liberalism would have it), fails on two counts: markets are not "free of politics," but are instead politically guaranteed and regulated and are capable of being reproduced only on the basis of this politically mediated order; nor is politics "free of the market," but is rather bound to the trajectory prescribed to the modern tax and welfare state by the economic system of the society (not to mention the privileged influence of economic interest groups or, indeed, corruption phenomena). As far as the idea that the unity of social life could rest upon "community" or "solidarity" is concerned, it is true that this notion is present alike in *populist* and fundamentalist protest movements, but it commonly amounts to a helpless political antimodernism – if not a "forcible communalization" – imposed by state terror.

Such negative findings make it seem advisable to deal less with "classical" solutions than with the nature of the problems themselves which the attained level of sectoral modernization raises, including the problems of those solutions that have introduced themselves evolutionarily in societies of our kind. A basic experience of intellectual and political elites in modern societies can be adequately if abstractly summarized with the following principle: on the one hand, nearly all factors of social, economic, and political life are contingent, elective, and gripped by change, while on the other hand the institutional and structural premises over which that contingency runs are simultaneously removed from the horizon of political, indeed of intellectual choice. The perfected capacity of the subsystems for ever new options for action is matched only by their inability to get under control, or responsibly to modify, the fatal relationships which they thus constantly create at the macro level. This conception stands in the background when Gehlen speaks of a "post-histoire," and makes itself felt when Horkheimer and Adorno in the *Dialectic of Enlightenment* write of the "freedom [to chose] the ever-the-same."[6] Only simple, not yet modernized, internally not yet very "option rich" societies – so it seems from a glance at the political revolutions that have taken place in the twentieth century – still might be revolutionized from within, while by contrast "complex" societies have become rigid to such an extent that the very attempt to reflect normatively upon or to renew their "order," that is, the nature of the coordination of the processes which take place in them, is virtually precluded by dint of their practical futility and thus their essential inadequacy. The weight of established facts, according to the doctrine of resignation, is greater than all reason: moreover, it is argued that the idea of an intentional and planned new construction of the social order or even its reform is misguided, because unintended consequences stand in the way of any will to change and, since they are foreseeable as such, they denude the will of its innocence.

There is indeed much to be said for the idea that there is such a thing as a principle of constant sums: the more options we open up for ourselves, the less available as an option is the institutional framework itself with the help of which we disclose them. This constant sum principle can be illustrated by the example of a highway, or of a transportation system based on the automobile. Under conditions of extraordinarily high (and, in comparison to rail-bound transport systems, with their comparatively rigid spatiotemporal schematization through train stations, schedules, etc., significantly increased) freedom of choice, in such a system every participant can at any time enter at every point within the street and highway system; at the same time, however, the system that permits this liquidity of movement is in purely physical (and of course in political and economic) terms an unremovable fact, as are its familiar physical and social effects. Simply due to the magnitude of the investments already made and now to be recouped, a tremendous resistance to revision is built into sociotechnical systems of this kind. They open all manner of options, but preclude for any relevant period of time the option of being able to do without them.

This would all be unproblematic to the extent that one could rely on these rigidities in their totality for having the characteristics of a "modern order," that is, that on the one hand they ensured freedom of choice, and on the other that they managed the problems of order and coordination created by the utilization of this freedom. In both respects, however, there exist the well-known contemporary doubts. Regarding the first criterion, both the theory of positional goods and everyday experience teach that the use value of options can rapidly sink or indeed become negative if the number of actors that make use of these freedoms grows. If *everyone* stands on their tiptoes, *no one* can see better, according to the well-known formulation of the problem by Fred Hirsch. Once again, one can illustrate the reality content of this formulation with the example of automobile transport: the more people simultaneously get behind the wheel, the less they can start on their way. One can also study the mechanism of the "endogenous loss of relevance," if not the self-liquidation of freedom of choice, with the example of institutionalized political participation, as Norberto Bobbio has convincingly shown.[7] In his analysis, Bobbio confirms the tendency – earlier diagnosed by Max Weber – of liberal-democratic systems to allow the formal rights of democratic participation of individual citizens to become materially empty by permitting quasi-autonomous "organs of mediation" of the "will of the people" to become dominant instead (in the form of bureaucratic parties, interest groups, political leaders, and parliaments); in addition, due to its own interest in the maintenance of its organizational possibilities, the bureaucracy of the state executive in modern democracies not only grows in bulk, but augments the barriers against the influence of individual citizens or of unorganized political publics. The more democratic rights the individual citizen enjoys, and the more citizens are drawn into the enjoyment of these rights, the more is the growth of organizations and prerogatives indirectly stimulated, in the face of which these rights (at least when they are used in conjunction with average material, informational, and temporal resources) decline in potential influence. The material meaning and political use value of these rights, Bobbio makes clear, are overwhelmed and drowned by formal organizational structures and procedures. The state power avenges the damages which threaten it from the side of the rights of democratic participation not by abolishing these rights, but by developing immunizing countertendencies that neutralize their actual efficacy and scope.

Horkheimer's and Adorno's theory of the "culture industry" is a model for the analogous dynamic in the relations between aesthetic culture and the valorization of capital: cultural autonomy is no longer the bulwark of individuality and freedom, but the welcome and thus less transparent pretext for their destruction. If one were to radicalize and generalize this idea, one confronts the not entirely misguided suspicion that, in a whole array of aspects of the modernization process, the gain in autonomy and subjectivity may have remained fictive and nominal insofar as it is neutralized by countertendencies of the "administered world." It is precisely on those paths broken by enlightenment that myth maintains itself. The permutations have been numerous. The Marxist critique of alienation and reification social theory had identified and elaborated those mechanisms through which modernity destroys and betrays its own emancipatory founding principles and achievements. In the name of progress it regresses to an "iron cage" (M. Weber) and organizes the "colonization of the lifeworld" (J. Habermas).

Reasonable doubts also exist regarding the second criterion. The *inefficacy* of the order and steering mechanisms is, next to the *losses of freedom*, the other frustrating basic experience that modern societies have of themselves. Steering capacity becomes deficient when in modern societies three factors coincide. First is the factor of growing differentiation, which increases the dependency and vulnerability of each social realm in relation to nearly every other, and thus raises the global *need* for coordination. Second is the inadequacy of the *available* means and mechanisms of coordination. And third is the *inflexibility*, the ponderousness and the resistances to revision, which available (but inadequate) coordination mechanisms put up against every attempt to close the gap between steering needs and steering capacities, between "design complexity" and "control complexity" through institutional innovations. Even political steering tasks of moderate proportions – say, a tax or pension reform that took into account all known facts, foreseeable developments, and recognized claims – appear such hopelessly difficult and time-consuming undertakings that the demand for coordination involved with any serious attempt to manage such problems narrows almost automatically to short periods, small circles of interested parties, and obvious central problems, while everything else is banished beyond the horizon of attention and consideration – that is, put off to a "second round" which is for that very reason more difficult. The principle being practiced here is that of "partial coordination through bracketing," which means coordination at the cost of third parties or the future. Coordination of extremely large steering problems which, corresponding to the nature of their object, cannot be managed within the framework of the nation-state – such as the military-strategic questions of peacekeeping, the management of problems of poverty in the Third World, and the maintenance of minimal ecological balances – thus seems completely futile. Such compatibility problems intensify by an order of magnitude if we make not just the functioning of systems but also their compliance to current norms a criterion as well. Thus we live today in the states of the Western alliance under conditions which include the organization of a military preparedness – in broad daylight, by a democratically constituted government, and in all of our names – which, in certain possible cases, foresees the commission of acts for which the characterization "nuclear holocaust" applies precisely; at the same time, the preparation for such an action (especially since it is an *empirical* question whether the appropriate causal conditions will in fact arise or not) is itself an act that can hardly be brought into discursive accord with ethical standards and demands that are current in the Christian Occident.

Organizations and state elites everywhere thematize the approaching danger or indeed the already achieved condition of their "ungovernability." In the face of such striking limitations of the collective capacity for action, the question forces itself upon us whether talk of a "modern" society is not rather an illegitimate euphemism, and whether we should instead speak more precisely of a society which, to be sure, has passed through manifold processes of sectoral increase of options and which therefore has at its disposal a truly modern administration and art, modern industry and communications networks, a modern military and pedagogy, but which *as* a society does not dispose over options as it does over this ensemble of partial modernities and their relation. There is rather the appearance that the "modernity deficit" of the society grows larger to the extent that the subsystems become more modern, and that at this macro level the helpless experience of blind fatalities becomes the rule to the extent that the rational increase of the subsystems advances. It appears that the modernization of the parts comes at the cost of the modernity of the whole. Precisely because of the "openness to the future" of the subsystems and of their innovation-intensifying sectoral rationalities, the society itself seems to have become incapable of conceiving its own future as a project or of reining it in according to elementary parameters. As the flip-side of modernization processes, there emerges a seemingly paradoxical entanglement in the status quo and an inflexibility of the overall society which no longer has anything in common with the fundamental motif of modernity, namely the ability to dispose over options and to choose.

II

The gain in freedom of expanded options is fictive, and the steering achievement of the global social system is deficient. These two experiences of disappointment fuel the theoretical as well as the political-moral critique of modernity by the neoconservative right and also by the intellectual camp that I would like to refer to as the "postindustrial left." The schemes of critique of the *neoconservative right* are familiar. First, the emancipatory value constellations of modernity are discredited as self-contradictory or scorned, and there follows a strict renunciation of "hedonism," the striving after progress, the "utopian expansion of horizons," the egalitarian motifs of "the happiness of mankind," etc. This basic motif of a modernity that has fallen out of step with its own moral impetus already dominated the 31-year-old Max Weber's programmatic inaugural lecture of 1895: "Abandon hope all ye who enter here: these words are inscribed above the portals of the unknown future history of mankind."[8] Unlike contemporary neoconservatives, however, Weber was in a position to give a *positive* point of reference from which, according to his conception, the system integration of bourgeois society would admit of being achieved (at least domestically). The idea of the cultural (*Kultur-*) and national state, which allows him to speak of "the solemn splendor of national sentiment,"[9] figures as such a model of social synthesis in Weber; to this idea corresponds, on the other hand, the famous formal principle of the "ethics of responsibility," which is supposed to enable the heroic individuals at the pinnacle of economic and political apparatuses to construct a synthesis (which itself however is not rationally reconstructible) of the divergent demands and value premises of the various social spheres of action. Beyond these two principles of synthesis, there is nothing but the unregulable conflict dynamic of cultural and social, economic, and military struggles. In comparison to this conception of a "liberal in despair" (Mommsen), contemporary neoconservatism operates more modestly yet less consistently. On the one hand, a colorful assortment of traditional "binding values" (family, nation, achievement, private property, religion) is reactivated and pressed into the service of disciplining demands, without, however, being able to name a common referent of values equivalent to the concept of the *Kulturnation*. Given the failure to demonstrate the self-evidence of such a global reference point, the advocates of these catalogs of virtues must confront the difficulty of having doubt cast upon the candor and sincerity with which they plead for the validity of moderating and binding values: how can they make persuasive the case that they are truly concerned with those virtues as a matter of ethical conviction, and not just as a pretense with which they actually strengthen privileges and intervene in distribution struggles in a regressive fashion?

On the other hand, however, the demands on such achievements of order as are at all possible are reduced so far that compatibility and securing continued existence are virtually interpreted as possible only as the result of forced sectoral modernization processes – whether of the technological and economic competition on world markets, or of the arms race: in other words, as the by-product of the satisfaction of a "capacity to prevail" that is pursued almost with the mania of an ethics of conviction. Taken together, the two lead to the familiar dilemma of neoconservativism, perceived by its critics in the fact that neoconservative politics wants in the same breath to be reactionary in cultural and social policy terms, and unrestrainedly modern in economic, technological, and military policy terms, whereas (it is at least suspected) modernism itself should have undermined the conditions of validity of this propped-up traditionalism. North American reality in the first half of the 1980s, meanwhile, shows that the juxtaposition of traditionalism and modernism (the coexistence of the death penalty, obligatory school prayer, the outlawing of abortion, "creation science," and other concerns of the Moral Majority with the mystification of "high tech," gene technology, and weapons-technological gigantism) can indeed attain a certain stability and become a seductive model for political forces in Western Europe. Only five years earlier, hardly anyone would have guessed the extent to which one can apparently and at least temporarily afford both: give a free hand to the logic of modernization and its built-in dynamic of an increase in capacities, while at the same time effectively putting the egalitarian and emancipatory ideas of modernity and their critical potential under quarantine.

In addition to the problem of the *sincerity* of its normative premises (that is, the question whether these rest upon moral arguments or rather upon interests), neoconservative thought must also deal with the problem of the *truth content* of its moral precepts, that is, with the problem of their rational persuasiveness and thus with their generalizability. How can the truth of such moral arguments be demonstrated? The answer is likely to be *either* in the discursive attitude of one who accepts no other vindication for one's position than the unconstrained assent of others, *or* by appeal to the self-evidence of moral truths and substantive imperatives. If one chooses the first course and commits oneself seriously to discourse, the inherent difficulty of the neoconservative critique of modernity would be clear with the first move: the critics of the values of subjectivity and reason would have to make use of just those media and premises the exclusive validity of which they wish to cast into doubt, and thus put themselves in the performative self-contradiction of one who in writing calls upon others to give up reading. But neither does the retreat to the nondiscursive alternative lead anywhere. The proclamation of explicitly "ungrounded" moral certainties is incapable of furnishing itself with the certainty of its own generalizability. In this situation, one may well be satisfied with the practice of each person's respective moral maxims; but, from functional perspectives, the limitation to this position appears inadequate precisely when one pleads for the adherence to principles – such as in the case of norms of moderation, renunciation, self-limitation, and constraint – the meaning of which can only be fulfilled if it is reasonable to expect that, at least tendentially, *all* will adhere to them. One must at least be able to reckon on the "diffusion effect" of good examples and one's own capacity to activate latent norms of reciprocity in others; for with respect to the socioethical norms in question here it is not only useless, but in the end downright self-destructive, if one subscribes to them (in the extreme case) only oneself. This consideration, which can be illustrated quite easily with numerous examples (such as the observance of speed limits), suggests the metaethical conclusion that problems of order can be "moralized" with less success the more one dogmatizes the corresponding moral principles and burdens them with "substantive imperatives," instead of keeping them discursively open.

The mirror image of the precarious mixing of the motifs of modernism and reaction can be found in the political forces and motifs of the *"postindustrial left."* The neoromantic protest of the new social movements is radically "modern" insofar as it is guided by the values of autonomy, emancipation, and identity. At the same time, this protest directs itself against those developmental results of the modernization of the technical-economic and of the political-military system where unregulated proliferation produces risks for autonomy and identity as well as for physical integrity and survival. The society is experienced and thus grasped theoretically as a "risk society"[10] in which a new politics of production and of producing becomes the central axis of conflict.[11]

One can view the new social movements, which represent a protest against consequences of modernization that is thoroughly "modern" in normative terms, as a phenomenon that takes on to a new level and continues the emancipatory bourgeois movements of the eighteenth and early nineteenth centuries, as well as the workers' movement of the nineteenth century and early twentieth century. The central concern pursued by the social and political movements of the bourgeoisie directed itself against the decision-making privileges and the *arbitrariness* of prebourgeois political elites. In contrast, the concern pursued by the workers' movement was directed against *poverty* and social inequality as the accompaniment to bourgeois-capitalist industrialization. The democratic constitutional state was the evolutionary achievement which flowed from the social movement of the bourgeoisie, partially in conjunction with the burgeoning workers' movement, and the Keynesian welfare state as we know it from the postwar epoch in West European industrial societies was the political-economic structure that was the result (if not necessarily the achievement of the aims) of the noncommunist workers' movement. Building on these movements and the structures which emerged from them, the new social movements concentrate on the themes of *pain and anxiety* that result from infringements upon or threats to the physical (or, in the widest sense, "aesthetic") integrity of the body, of life, or of a way of life. The protagonists of this protest theme thus stand in continuity with motifs and achievements of the bourgeois-democratic and proletarian-socialist movements. Without their accumulated achievements, there would have been neither the occasion nor the possibility of making injuries, infringements, and the experience of suffering, or the defense of life and way of life against such infringements, into a successful mobilizing theme. International organizations such as Amnesty International and Greenpeace signify today in the Western countries – far ahead of "green" and "alternative" political initiatives and experiments – the urgency of these themes and experiences.

On the other hand, this continuity of old and new sociopolitical movements is not unbroken. I find three discontinuities. First, at least so far, the ecological, pacifist, feminist, regionalist, and neighborhood autonomy movements are far from having developed even the outlines of a program of social transformation with the same degree of consistency and comprehensiveness that characterized the earlier sociopolitical movements. I find another rupture in that in their critique of modernization – with thoroughly emancipatory intent – these new social movements are not entirely immune from the temptation to revert to unmistakably *pre*modern ideals and to base their critique on particularistic, communitarian, libertarian, anarchistic, ecological-biological, or similar fundamentalisms. One might, of course, suspect in these symptoms of a normative regression a *general* characteristic of sociopolitical movements with parallels in early bourgeois romanticism and in the "guild" conceptions of the early workers' movement, especially in the Latin countries. The third and most important discontinuity seems to me to lie in the fact that the new social movements have taken as the object of their critique precisely those institutional arrangements of political rule, material production, and scientific-technical innovation with the help of which the demands of the older movements could be satisfied to begin with. For the critique is directed against the dynamics of industrial *growth* and scientific-technical change which has become autonomized and escaped all effective social ties of responsibility, on the one hand, and against the functioning of a "welfare–warfare state" committed to the central value of (social and military) *security* on the other.[12] Out of this discontinuity there arises the peculiar difficulty of the intellectual and political task of reconciling the partial rationalities of technical-economic efficiency and state-bureaucratic security measures with the new sensitivities to suffering and the claims to inviolability, without at the same time negating their relative importance and their practical indispensability. What must be made "socially acceptable" and compatible with life conditions, according to the demands of the new social movements, are precisely those political-economic structures that appeared to the predecessors of the contemporary social movements as the guarantee and securing of *their* life conditions.[13]

Two internally driven political-theoretical positions concerning the disappointing experiences and results of the modernization process thus confront one another today, while it appears that the middle ground of those who, *in good conscience*, advocate further modernization and presuppose a continuity of technical and social progress on the old socialist model is occupied by fewer and fewer all the time. On the one side stand the apologists for modern structures, who, to be sure, hold forth with their pleas for the further unleashing of technical, economic, military, and bureaucratic increases in capacities by recourse to premodern and antimodern catalogs of virtues and duties. In mirror image stand in bright-plaid intellectual formation a wide array of contrasting positions which all rely upon the emancipatory and autonomy-enhancing initial motifs of modernity, but which for just this reason sharply criticize the achieved condition of modernization with the familiar arguments of the critiques of growth and technology, of bureaucracy and the professions. But the advocates of this position run the danger of committing the error which the advocates of the neoconservative apology commit without a second thought: namely, of falling back with doctrinaire absoluteness on principles of order that are derived from an alleged "essence" of human beings (or of women or men), of society, of nature, or whatever, in a supposed effort to strengthen their critique of the established structures of modernization. In the hands of such zealots of the simple life or of life true to human essence, the critique of modernization threatens to forfeit the modernity of its impulse. A schematic representation of this constellation of forces would yield something like the matrix in figure 1.1.

| | | VALUES OF MODERNITY | |
POSITION TOWARD		positive	negative
MEANS OF MODERNIZATION	positive	"social democratic mainstream"	"neoconservative right"
	negative	"postindustrial left"	"postmodern" regressive particularistic potentials

Figure 1.1   Means and values of modernity

III

In conclusion I would like to deal with the rather immodest and thus only quite incompletely treated question: how can the regressive potential – which the rightwing apologia of modernity brings in its train with an untroubled conscience while the leftwing critique of modernity carries it along with a rather bad conscience – how can this potential be shaken off at least in the case of the latter. I thus return to the previously substantiated thesis that the prevalent self-characterization of our societies as "modern" societies is actually a euphemism. "Society" is not "modern" in the sense of "open for options"; rather, this applies only to its constitutive subsystems of material production, cultural reproduction, political public sphere, and state domination. The manner in which these subsystems are related to and affect each other must instead be considered extraordinarily rigid, fatal, and sealed off from any freedom of choice. But not only that: in addition to their rigidity and lack of optionality, the integrated circuits of coordination are characterized by their inadequate efficacy, which is decried on all sides. That means that partial processes have effects on other partial processes in substantive, temporal, or social respects which are either completely unknown or unforeseen, and/or cannot be neutralized or held under control to an extent that would "really" be demanded by normative parameters and functional equilibrium conditions of the affected (or other) subsystems. In systems so constructed, it is extremely risky to rely on the assumption that what is complementarily required will actually have already occurred, and thus on not having to reckon with truly unassimilable effects of the actions taking place elsewhere. The situation can be likened to one in which airplanes are starting up everywhere before the runways of the destination airports are in operating condition – an analogy which, given the happy-go-lucky adoption of "modern" energy technologies long before the resolution of the storage and disposal problems for the radioactive wastes, should not be considered overly dramatic. In all spheres of life, one is increasingly forced into the reliance, which is by no means immune to disappointment, that by some kind of providential arrangement or far-sighted measure (but whose?) the right actors will do the right thing at the right time.

I would describe such problems of fine-tuning coordination and steering as modernization problems of the second order. They are not subsidiary in urgency to those modernization problems of the first order which strike any West European visitor to developing countries, such as the search for drinkable water or a functioning telephone. Modernization problems of the second order, the core of which concerns the rationalization of the interplay between already rationalized subsystems, today occupy the social sciences on a broad front (for instance in the theory of collective goods, corporatism theory, social-scientific systems theory, but also in the "theory of communicative action"). Max Weber was of the opinion that the problem of bringing the divergent partial rationalities into a tenable synthesis could be dealt with in ethical categories and could find its solution in the "ethics of responsibility" of the political leadership of organizations and states, where a "sense of proportion" and "passion" were supposed to undergo an individually specific combination. A solution of this "ethical" type has today become problematic, because it is difficult to uphold the Weberian premise that responsibility today can anywhere actually be exercised by charismatic figures, that is, by political leaders who have all the relevant variables "in hand" (or at least in view). If that cannot be presumed, one can obviously no longer rely on an elite ethic or elite consensus, and the problem becomes transformed into the question how "responsibility" can be secured through an appropriate institutional design.[14]

For purposes of overcoming the modernity deficits that stand out in (incorrectly so called) "modern" societies, three methodical approaches come into consideration for the construction or improvement of such a design. Their common problem is, as I mentioned, the opening up of new and, at the same time, legitimate possibilities of action in the management of problems of order and coordination. One can in this respect proceed by attempting to expand the capacities of the already available media of coordination, that is, for instance, by making administration more effective, the market mechanism less disturbed, or the communicative processes of enlightenment and education of the political public sphere more widely diffused.[15] A second possibility is to redesign the spheres of application of these diverse steering mechanisms and thus to achieve new "mixes" between market, state, and consensus. Third, it is imaginable that one could approach the matter from the demand side, the other way round so to speak, and so *reduce* the requisite degree of capability for coordination and the securing of compatibility in such a way that one actually manages with the available steering capacities. The available alternatives are then the *enhancement*, the *recombination*, and the *unburdening* of social steering mechanisms.

First, as far as concerns the strategy of *enhancement*, the issue can well be said to consist in the attempt to reconstruct the functional primacy of a social subsystem, whether it be the market, the state or the community, and to raise this to the level of a global sentry of order. Precisely in those societies whose subsystems are already highly modernized, particularly bad experiences have already occurred with such single-minded approaches to problems of sociopolitical order. This is especially true of those attempts to secure the fabric of social life by means of state administration and legal regulation; but it is also true for those attempts to entrust the self-regulatory logic of the market with macrosocial steering tasks. The experience which one quickly encounters, however, in face of the doctrinaire one-sidedness of such puristic injunctions of political order is that with the regulations already in existence the outstanding need for regulation grows rather than declines: the more bureaucratic regulations there are, the more is action *other* than what is motivated by such rules discouraged, and the greater grows the gap which must then be closed by further specific regulations. One can theoretically prognosticate quite analogous phenomena of continuous self-overtaxing for the cases of pure market steering or pure community coordination.

The second alternative to increase the capacity of global social systems for "responsible" action takes a different approach. In the case of the *combination* of various steering mechanisms, the attempt is made to redesign their respective "jurisdictions" according to various substantive, social, and (business) cylical parameters in such a way that their interpenetration and "mix" leads to a tolerable degree of stability and "normality." As soon, however, as one gets serious about combination recipes like "as much market as possible, as much state as necessary," or, worse, if one seeks to incorporate a bit of "common sense" into the complex steering design, one confronts significant mutual intolerances and rivalries between these media, if not imperialistic claims of exclusive authority. A cornucopia of contemporary economic, social, labor market, and pedagogical controversies provides an excellent illustration of how difficult it is to shift the limits of authority even slightly in one or the other direction – say, between the employment prerogatives of employers and welfare state authority, or between parental rights and egalitarian demands in the area of educational policy. The sphere of market-regulated social processes in particular proves especially sensitive to such gradual impairments, and minimal impairments of its sphere of authority can lead to far-reaching and self-intensifying collapses of equilibrium and drives toward disinvestment. One has ironically pointed to the (apparent) contradiction in the fact that the most devoted advocates of market competition reveal the strongest aversion as soon as competition no longer takes place *in* the market, but rather *between* the rival steering approaches of the market, of state authority and solidaristic (for example, cooperative) production and labor processes. In any case, it is apparent that formulas like "as much X, Y, Z as necessary/possible" are so difficult to implement because operative and consensual criteria are so hard to come by for what is supposed to be "necessary" or "possible" in the given case.

In the face of these (admittedly briefly stated) negative findings, it would be useful, I think, to consider more closely the remaining third alternative of *"unburdening,"* and to look at measures and strategies that can make manageable the problem of coordination and compatibility not just through the enhancement of steering capacities but through the *reduction of steering needs.* As we have seen, the sectoral modernization processes and the substantial gain in economic, political, aesthetic, bureaucratic, and military options rest upon the social principle of differentiation and specialization. The result is the correspondingly increased mutual "recklessness" of the spheres of action toward one another; their internal rationality gain and their growing freedom of choice give rise to the dilemma that they mutually burden each other with externalities and all kinds of "social costs." In addition, their interdependence grows; the action systems lose their autarchy because they must rely upon preliminary and complementary achievements in relation to one another. From this context derive the familiar steering problems, the nature of which in many spheres of policy (from geostrategic to banking regulations) is frequently characterized by the metaphor of the "domino chain." The solution of such problems would appear to consist in securing a sufficient degree of independence of these elements from one another and – to stick with the metaphor – to enlarge the distance between the groups of dominos. If the solution of this (systems-theoretically reformulated) problem of responsibility fails, this damages the use value and welfare value of the options opened up in the individual subsystems. To be sure, each may continue along the path of modernization and the sectoral increase of capacities, but if the aforementioned steering functions do not keep pace in their capacity to perform, that suboptimal situation emerges which in another context has been characterized as "collective self-injury" and which game theory models as prisoner's dilemma situations.

In the sense of a rational calculus, then, the issue would by no means consist in putting sectoral modernization gains under restrictions *as such,* but in balancing them off against the losses of well-being which strike back in the form of steering deficits, and not just at the society as a whole, but against each individual actor as well. We lack, however, a unit of reckoning or an accounting framework which would help such a calculation to be made. Above all, we lack the practical possibility of actually choosing those "zero options" which would protect against a further escalation of unmastered steering problems, especially in those cases where clear intuitions indicate that the gain in utility from the exploitation of further options would be negative. For most citizens do not realistically dispose of the chance to opt *for themselves alone* against a further increase of their options, that is, to uncouple themselves from the virtually objective processes of the further growth of automobile transport, agricultural chemicalization, cable media, the arms race, international technological competition, etc. – not even if they were persuaded that the preconditions of "responsible action" lay in this course. The real utopia today lies in the freedom of the calculated zero option, of rational self-limitation in the face of the exponentially growing risks of interdependence.

The suspicion that in many spheres of life and of action further differentiation, further increase of capacities, and further modernization really wouldn't be "worth it" because the risky steering problems thus engendered would, at least in the long run, destroy the corresponding gains in welfare is today perceptible just beneath the surface of many sociopolitical discourses. What keeps this suspicion *under* the surface in most cases is most likely the concern that, given existing technical, economic, and military interdependencies and relations of competition, every zero option actually embarked upon meets with the punishment of severe *losses* of welfare. The fear, usually quite well grounded under circumstances of high interdependence, is that the renunciation of *marginal* advantages could entail *in*calculable disadvantage. If (as in war and in Darwinism) the second-best solution is no longer distinguishable from the worst, zero options become intolerable. The nature of the already extant interdependencies would, on this model, force us to erect ever greater interdependencies beyond all responsibility; and modernization would then be, to paraphrase Max Weber, no "horse-drawn carriage which one could climb out of at will."

But perhaps one can change vehicles, or rebuild the vehicle in such a way that the penalty which until now has deterred the decision for zero options can be reduced to a tolerable level. I think that the gradual loosening of relations of interdependence would indeed be the way to remedy the egregious modernity deficit on the level of society, and to enhance our capability for dealing with the problems resulting from sectoral modernization. I know of no argument which states that the degree of interdependence which itself becomes the stimulus for new, risky interdependencies could not in principle be made into an object of strategic influence by society upon itself, and thus also into an object of gradual transformation. To name one example, one could make a connection between the comparatively quite auspicious labor market situation in evidence in 1987 in the four West European industrial nations of Norway, Sweden, Austria, and Switzerland and the independence of these countries alone – unlike those of the Common Market – from any supranational political-economic alliance system. The gain in options to be reaped from opening up assimilable and tolerable zero options (for example, from the interdependencies resulting from Common Market membership) is obvious: it consists in the enhancement of the capacity to deal responsibly with the consequences of one's own actions. Of course, zero options are only rational when the renunciation of options brings with it at least an equally great gain in global control, or at least in structural chances for responsibility. In order to realize this gain in control, it would be necessary to put up "dividing walls," so to speak, between social subsystems which, on the one hand, were relatively impermeable to negative external effects, and which, on the other hand, also diminished the dependence of these subsystems upon the requisite inputs and services of other action systems. Naturally, this cannot amount to the dividing up of functionally differentiated social complexes into a structure of self-sufficient monads, but instead entails the cautious reduction of the substantive, social, and temporal distance between actions and their consequences to such a degree as would first make it possible cognitively to comprehend and somehow politically-morally to judge the quality of that complex. Social, political, and economic action systems can indeed be refashioned in such a way that reflection upon the subsequent effects of their actions and their defensibility is made clear to actors, and so that, vice versa, they are released from direct dependence upon the limitations of other action systems.

Such an attenuation of externalities and dependencies is increasingly discussed in social-scientifically grounded steering conceptualizations with concepts such as "self-reliance" or "auto-centered development" (in development sociology), "loose coupling" (in the sociology of organizations), and decentralization or "devolution" (in political sociology). The common basic idea here is to refashion social systems in such a way that they burden their environment less with economic and political externalities and at the same time become more autonomous vis-à-vis their environment, from which on the whole some gradual moderation of problems of coordination and steering needs can be expected. This suggestion is unequivocally distinguished from libertarian or romanticizing conceptions: for here the issue is not to plead for the "natural right," or essential priority of individuals or "small" units, but rather to use the specific capacities of action systems, which have been released from stifling relations of interdependence and which thus develop potentials for "responsible" action, for macrosocial steering processes.

The problem of self-limitation of the radius of effects of actions and decisions in the temporal dimension seems to me particularly pressing. Consideration of this perspective would entail that a bonus be methodically calculated into decisions for those alternatives whose potentially problematic consequences reach less far into the future.

Putting such a premium on short temporal chains of effects and on reversibility could prevent present gains in options from returning as future steering bottlenecks; this standpoint is of some relevance, for instance, in the area of renewable energies, but also in quite different areas such as urban development and social security reform. It would be consistent with such a criterion of rational decision, disciplined in the temporal dimension, if the method of taking decisions prescribed that they were not taken under the time pressure exerted by competing decision-makers, but rather were taken – for instance, through the introduction of moratoria[16] or iterative decision procedures – with the time necessary to enable evaluation of possible subsequent effects of the decision and to avoid rashness. In the social dimension, the same basic notion of the "rationality of shortened chains of effects" would entail the reduction of the social ramifications of bureaucratic and managerial decisions through the strengthened protection of constitutional rights or indeed protection against layoffs, or through the introduction of local autonomy and veto rights, thus preventing subsequent effects from decaying into the uncontrollable.

It is incontrovertible that, at least in many cases, the substantive, temporal, and social self-limitation of actors leads to certain losses of welfare and renunciations on their part. Through renunciation of further modernization of their field of action they subsidize, so to speak, the modernity and steering capacity of the overarching societal whole. But it is just as little obvious why such a renunciation cannot be made tolerable or perhaps indeed attractive through countervailing "subsidies" or guarantees of continued existence and of protection. With the modernization of subsystems, in particular of the productivity of commodity production, as far advanced as it is today in West European industrial societies, it is not clear why in principle there should be a shortage of those resources which the society can use to compensate its members for *renouncing* a further increase of particular options and thus achieve a further modernization of its macrosocial steering system as a whole. An example of this connection, which appears in the contemporary debate over social and labor market policy, is the suggestion that participation in the labor market and distribution of income should be uncoupled from one another in such a way that those persons who have decided upon a zero option with respect to labor force participation should not be punished with severe losses of income, but rather should be able to claim a "basic income." In this manner, economic, technical, or demographic (consider old age insurance) discontinuities can be prevented from being externalized in a way that is unmediated and decidedly to the disadvantage of those who lose their jobs or their claim to transfer payments; in other words, relief can be had from substantial economic and sociopolitical steering problems.

If one puts the problem in this fashion, as a problem of optimization where the solution entails the exchange of marginal renunciation of enhancement of options for a gain in steering capacity (or, more precisely, for a marginal saving of steering problems caused by unforeseen later consequences and results of action), then the occasions and temptations for an antimodern ideologization of the vote for zero options fall away. Smallness, nearness to nature, simplicity, modesty, autarky, leisureliness, solidaristic self-steering, etc., are by no means self-evident moral or aesthetic virtues; rather, they *could* be a worthwhile and rationally justifiable price to pay, insofar as, by paying it, one can save risky further increases in complexity and problems of steering related to this complexity which are correspondingly more difficult to manage. "Small" is by no means necessarily "beautiful": but perhaps at times it is indeed "intelligent." If such calculations are to become relevant for action (beyond the circle of the ideological proponents of zero options), it would be necessary to presuppose that a balancing of costs would be politically organized in such a way that the expense for the *collective* benefit of the renunciation at least need not be carried *individually* by those who create the preconditions of this benefit through rational self-limitation. The rationality of an "ethics of responsibility" of self-limitations will, instead, only admit of realization to the extent that zero options are made assimilable and tolerable in a further, reflexive step of political modernization. This could have the result that societies subject the achieved condition of their modernization to a thoroughly "modern" revision and put themselves institutionally in a position to deal more selectively with further modernization processes.

These reflections on models and examples of application should have made clear that in "modern" societies a *fundamentally* paradoxical relationship exists between the sectoral enhancement of capacities and options on the one hand, and global rigidity and immovability on the other. The more responsive the subsystems become, the more fatal grows the problem of their viable coherence. In this sense, the pessimistic perspective is not to be dismissed that, precisely as a result of rapid modernization and rationalization processes, societies can regress into a condition of mute condemnation to fate and inflexibility, the overcoming of which was the original motif of modernization processes in the first place. But it should have been equally clear that *between* the extremes of modernized yet rigidified, and "primitive" yet revolutionizable societies there lies a plethora of intermediate combinations in relation to which the limited advantages of expanded options for action and increased steering capacity can be "netted out" against and reconciled with one another.

Notes

1 W. Zapf, "Die soziologische Theorie der Modernisierung," *Soziale Welt* 26 (1975), p. 217.
2 Ibid, p. 44.
3 Ibid, p. 212.
4 J. Berger, "Der Kapitalismus: Ein unvollendbares Projekt?" in B. Lutz (ed.), *Verhandlungen des 22. Deutschen Soziologentages* (Frankfurt, 1985), pp. 488ff.
5 M. Weber, *The Protestant Ethic and the Spirit of Capitalism*, trans. Talcott Parsons, introd. Anthony Giddens (New York, 1976), p. 182.
6 M. Horkheimer and T. W. Adorno, *Dialektik der Aufklärung* (Amsterdam, 1947), p. 198; trans. as *The Dialectic of Enlightenment* (London, 1979).
7 N. Bobbio, "The Future of Democracy," *Telos* 61 (Fall 1984).
8 M. Weber, "The National State and Economic Policy," *Economy and Society* 5:4 (Nov. 1980), p. 437.
9 Ibid., p. 448.
10 Cf. U. Beck, *Risk Society: Towards a New Modernity* (London, 1992).
11 Cf. H. Kitschelt, "Materielle Politisierung der Produktion: Gesellschaftliche Herausforderung und institutionelle Innovationen in fortgeschrittenen kapitalistischen Demokratien," *Zeitschrift für Soziologie* 14 (1985).
12 Cf. C. Offe, "New Social Movements: Challenging the Boundaries of Institutional Politics," *Social Research* 52:4 (1985).
13 Cf. J. Habermas, *Die neue Unübersichtlichkeit: Kleine politische Schriften V* (Frankfurt, 1985), pp. 156ff.
14 Cf. U. K. Preuss, *Politische Verantwortung und Bürgerloyalität* (Frankfurt, 1984), pp. 145ff.
15 Cf. C. E. Lindblom, *Politics and Markets* (New York, 1977).
16 In many countries, the doors of banks are equipped with a mechanism which holds the door closed for several seconds after the handle has been turned. Obviously it is assumed that the forfeitures of freedom imposed on the bank customer by this moratorium stands in a completely acceptable relation to the increased security against bank robberies.

2

Bindings, Shackles, Brakes: On Self-Limitation Strategies

From the point of view of the social sciences, the great appeal of Habermas's program stems from the fact that he explicitly asks what conditions of society and of socialization would provide the most fertile ground for a practical confirmation of the insights of his practical philosophy. Hegel concludes *The German Constitution* of 1802 with the pithy moral-sociological thesis that "thinking and insight into necessity are far too weak in themselves to become effective in action. Thought and judgment carry with them so much self-mistrust that they have to be validated by force, and only then does man submit to them."[1] It almost seems that Habermas is paraphrasing this passage when he writes that "uncoupled from concrete, everyday ethical life, moral insights can no longer simply be assumed to have the motivational force that would allow them to have a practical effect."[2] Thus, in contrast to the tradition of formal ethics, Habermas concedes that "leaving subjects alone to resolve [problems of moral judgment] places too great a burden on them" and that "the *rationality of a life-world* ... is measured by the extent to which it meets individuals halfway in solving these problems."[3] At the same time, and in opposition to Aristotelian moral philosophers, he insists that a specific local and historical context of a given form of life does not in and of itself constitute a standard for moral justifications. For no matter how robust the habitual nature of that form of life, this cannot guarantee that it is also rational. Similarly, cultural traditions, social structures, and conditions of socialization by themselves do not determine the content of practical reason, but only enhance (or impair) the ability of individuals to judge that content autonomously and, in accord with the mutual agreements thus arrived at, to bind themselves in a morally rational way. With an astonishing degree of confidence, Habermas believes that favorable contextual conditions for the development of this capacity are "structures of the lifeworld" that "do in fact appear in modern societies and are proliferating."[4]

According to the logic of this construction, that would be a happy, albeit not a necessary, coincidence of circumstances. In what follows I want to distinguish three variables, the respective manifestations of which would have to be mutually compatible in order for this "coincidence" or "meeting halfway" to be the case.

The first variable is the (very difficult to operationalize) degree to which a given social system has a functional "need" for its members to be morally orientated by their own autonomous insights. Different historical social formations are more or less "demanding" in this respect because, for instance, owing to a lack of functional equivalents and substitutes for "morality," they are more or less functionally dependent on individuals reflectively orienting their actions by a standard of practical reason (even if they are morally motivated thereby and do not take the satisfaction of these functional requirements as their *goal*).

The second variable that determines whether the political equilibrium between practical reason and form of life obtains is the degree to which a society's typical processes of socialization foster a capacity for reflection in its members, that is, the degree of their autonomy and the "stage" of moral consciousness they have attained or that is structurally attainable for them.

Finally, if the demands of practical reason are to "coincide" with a form of life and a constitution of society that "meet them halfway," it is important that the societal forms of association and structures of collective action, as well as the interpretations of collective identity, be such that they do not overburden individuals, in the sense of requiring them to take "unreasonably" high risks of falling victim to deceit or exploitation by third parties when following their moral insights in practice.

I shall touch briefly on the reasons why, under certain social conditions, particularly high demands are placed not only on the capacity of individuals to bind themselves autonomously and rationally, but also on their power of moral judgment. If the burden of meeting these demands of moral rationality were "met halfway" by the lifeworld, these conditions would at the same time give rise to contexts conducive to making individuals capable of coping with those demands, individually as well as collectively. This benevolent circle would clearly be advantageous not just to anyone whomsoever, but especially to the moral philosopher, as he or she would no longer have to rely on nothing but how compelling his or her theoretical constructs and criteria were, or on the polemic success of the moral goods he or she advocates. Instead moral philosophy (in some formal analogy to the Marxian model) could rely on the forces and tendencies of a real social development that strives toward its results, as it were, and gives it compelling force.

As theoretically captivating and practically attractive as this integration of moral and social theory is, there are, needless to say, alternative social-theoretical doctrines on offer that trace the processes of moral development to the micro level of "formative games." At that level, they raise the critical question of whether we can expect a convergence between (a) the moral capacity of individuals for responsible self-binding, and (b) a given set of social-structural problems that can be dealt with only morally. If so, what are the *institutional* conditions that must be met? And what are the *dilemmas of rational action* that need to be resolved in order for this to happen?

Self-Limitation as Method and as Result

As a broad summary of the main theses of Ulrich Beck's *Risk Society* clearly and succinctly shows, the success of that book rests without a doubt on its opening up of a number of new ways of thinking. We no longer live in a class society, but in a risk society. This fits with the finding that the "game" of accumulation and "exploitation" that pits capital against labor – a game which shows a positive sum in the form of a "growing pie" – has been replaced by a negative-sum game of "collective self-injury." In this game, everyone inflicts injury on himself or herself as well as on everyone else without any net gain: "circular endangering effects lead to a unity of perpetrator and victim."[5]

This picture becomes more complicated and, presumably, more realistic once we take into account that there might be an unequal distribution of damages without a reciprocal unequal distribution of privileges *resulting from it*. Those accumulating damages would be "marginalized," but not "exploited" and turned into a means for the enrichment of others. In place of becoming richer, the latter could shift part of the damages on to the marginalized group: "my" advantage would in fact simply be my reduced disadvantage – reduced, that is, by the amount of damages I manage to shift on to others.

This congruence of the roles of perpetrator and victim in post-class society has two important consequences. First, in a society that fits this model, there would be no privileged points anymore from which to initiate a *causal* therapy as was possible in a class society. In the latter type of structure for inflicting damages, it is obvious that something (such as control of material resources, privileges, political power) must be taken away from the exploiters for the problem to be resolved. Conversely, the exploited must fight in order to be compensated with the requisite goods and advantages. Yet if social conditions approximate a state of collective self-injury, then everyone involved gains and loses (more than he or she gains) at the same time. In addition, marginalized social categories may accumulate losses but their suffering may not profit others. Under these conditions, there is nothing that can be done to combat this completely irrational structure from the executive heights of state politics (be they conquered by revolution or reform).

Instead of being subject to governmental redistribution of rights and resources, the required controlling mechanisms in such a constellation are subjectivized, as it were. They drift away from the stage of national politics and take effect immediately among "the public," that is, in the practical lives of those willing and able to orient their actions to rules of collective and responsible self-binding. The functional role of these actors is now revalorized, and government regulation can at best offer points of orientation to them, but it cannot assume sole responsibility for setting and enforcing norms.

According to Beck's model, a risk society is so arranged that constitution, law, and state politics, as protectors and trustees of collective reason, generally play a diminishing, sometimes even a negative, role. This kind of society virtually does not respond to Hobbesian solutions anymore. But where the *state*-produced rule of law fails as the guideline for determining an interest that all reasonable individuals are capable of, and indeed coerced into, recognizing as their common interest, the "problem of order" is apparently put back into the hands of individuals and their associations and organizations. Precisely because there is no other force sufficiently "sovereign" to impose a common good on them, they must control *themselves*, apply their capacity for practical judgment, and appeal to the cultural traditions of their form of life – they must, so to speak, substitute for a notoriously overburdened state power. The state-instituted media of law and money are capable, at best, of regulating conditions of exploitation and of altering structures of privilege that have become untenable *within* national societies. They are certainly not capable by themselves of laying to rest a whole series of contradictions and questions of justice in the *international* "risk society." At the very least, they need to be supplemented by an increasing participation on the part of citizens whose actions and self-binding are oriented toward enlightenment, solidarity, and responsibility.

Beck's diagnosis of society suggests the following second inference. What is lost is not only the Archimedean point from which "causal" therapies can be carried out *in practice*, but also any reliable *theoretical* knowledge of which actions and inactions place a heavy burden of risks on whom, and in what temporal horizon. To the extent that the practical mitigation of collective self-injuries becomes "morality dependent," whatever knowledge and certainty we have of the causes, effects, and possible remedies of material need may themselves fall prey to arbitrary interpretations as soon as we are dealing with the causes, effects, and remedies of smog or of dying forests. The controversies arising from a politics of prophecies, interpretations, causal explanations, and attributions of blame can no longer be settled by the authority of the special sciences. In any event, "the very claim of the sciences to be rational permanently disempowers them so that they cannot investigate the degree of risk involved *objectively*."[6] In the end, the public, comprising citizens and lay persons, depends not only on practical self-help but also on the actors' own cognitive *interpretation* of the situation – along with the fairly obvious consequent risks of myth formation, panic mongering and "*Angst* communication."

The general formula invoked in response to this dual practical-theoretical problem is neither surprising nor controversial. At least rhetorically, everyone participating in or affected by the issue appeals to it, with good intentions and demands for self-restraint, self-limitation, responsibility, and moderation. According to all these formulas, the debate turns on the meaning of the metaphors of brake and shackle, that is, on the intentional self-prevention of "wrong moves," given that any authority accruing to specific institutional sectors – be it organized science or state politics – to determine what the "right" moves are in theory or to execute them in practice is largely depleted.

Discourse ethics fits this sketch of social structures and problems because – at the cost of methodically renouncing philosophical hypotheses on the substance of "progress" or "liberation" – it establishes the rules and procedures of sincere, fair, and open-minded communication, but without claiming to morally qualify the material results of these rules in advance. Discourse ethics proceeds reconstructively, not constructively. It is concerned with procedures, not with results. The goal of argumentation is not the positive determination of the "good," but the negative elimination of particularistic prejudices, preoccupation with strategic interests, and cognitive narrow-mindedness from practical discourse.

Discourse ethics establishes a *procedure* of self-control. Basing itself on the norm of rationality of mutual understanding inherent in linguistic communication, it justifies the criteria of rationality and the procedural norms derived from it. According to these norms, whatever a speaker honestly brings up, having checked it against reality and without assuming any (socioeconomic or cognitive) privileges, may count as a valid argument. The *results* of discourse ethics are congruent with this process of self-control. The "autonomous public spheres" that follow its laws apply rules of "intelligent self-limitation,"[7] the material content of which cannot be judged by substantive criteria but only by procedural ones. In light of the fact that every attempt to determine a substantive ethics is soon hopelessly mired in the failure to survive ultimate validity tests, Habermas is convinced that

> negative versions of the moral principle seem to be a step in the right direction. They heed the prohibition of graven images, refrain from positive depiction, and, as in the case of discourse ethics, refer negatively to the damaged life instead of pointing affirmatively to the good life.... Moral philosophy does not have privileged access to particular moral truths.[8]

Note that connecting the theoretical principle of the "prohibition of graven images" with the practical principle of procedural duties that have moral content because they guarantee fairness and rationality in argumentation is characteristic of an orientation similar to that of leftwing political theory. The left (not only in developed capitalist countries but also in the Third and Second Worlds) has been leaning in this direction ever since the experience of the movements of the 1960s, as well as after having run into various antinomies and dead ends in its own policies. First, as far as the prohibition of images is concerned, we can say without hesitation that nowadays the concept of "socialism" as a comprehensive structural formula for a truly emancipated social order is operationally empty – and has been for some time.[9]

The political left has therefore replaced this global formula for structures and goals by an alternative project of *guaranteeing minimums* instead of realizing maximums, and of using appropriate procedures and institutions to brake and shackle the destructive effects of the dynamics of technological, military, economic, bureaucratic, and ecological modernization by applying principles of responsible self-limitation. This is by no means a more modest, but simply a more fitting, reinterpretation of the "leftist" project, one that follows the negative principle that no one, neither individuals nor social categories, nor any society as a whole, is to be deprived of material means of subsistence, of human and civil rights, or of opportunities for political and social participation. Nor should anyone become a victim of military and ecological disasters. Avoidance criteria of this sort cannot be objectively established once and for all; they can only be defined case by case and applied according to the available options by means of the appropriate *procedures* and institutions. The latter would have to underwrite moral sensibility, a sense of reality, and critical thought within extended temporal horizons. In order to claim moral evidence, this policy of guaranteeing minimal standards should not be protectionist and concentrate on *specific* sectors, social categories, and needs. Rather, it should strive for flexibility and focus its resources on areas facing the greatest needs and the greatest threats.

This methodology of the left, which no longer seeks to attain certain concrete final ends but to establish universal negative criteria of avoidance instead, not only makes good sense in the context of the model of a "risk society" and its chronic need for the capacity of "intelligent self-limitation"; it also offers a clear-cut antithesis to proliferating neoconservative and postmodern political projects. Whether in the sphere of economics, state power, the military, or echnological development, whether in the sphere of cultural norms and traditions, these projects can be characterized by their common goal of breaking down limitations and replacing them with the free play of an arbitrariness that deems itself above reason (strategic or critical). Thus, "active," interventionist forms of public policy are giving way on the right as well, though not to an alternative that would more resolutely ensure minimal standards in the dimensions mentioned above. On the contrary, they are giving way to an uninhibited play of the forces of evolution. Policy takes on the aim of facilitating adaptation and modernization processes whose substantive content escapes political regulation and goal setting. The dominant pattern might be described as "releasing the brakes": deregulation, liberalization, flexibility, increasing fluidity, and facilitating transactions on the financial, real estate and labor markets, easing the tax burden, etc.

This conservative-postmodernist syndrome is mirrored by both the procedurally very ambitious, yet materially just as "frugal" approach of discourse ethics and the parallel project of a modern left-wing politics that is just as clearly based on the prohibition of images and on ideas of procedural justice. Together, the two lead us to ask what are the conditions for and motives behind the self-limitations actors assume as their duty. What are their consequences and what dilemmas of rationality do they give rise to? I wish to explore these complex questions by first examining several, primarily philosophical, texts whose authors make use of the metaphors of "shackle" or "brake."

Precautions against "False Moves": A Collage

Elster's Ulysses

As Jon Elster sees him in *Ulysses and the Sirens*,[10] Ulysses, having himself tied to the mast of his ship, is the model of rational compensation for irrationality. His irrationality consists in "being weak and knowing it" (p. 36). Ulysses can react to the anticipation of his own weakness in one of three ways. First, he can react *opportunistically*, that is, alter his preferences according to circumstance so that he no longer considers his "weakness" to be such. Second, he can react *"morally,"* that is, change into a person capable of doing the right thing even without formal self-binding. As a matter of fact, since he disdains the first option and does not believe himself capable of the second – or also because, on the first alternative, intentional self-manipulation of one's own preferences is ruled out in principle since they are uncontrollable "by-products"[11] – he chooses the middle road: he makes sure that the *undesired* action becomes *impossible* for him due to external circumstances; or, on a weaker reading, becomes costly enough to be a deterrent. He succeeds by evading a foreseeable excessive moral demand and exposing himself to conditions that "accommodate" his moral willpower. One might say he protects himself from himself by giving himself a *constitution*, installing a causal force (pp. 42ff.) and in this way enters into what Elster calls a "precommitment" or "self-binding."

Elster is primarily interested in the second of two objections that can be raised against this conception of the rationality of moral action as prudent manipulation of one's self. First, one might think that Ulysses harbors rather exaggerated fears concerning the weakness of his will.[12] In the political context, he would be seen as inscribing at the *constitutional* level a condition that could be attained just as well by mere *legislation*.[13]

The limits of indirect rationality that Elster highlights, however, concern the second case, namely, when the agent has good grounds to undo the shackles but has ventured into a trap so that he or she is no longer capable of doing so. These good grounds, which are difficult if not impossible to know from the outside and are subject to self-deception, can be of two kinds: either the *world* changes in unanticipated respects so that "one may be prevented from making the right choice in unforeseen circumstances,"[14] or the *agent* himself or herself experiences a change of preferences and now begins "authentically" (rather than opportunistically) to prefer the previously censored preference.[15] Obviously, these considerations necessarily lead to the conclusion that self-binding is not a question of maximization but of optimization, and that in the very practice of self-limitation, self-limitations are in order. However, this problem of optimization can no longer be solved by means of prudence; it can only be solved by appealing to emergent ideas of justice to which there is no access from the subjective sphere of the rationality of action.

Ulysses in the Dialectic of Enlightenment

On Adorno's interpretation of Ulysses in the *Dialectic of Enlightenment*,[16] "the hero of the adventures shows himself to be a prototype of the bourgeois individual" (p. 43), insofar as self-affirmation and self-denial coincide in the latter: Ulysses' "self-assertion ... as in all civilization, is self denial" (p. 68). His attempt to escape his own weakness by prudently applying indirect rationality falters on his "sacrifice of the self"; it is "almost always the destruction of the subject." Ulysses "struggles at the mast," but this "technically enlightened ... man's domination over himself" is a "renunciation" leading to a "mimesis unto death": the ruse that conquers the self as "irrationality of *ratio*" (pp. 54ff.). Unlike for Freud, then, this self-denial is not, *qua* sublimation, a necessary tribute to civilization but an indication of its return to a "coercive circle of the natural context." Adorno leaves no doubt concerning the repressive character of the Ego-principle nor about the "coercive character" of identity as he is to express it later.[17] The radical nature[18] of this critique is based on his certainty that with the self-limiting "denial of nature in man not merely the *telos* of the outward control of nature but the *telos* of man's own life is distorted and defogged ... all the aims for which he keeps himself alive – social progress, the intensification of all his material and spiritual power, even consciousness itself – are nullified" (p. 54).

In order to escape sacrifice, man sacrifices himself. This critique of instrumental reason dramatizes the model of the circle, in which the ruse of self-preservation by self-domination can lead to nothing but self-denial, to indifference with respect to means and ends, and finally to "open insanity." Adorno's model – like the rest of early Critical Theory – blocks every road toward a theory of rational morality. Because of the radical mistrust toward the practice of self-limitation, moral precepts are valid only if they themselves appear in the unrationalized form of an intuition or an "impulse." These precepts "must not be rationalized; as abstract principles, they would immediately fall prey to the bad infinity of their derivation and validity."[19] In support of this radical critique of "indirect" rationality, one might cite the guilelessness with which, only a few years earlier, Joseph Schumpeter had praised the rationality of self-limitation.

Brakes as Lubricants of Capitalist Development

Schumpeter defends the practice of self-limitation from a strictly functionalist perspective and accordingly dispenses with its ethical justification. As a century before him Tocqueville had done at the level of democratic theory, he advocates, at the level of economics, elements of a static inefficiency in the name of the dynamic efficiency of capitalism. These elements can consist in limitations on price formation, market access, and the freedom of contract. Following his analysis, the capitalist dynamics of growth and wealth do not rest on free price competition and on the unfettered development of market conditions, but on their shackling by monopolistic practices (such as cartel formation), as well as on state regulations and interventions. Such monopolistic "restrictions," Schumpeter writes, are the carriers and triggers of a "long-term process of expansion which they protect rather than impede. There is no more of a paradox in this than there is in saying that motorcars are travelling faster than they otherwise would *because* they are provided with brakes."[20]

This conception raises a whole host of questions. Is every sort of static inefficiency (such as market limitations) going to pay off in the sense indicated? What are the underlying reasons for the desirability of the results of this dynamic efficiency? What is the time frame and the degree of certainty with which these increases in welfare will take effect? And, correspondingly, what will be the motivating and legitimating effects of such increases? What is the relationship between the motives of cartel formation (monopoly income, and more generally, the securing of power and wealth) and their supposed functions (a *universal* increase in welfare)? How can the motives of cartel formation be stabilized in the face of the problem of the collective good so that every member of a cartel has an interest in every *other* member abiding by the stipulated rules (quantity and price limitations), only in order to be able to draw an even greater profit itself from its own *violation* of these rules? Because the argument does not examine, let alone resolve, these consequent problems, it can offer no prescriptive conclusions concerning the nature of the rational action of citizens, entrepreneurs, and political elites. All that it allows for are defensive moves against objections focusing on competition from orthodox market economists. Self-limitation is praised on grounds that do not motivate it but that can offer only (weak) justifications for the circumstances in which it is already being practiced.

Reaching for the "Emergency Brake" as a Revolutionary
Suspension of Progress

In his two final manuscripts ("Central Park," "On the Concept of History"), Walter Benjamin formulates an antithesis between progress and revolution – an idea that until then would have been considered oxymoronic. "The concept of progress is to be grounded in the Idea of the catastrophe. That things 'just go on' *is* the catastrophe."[21] He confesses to his "ferocious animosity toward the blithe optimism of the leaders of the Left."[22] Social democracy takes pleasure in "assign[ing] to the working class the role of the redeemer of future generations," while it is clear to Benjamin that revolutionary virtues "are nourished by the image of enslaved ancestors, rather than that of liberated grandchildren."[23] Marked by fundamental motives of Jewish theology, the idea of a "recruiting critique" lies at the heart of the concept of revolution that Benjamin opposes to the stubbornly grinding wheels of progress (always that of the forces of production as well as of emancipation[24]): it is the job of revolutionary acts to "shatter" history's continuity, to take the "origin" as the end, to bring events to a standstill in the "remembrance" of history. In Benjamin's manuscript, the following sentence is crossed out: "A classless society is not the final goal of progress in history; rather, it is its so often failed and at last successful interruption." However, he retained the famous sentence with the same meaning: "Marx says revolutions are the locomotive of history. But perhaps this isn't so at all. Perhaps revolutions occur when the human species, travelling in this train, reaches for the emergency brake."[25]

This vision obviously does not focus on purifying and defusing the rationalization of modernity, on overcoming its contradictions and continuing to develop in accord with the standards of its better possibilities; it focuses instead on a revolutionary act in which the entire dynamics of modernity is brought to a standstill. Reason does not self-correct in order to find a way out of the circle formed by civilization and nature; rather, in one final act, it applies its unequivocally destructive force to itself.

The fragments of the problem of self-binding action contrasted here stem from highly heterogeneous theories and traditions. While a comparison of these fragments with the approach of a strictly procedural ethics of self-binding based on duties of argumentation and principles of universalization is beyond the scope of the present chapter, it would have the following results: (1) that discourse ethics claims to close the gap that Elster's model finds between the rationality of action and intuitions about what is just;[26] (2) that discourse ethics –

pace Adorno – insists that moral precepts can be justified beyond a brute "impulse" and are moreover in no way caught in the aforementioned circle; (3) that, contrary to Schumpeter's functionalist derivation of the practice of self-binding, discourse ethics proceeds from an autonomous motivating force that supports this practice; and (4) that, in diametrical opposition to Benjamin, it relies on the ability of practical reason to self-correct its own practice.

Associative Relations and "Societal Constitutionalism"

In addition, Habermas believes that there are cultural, socializatory, and legal-political conditions and forms of life that converge with the social preconditions of a practice corresponding to discourse ethics. He proceeds from the assumption that at least the seeds of these conditions are present in modern Western societies and that they can be developed further. In order to examine the question of whether or not there is such a convergence, I want to contrast the global categories of form of life and lifeworld, which are supposed to secure a beachhead for discourse ethics in the social world, with more sociological categories. To this end, I want to apply the – no doubt still precariously fuzzy – concept of "associative relations." This concept is supposed to encompass societal commonalities and differences that take institutional forms, as well as the processes of conflict resolution among social categories of people. The starting assumption is that the institutional character of such *internal differentiations* within a lifeworld shared by the members of a society (or speakers of a language) as a whole offers either favorable or unfavorable conditions for the presumed convergence of form of life and moral demands – and thus for the solution of what is ultimately an empirical problem.

If conditions are *unfavorable*, the effects of discouragement, the risks and costs, that emanate from associative contexts and the "games" they define (from configurations of actors, preferences, expectations, incentives, and interdependencies) can be such that, as a matter of fact, only one of two diametrically opposed alternatives remains. *Either* we are left at one extreme, with "realistic" moral insouciance, dominated exclusively by individual utility categories. This insouciance could be interpreted as a residue of insufficient structural moral demand made upon individuals. *Or*, at the other extreme, we are left with fundamentalism, that is, the deformed residue of practical reason preoccupied with reveling in its own righteousness.[27] In fact, the monomaniacal thirst for *ideal* enrichment of one extreme is no different than the thirst for material enrichment of the other.

In contrast, if conditions are *favorable,* the institutional and procedural context can be such as to imply that "responsible" action can reasonably be expected by demanding, or at least permitting, continually and in a more or less comprehensive manner, that the principles governing actions and decisions be subjected to validity tests. The structural principles and institutions of political order, especially the determination of the latter's democratic, representational and constitutional forms, are necessary but not always sufficient conditions for realizing such a challenge. Thus, for example, legal coercion is the classic means for dealing with the free-rider problem: "Even morally well justified norms are reasonable only to the extent that those tailoring their practice to these norms can expect that everyone else will behave in conformity to them as well."[28] This is precisely what is accomplished through "legally binding" norms.

However, whether the results of determining the forms of legal and parliamentary-democratic processes like this meet the ambitious criterion of securing "the equal consideration of all interests concerned and of all the relevant aspects of any given case"[29] is a question the affirmative answer to which demands a heroic idealism nowadays. Habermas does indeed respond with muted confidence, but qualifies his answer by introducing two requirements: (1) that the procedural rules mentioned be adhered to, and (2) that the political public sphere make active and self-conscious use of these procedures. Thus, "the rational quality of political legislation also depends on the level of participation and of education, on the level of information and of the clarity with which disputed issues are articulated among the general public."[30] In other words, it depends on the will and consciousness of the citizens of the state as they arise from the prevailing conditions of socialization.

But whether democratic-constitutional procedures, even if combined with the appropriate cognitive and moral dispositions on the part of the public, that is, with widespread virtues of a republican political culture, are enough to not only help the "better" argument to be recognized as valid, but also to generate (sufficiently) "good" arguments is another matter. The answer to this question is determined by the nature of the "games" in which actions are taken and decisions are made. By "sufficiently good" arguments I mean arguments that take into consideration the substantive, temporal, and social interdependencies and consequences of action so comprehensively that they do not lead to just any self-binding but only to "appropriate" self-binding, such that the actions and decisions following from it can be considered responsible and nonregrettable in anticipation of a future point in time at which we might look back upon them. To act responsibly, then, is for the agent methodically to take, vis-à-vis his or her own actions, the critical perspectives, simultaneously and in the *futurum exactum*, of the expert, the generalized other, and of himself or herself. By assuming this triple perspective, the actor validates the criteria of action substantively, socially, and temporally.

"Public Spirit"

Social systems seem to differ in the degree to which they *depend* on the autonomous moral self-discipline and civilized self-control of their members (or, conversely, in the degree to which they can*not* sufficiently *compensate* for the absence of such self-control by applying the media of legal coercion and of (the incentives of) money. In this dimension, complex societies and the partial systems that constitute them exhibit a prominent functional need for orientations toward an ethics of responsibility not just among elites or experts, but among the masses. As examples of this need, consider seemingly trivial contexts of action in the areas of education, health, consumption, and transportation, and, more generally, the regulation of relations between genders, between generations, between indigenous and immigrant populations, between professionals and their clients. There are countless other cases where so-called problems of the collective good and of systemic control cannot be resolved by price regulation or by legal coercion (no more than by the knowledge and professional practice of experts). If such problems can be resolved at all, it can only be by the informed and circumspect, yet abstract development of solidarity and of a civilized public spirit. In all these spheres of action, the common moral problem resolves around the constitutive "vulnerability"[31] of individuals, and the need to compensate for it by protecting their physical integrity and respecting their dignity.

The dispositions toward an ethics of responsibility that activate this public spirit have the quality of moral norms. They differ from the precepts of a merely habitual everyday ethical life in that one cannot get by in the spheres of action that I mentioned with traditional norms, stereotypes of conflict resolution, and particularistic status rights alone. Similarly, they differ from mere rules of prudence in that acting in conformity with norms often contributes very little to gaining privileges (or to avoiding disadvantages); what little effect there is is uncertain and geared toward the long term. Hence such calculations of profit alone could hardly motivate the corresponding actions to the "required" extent. Most of all, however, these orientations toward an ethics of responsibility have the character of norms because, however great their importance for the continued viability of complex social systems from functionalist points of view, they are nonetheless not *motivated* by this functionality but spring forth from the actors' uncoerced and indeed uncoerceable moral self-binding. Motive and function are thus separated, and the dispositions mentioned are motivated by something *other* than by the rational solution of systemic problems.

On the other hand, they are – at least in a negative respect – *not independent* from social and institutional structures: the origin and development of the moral orientations in question can be inhibited by perceived risks and burdens which may prevail within unfavorable structural contexts. The best way to analyze these is by means of game theory, which is able to demonstrate how, the more unfavorably the associative context is constituted, the more the action embedded in it becomes susceptible to noncooperative strategies.

The *capacity* for moral self-binding, not merely the *dependence* of social systems on it, must thus be seen as empirically contingent – contingent at first vis-à-vis what I have labeled, in contrast to the "conditions of socialization" of a historical form of society, its "associative relations." A society's associative relations are determined by the structure of the division of labor, on the one hand, and by the thematic and social pattern of institutions of collective action, that is, by the mediation and aggregation of interests, on the other. And third, they are determined by established procedures of conflict resolution.

Institutions as Filters

Here, I merely want to argue for the fecundity of a particular research perspective[32] for the social sciences and to support my claim with a few examples. From that perspective, associative relations fulfill the function of a filter vis-à-vis the moral dimension of action. The selectivity of this filter determines whether and to what extent the application and development of legally guaranteed freedoms of action plus cognitive and moral capacities of individual actors, as constituted in socialization processes and by cultural transmission, are encouraged and fostered; or whether, on the contrary, they lay fallow and fall into disuse – either because these capacities are insufficiently activated, or because the expectations being placed on them are overly demanding. If this point of view carries any plausibility, it means that not only the procedures of an open, fair, and argumentative will-formation and decision-formation that are laid down by *constitutions*, and not only the capacity for postconventional moral judgment-formation that is constituted in socialization processes, but also *the social-structural and institutional conditions of collective action* within civil society, that is, its pattern of the *division of labor* and its "associative design," are significant factors in the development of moral competence.

The perspective I am defending might be turned into the following "strong" hypothesis. Where empirical associative patterns do not favor or at least make affordable moral considerations, and where there is no modern equivalent for the central political categories of historical materialism that have become empty (namely, the categories of "class" and "party" as structural or institutional carriers of collective action and moral consciousness), a society's legal, constitutional, and socialization conditions may well be highly developed; but in the absence of corresponding institutions representing collective identities and associative "bearers" of the "moral point of view," the potential of moral capacities will still not be realized, let alone exhausted, because, taken by themselves, the bonds existing in a community between those participating in no more than a common *language*, a common *public sphere*, and a shared *lifeworld* are too weak to release the potential for acting in solidarity. The following reads like a concession to the suspicion that the mere combination of constitutional guarantees and civic courage (plus the synthesis of the two into "constitutional patriotism") requires a third element in order to give rise to a strong civic spirit, namely favorable associative patterns of collective action:

> any universalistic morality is dependent upon a form of life that *meets it halfway*. There has to be a modicum of congruence between morality and the practices of socialization and education. The latter must promote the requisite internalization of superego controls and the abstractness of ego identities. In addition, there must be a modicum of fit between morality and sociopolitical institutions. Not just any institutions will do. Morality thrives only in an environment in which postconventional ideas about law and morality have already been institutionalized to a certain extent.[33]

At the very least, this can be read in the sense that the "socially integrative force of solidarity"[34] can be enforced against the two other controlling resources – money and administrative power – only if solidarity is given a chance to develop in the relative safety of appropriate associative contexts which serve as its home base and which it can subsequently go beyond. I would like to provide a few points of reference to support this suggestion.

Today, there are many contexts in which solidarity is precariously problematic, not only in the societal dimensions, that is, the dimension concerning the fair consideration of the needs of our contemporaries, but especially in the temporal dimension,[35] that is, the dimension concerning our unbiased respect for the needs of future generations whose welfare is affected, positively as well as negatively, by our actions. If even the weak tie of contemporaneity is clearly insufficient to motivate solidarity in action, what can intertemporal community rely on? The idea that the horizon of our future-directed solidarity might be limited by the fact that, at most, we can encounter our great-grandchildren in person stems from Max Frisch. If we think exclusively in terms of individuals and their family ties, any cause for exerting our moral capacity for intertemporal solidarity drops out beyond their generation – considering that those alive today can feel entirely impervious to the sanctions and moral reproach of future generations. This indifference is altered once we think in terms of a *nation qua* institution whose continuing identity connects the "inhabitants" of time t_0 with those of almost any future time t_n, thereby letting the latter enter the circle of possible objects of moral action. A similar connection appears when future generations are considered as participants in a divine scheme for salvation or – already in a considerably more limited fashion – simply as members of a profession, a scientific or artistic discipline etc., who are capable of judgment and in whose judgment those acting today want to be considered worthy ancestors.

To this extent, institutions such as religious communities, nations, or professions mediate the temporal range of solidarity. The same holds for historical cross-sections: valid and institutionally shaped interpretations of the relevant totality of "kin," for instance, determine whether we regard species of animals and plants (or even individual exemplars of these) as objects of instrumental action or, on the contrary, as creatures of divine creation that are candidates to be objects of our morally binding sympathy. Conversely, the highly restrictive definition of the domain of a trade union may result in the complete exclusion of the problems of the unemployed, even of part-time workers, so that solidarity toward them remains a matter of individual engagement which is not only ineffective but can also be quite risky.

Even the concept of those "affected," which serves to define the universe of everyone whose interests and arguments merit fair consideration on a given issue, is to be elucidated not by analyzing the issue itself, but only with a view of demarcating the institutional arena that mediates and limits the claim to be "affected." Such a connection might even be drawn in retrospect. In forming judgments about historical moral issues, we find that they may be posed differently from within the persisting framework of a nation than from the external perspective of someone who does not share the relevant history. If, however, as in the game-theoretic model of the "prisoner's dilemma," the interacting partners are authoritatively *dis*sociated, and if, moreover, they are prevented from spontaneously generating solidarity – because of the expectations and incentives built into the pay-off matrix – then we have reached the limiting case of an associative context that virtually precludes moral action.

To be sure, associative relations against the background of which individuals can code themselves as "members" may clearly also fulfill *restrictive* functions that can fall significantly short of the criteria of a universalistic moral theory. This happens if organized collectivities mediate particularistic local traditions and moral ideas that are tied to a given milieu and do not live up to universalistic standards. This reservation notwithstanding, the catalyzing function of associative relations must not be underestimated. They constitute environments of action that, on one hand, allow questions of fairness and mutual obligation to be raised,[36] if only among the members of narrow communities, while, on the other hand, they allow participants to be shielded from unreasonable expectations and the risk of standing alone with the "right" kind of action. This catalyzing function of activating at least some capacities for moral judgment is fulfilled by associations and other institutions of social representation and mediation of interests. They do so by generating as their by-product, from a social, substantive, and temporal point of view, the assurance of stability and conditions of trust. The absence of the latter would place too heavy a burden on moral capacities, whereas their existence does not *necessarily* result in a permanent limitation of these capacities to the horizon of the local concrete ethical life. As in a "hidden curriculum," institutions and procedures "evoke" certain preference orderings, yet without manipulating them or paternalistically deciding in advance what they are. In this connection, Goodin talks about "multiple preference orderings actually operative within the individual . . . which he applies differently according to the context . . . The social decision machinery changes preferences in the process of aggregating them . . . An individual's response depends on the institutional environment in which the question is asked."[37]

In the social dimension, intermediate associations within civil society can ensure that the binding force of valid rules is generalized internally so that none of those complying with them need fear that his or her own rule-bound actions remain unreciprocated or are exploited by others.[38] In the temporal dimension, expectations are stabilized to the extent that associations are capable of creating a basis for the confidence that existing rules and preferences will continue to be valid in the future, and insofar as the future selves of those involved will be sufficiently like their present selves so as to minimize the likelihood of unpleasant surprises down the road. One counts on "seeing one another again," and for that, much depends on one's still being "the same." Finally, in the substantive dimension, institutional carriers of collective action fulfill the function of putting at the disposal of the participants interpretations of reality that are mutually consistent, are cognitively adequate, and encourage sincere (as opposed to strategically falsified) communication of information. This more or less guarantees that such information is reliable, which in turn has the function of keeping the appearance of moral orientations from becoming unreasonably risky.

Moral Evaluation of Institutional Arrangements?

In order to shed light on the highly variable extent to which these functions are actually fulfilled by different institutional arrangements for the aggregation of interests and preferences, it will be useful to remind ourselves that associations have the potential to encourage and foster the adoption of a moral point of view. For the moral capacity of individuals does not depend on the structures of personal identity they have acquired in their primary socialization process alone. Nor does it depend exclusively on the legally institutionalized framework of rules provided by the law and the constitution. How much of this capacity is developed and applied in practice depends on the nature of the "games" in which the prevailing forms of collective action of a given situation involve them.

The motivation to help, for example, is likely to be more effectively activated where help is solicited in direct confrontation with the concrete needs of other people as well as in contexts where others are visibly helping, as opposed to a situation where the relation between the helper and the needy is mediated by legal, bureaucratic, or professional procedures.[39] For such procedures are likely to discourage potential helpers due to the fourfold reservation or suspicion that their active help would be useless (because isolated), or ineffective (because unprofessional), or superfluous (because the case is already under the jurisdiction of some "competent authorities"), or, finally, susceptible to exploitation (because the recipient might not "really" be in need of help).

Effective motivations to justice and solidarity are activated under the institutional, contextual conditions of the political or associational public sphere, whereas in party competition they are most likely to be neutralized and treated as insignificant in the context of the individual act of voting. In a game where everyone votes at the same time and in secret, "I" am not only protected from the threat of sanctions by "everyone else," but I also have neither cause nor occasion to take a responsible stance toward them. At the same time, I find out how everyone else has acted only after my own act of voting has been completed, at which time I therefore no longer have the opportunity to react to their actions by adopting a cooperative strategy. Moreover, the social, temporal, and substantive "real abstraction" that separates the voter from those he or she votes for, from the disputes that those elected are to decide, and from the future realities that will emerge in the course of their mandate helps to establish a "game" that does not place any significant demand on the ability of individual voters to consider moral viewpoints in their electoral decision and therefore discourages the electorate as a whole.

To a certain extent, a responsible and adequate consideration of the vulnerability of human life and its natural bases is no doubt possible legally by means of regulatory policies (for instance, protecting the labor force, the environment, and health). The question, however, is whether the moral capacities that are activated by *this* mode of society's legally mediated self-binding are not inferior to other equally practicable institutional arrangements.[40] In a paper on the limits of guaranteeing security by means of legal rationality, Preuss has shown that according to the binary scheme of the rule of law, everything that is not explicitly prohibited is permitted and that in environmental protection law "technical standards ... [thus have] the function of rights to pollute the environment."[41] To that extent, regulatory legislation would explicitly exonerate actors from reflecting on the extent of their responsibility for what they do, as long as what they do remains below the (usually technically though not normatively justified) standards. Even beyond this limit, at least as long as penal provisions (and the probability of enforcement) are not truly prohibitive, there is room for morally neutralized, unremonstrable cost–benefit calculations. Such a construction evidently lends itself to cutting the level of regulation off from "social contexts, probability assumptions, values and interests and reflection on them in ... social discourse," and to making the "mutual understanding of the risk the society can reasonably enter" appear to be dispensable to a greater degree than might be the case in alternative forms of regulation.

The practically effective motivations toward justice and solidarity, as well as the range of social, substantive, and temporal applications to which these motivations extend, depend on the concrete forms of institutionalized class conflict, especially in the case of the representation of workers' interests by labor unions. It is instructive to compare West European systems of industrial relations on this point. In the extreme case of Great Britain, we find a loosely federated system of professional and sector unions that are almost exclusively substantively limited (that is, limited with respect to the substantive domain in which they act as representatives) to the distributive interests of their members in (guaranteeing) real wages and in job security. Since they partly compete against each other for members, they are incapable of long-term income policies because, in case of conflict, securing membership enrollment always takes precedence. Given these parameters, the result is as predictable as it is tragic: the British labor movement is almost completely incapable of entering into and keeping "social contracts," of maintaining its profile as trustee of universal political-moral demands and – in light of the growing defenselessness against the onslaught of the Conservative government's policies – to use labor power without letting that power dissipate (for instance, in the printing or mining industries) in what are manifestly counterproductive outbreaks of local militancy.[42]

On the other end of the continuum, we find the Swedish system of industrial relations. The wage policies of Swedish labor are highly centralized, and explicitly foster solidarity. There is a program to implement egalitarian and "active" labor market policies, in professional training, in social and taxation policies – all in cooperation with the (ruling) Social Democratic Party (SAP). These elements, as well as labor's elaborate policies concerning *production* (and not just distribution) yield a system in which moral questions concerning the continued development of social conditions according to ambitious standards of solidarity, justice, and responsibility come under the scrutiny not only of labor, but also of the public at large, as freely as they do necessarily.[43]

To be sure, the explanatory power of the institutionalist model of analysis briefly illustrated here must not be overestimated. The negative aspects of the "force" of institutional structures which unfold in the intermediate realm between individual citizens and the state's constitutional order are rather more noticeable than its positive aspects. "Unfavorable" institutional contexts will inhibit the emergence of moral discourses relatively effectively, whereas "favorable" conditions by no means guarantee their generation but – like the telos of mutual understanding built into linguistic communication – at best have the power of some "weak necessitation." The social sciences therefore cannot dispense with supplementing institutional analyses with actor-centered ones.[44]

But even if it were possible to strictly document how institutional structures and associative relations positively determine the degree to which the decisions made under these conditions measure up to standards of universalism, this would neither necessarily nor effectively lead to the recommendation of a specific institutional "design," that is, to proposals of a sectoral constitution according to the criteria mentioned above, a constitution that would ideally "match" specific interests, actors, and conflicts and would activate a maximum of moral resources. For this proposed constitution would stand in just as tenuous a relationship to the given institutional reality as a reforestation plan to an actual forest.

"Better" institutional arrangements can be introduced strategically only to a highly limited extent. This distinguishes them from organizations. The best way of trying to change institutions, as Scharpf has incisively put it, is "institutional gardening," not "institutional engineering." One of the reasons for this is the "path dependency" of the development of national and sectoral institutional orders: once a path has been chosen, it demotes any other path, which *initially* may have looked just as good, to a wrong path because the transition to the rejected path would lead across untrodden territory and would hence involve deterringly high costs; and the longer the path, the higher the costs. But this "conservatism from complexity" is not the only explanation for the noncontingency of established associative patterns and procedures. As the example of the institutional order of industrial relations shows, social power is an equally important factor. As soon as constituted social interest groups allow universalistic demands for justification and criteria of responsible self-binding to be applied against their goals and strategies, they often lose flexibility and with it the chance to prevail against their partners, opponents, and members.[45]

Suppose trade unions were to take as strong an initiative on the front of industrial policy (concerning location, technical design, labor productivity, external effects of production) and on the front of consumer policy (concerning use value and harmlessness of the products) as in their "native domain" of distribution policy. As a consequence of this broadening of its substantive domain, labor would immediately be weakened as a collective actor because the added complexity and burden of deliberating on standards of widespread, international and intertemporal solidarity would go hand in hand with a loss of strategic rationality and calculability (for opposing interests as well as for labor's own basis). This certainly holds where unions are opposed by employers' associations with the structural capacity to effectively reject the demand for an unprejudiced scrutiny of moral questions with reference to economic rationality, international competition, and the legal foundations of private ownership and investment.[46] Because of these implications for their power, only very strong unions (those that are backed by a social democratic government, as in Sweden, for instance, or by a regional communist government, as in Italy) can afford to open up their policies more or less without reservation to norm-generating discourses – or, on the other hand, very weak groups of the fundamentalist sect variety, that have nothing much to say anyway in the realm of power, and hence compensate for their lack of power by proclaiming virtues without having to take upon themselves opportunity costs by doing so.

The relations of power among social classes therefore also determine whether and to what extent institutions can be developed that provide favorable conditions for the demands of discourse ethics. In addition, political legislation and planning have only limited access to a society's institutional forms of association, interest aggregation, and conflict resolution – forms in which individuals encode their allegiances and oppositions. These institutional forms are all the more exposed to the destabilizing challenges of sociostructural and cultural change. Institutions must "fit" the social, interest, and value structure which they encounter in their respective environments and which they are supposed to embody and constitute – otherwise they all dry up and become quite implausible. This lack of structural fit is illustrated by the examples of traditional sports clubs trying to keep up with commercial fitness centers in the context of a metropolitan middle-class culture, of local social democratic clubs, large family networks, traditional academic associations, or of an institution such as the work-free Sunday.[47] Such structural changes force the elites, members, and ideological leaders of such forms of association to reflect on these discrepancies and to seek possibilities of survival and renewal.

A standard problem with these endogenously produced quests for appropriate institutional designs is how to absorb and connect heterogeneous elements; this can only be done successfully if associative structures themselves are appropriately transformed. In a negative regard, this means that socially and substantively, they must stop specializing in sharply delimited domains within the system of the social division of labor, and weaken their internal requirements for ideological consensus and cultural homogeneity. Positively, such transformations – which may be very painful in terms of organizational politics – can lead to internally pluralized networks and coalitions that reach a certain level of "abstraction" from any concrete social basis by not only allowing but even encouraging a mixture of membership motives.[48]

The dynamics of these quests for new forms of incorporating collectivities can be widely observed, and may, I believe, be inspired as well as rationalized by the moral-theoretic arguments of discourse ethics if the latter is open to institutional analyses and, in particular, begins to map out the philosophical concept of the lifeworld in sociological terms. A closer look at concrete institutions of interest mediation and political will formation may thus render the perspective of discourse ethics fruitful for a differential diagnosis showing which institutional arrangements, under the prevailing structures and conditions of the social division of labor, help agents to bear the burden of meeting the criteria of fairness, justice, and solidarity better than which other arrangements, and why. The question of which associative contexts are more conducive to the development of a decontextualized capacity for moral judgment than others may sound paradoxical, but without this kind of evaluation of associative relations, it seems, the critical potential of discourse ethics will not be fully utilized.

Notes

1 *Hegel's Political Writings* (Oxford, 1964), p. 242.
2 J. Habermas, "Wie ist Legitimität durch Legalität möglich?," *Kritische Justiz* 20:1 (1987), pp. 13f.; cf. also J. Habermas, "On Hegel's Political Writings," in Habermas, *Theory and Practice* (Boston, 1972), pp. 170ff.
3 J. Habermas, "Über Moral und Sittlichkeit – Was macht eine Lebensform rational?" in H. Schnädelbach (ed.), *Rationalität* (Frankfurt, 1984), p. 228, my emphasis.
4 Ibid., p. 231.
5 U. Beck, *Risk Society: Towards a New Modernity* (London, 1992); see p. 50 of the original edn, *Risikogesellschaft: Auf dem Weg in eine andere Moderne* (Frankfurt, 1986).
6 Beck, *Risikogesellschaft*, p. 38.
7 J. Habermas, *The New Conservatism* (Cambridge, 1989), p. 67.
8 J. Habermas, "Morality and Ethical Life: Does Hegel's Critique of Kant Apply to Discourse Ethics?" in Habermas, *Moral Consciousness and Communicative Action* (Cambridge, 1990), pp. 205, 211.
9 In order to defend the opposite thesis, one would have to respond to at least the following points: we do not know how the political and economic institutions of socialism are constituted; even if we did know it, we wouldn't know how to attain them; even if we knew that, relevant segments of the population would not be willing to embark on such a path; even if they were, there would not be sufficient warrant for thinking the conditions thus established would be workable and immune to regression; and even if that were to be the case, a large part of the social problems politically thematized today would remain unresolved.
10 On the following, see Jon Elster, *Ulysses and the Sirens*, rev. edn (Cambridge, 1984), pp. 36–111.
11 On this thesis, see J. Elster, *Sour Grapes* (Cambridge, 1983), ch. 2, as well as his "The Possibility of Rational Politics," *Archives Européennes de Sociologie* 28 (1987), p. 71.
12 Adorno mentions Ulysses' option "to listen freely to the temptresses, imagining that his freedom will be protection enough." Max Horkheimer

and Theodor W. Adorno, *Dialectic of Enlightenment* (New York, 1972), p. 59.

13 The critique of the excessive legislation of labor and its role in the distribution struggle between capital and labor follows the logic of this objection. Underlying this critique is the worry that endowing labor with secure legal status could deprive it of the ability to "rely on its own power" – in the worst-case scenario, to the point of not even being capable of successfully warding off attacks against this legally guaranteed status. On this debate, see R. Erd, *Verrechtlichung industrieller Konflikte: Normative Rahmenbedingungen des dualen Systems der Interessenvertretung* (Frankfurt, 1978). An analogous skepticism emerges with regard to the implicit mistrust that the constitutional order of the *Grundgesetz* not only professes toward the people (which is why it strengthens parties and parliaments), but also harbors against parliament itself, which is therefore placed under the supervision of the Constitutional Court. On this, see U. K. Preuss, *Legalität und Pluralismus* (Frankfurt, 1973); P. Hammans, *Das Politische Denken der neueren Staatslehre in der Bundesrepublik* (Opladen, 1987), esp. pp. 117ff. ("autoritäretatistisches Verständnis streitbarer Demokratie"); as well as O. Jung, "Volksgesetzgebung in Deutschland," *Leviathan* 15 (1987).

14 Elster, "The Possibility of Rational Politics," pp. 81ff.

15 On this variation, however, the question of how to distinguish between breaking the rules for good reasons and breaking them for bad reasons simply remains undecidable from the observer's perspective (*Ulysses and the Sirens*, pp. 108ff.).

16 Page numbers cited in the text are from the edition cited in note 12 above.

17 T. W. Adorno, *Negative Dialectics* (New York, 1987), p. 299.

18 On this, see J. Habermas, *The Philosophical Discourse of Modernity* (Cambridge, 1990), ch. 5.

19 Adorno, *Negative Dialectics*, p. 285.

20 Joseph A. Schumpeter, *Capitalism, Socialism and Democracy* (New York, 1950), p. 88.

21 W. Benjamin, "Central Park," *New German Critique* 34 (Winter 1985), p. 50.

22 *Briefe*, ed. G. Scholem and T. W. Adorno (Frankfurt, 1966), p. 840.

23 W. Benjamin, "Theses on the Philosophy of History," in Benjamin, *Illuminations* (New York, 1969), p. 260.

24 Cf. J. Habermas, "Walter Benjamin: Consciousness-Raising or Rescuing Critique," in *Philosophical-Political Profiles* (Cambridge, Mass., 1983), esp. p. 157.

25 W. Benjamin, *Gesammelte Schriften* (Frankfurt, 1974), vol. 1.3, pp. 1231f.

26 This is Elster's thesis in "The Possibility of Rational Politics."

27 Cf. Hegel's critique of fundamentalism in G. W. F. Hegel, *Phenomenology of Spirit* (Oxford, 1977), pp. 403–5: "the consciousness of duty maintains an attitude of *passive* apprehension ... It does well to preserve itself in its purity, for it *does not act*; it is the hypocrisy which wants its judgment to be taken for an *actual* deed, and instead of proving its rectitude by actions, does so by uttering fine sentiments." The moralizing fundamentalist follows an "urge to secure his own happiness, even though this were to consist merely in an inner moral concept, in the enjoyment of being conscious of his own superiority and in the foretaste of a hope of future happiness ... [this consciousness that sets] itself above the deeds it discredits, and want[s] its words without deeds to be taken for a superior kind of *reality*."

28 Habermas, "Wie is Legitimität durch Legalität möglich?" p. 14.
29 Ibid., p. 16.
30 Ibid.
31 Habermas, "Morality and Ethical Life," p. 199.
32 In connection with Habermas, compare Talcott Parsons and the American legal theorist D. Sciulli, "Voluntaristic Action as a Distinct Concept: Theoretical Foundations of Societal Constitutionalism," *American Sociological Review* 51 (1986).
33 Habermas, "Morality and Ethical Life," pp. 207–8, emphasis added.
34 Habermas, *The New Conservatism*, p. 65.
35 U. K. Preuss, "Die Zukunft: Müllhalde der Gegenwart," in B. Guggenberger and C. Offe (eds), *An den Grenzen der Merheitsdemokratie. Politik und Soziologie der Mehrheitsregel* (Opladen, 1984); H. Hofman, "Langzeitrisiko und Verfassung. Eine Rechtsfrage der atomaren Entsorgung," *Scheidewege* 10 (1980).
36 Cf. *Hegel's Philosophy of Right* (Oxford, 1967), §254ff., p. 154.
37 R. E. Goodin, "Laundering Preferences," in J. Elster and A. Hylland (eds), *Foundations of Social Choice Theory* (Cambridge, 1986), p. 87.
38 This problem and the possibilities of dealing with it by means of norms, contrasts, and institutions is the subject of a broad "micro-Hobbesian" literature. Cf. M. Olson Jr, *The Logic of Collective Action* (Cambridge, 1965); E. Ullmann-Margalit, *The Emergence of Norms* (Oxford, 1977); R. Axelrod, *The Evolution of Cooperation* (New York, 1984); and M. Taylor, *The Possibility of Cooperation* (Cambridge, 1987).
39 On the motivating effects and transaction costs of institutional arrangements of the social welfare state, see R. G. Heinze, T. Olk and J. Hilbert, *Der neue Sozialstaat: Analyse und Reformperspektiven* (Freiburg, 1988); chapter 8 below; as well as, more generally, Habermas, *The New Conservatism*, esp. pp. 48–70. These findings have also led to proposals of explicitly particularistic, not just antibureaucratic, but also antiegalitarian solutions; e.g., P. L. Berger and R. L. Neuhaus, *To Empower People: The Role of Mediating Structures in Public Policy* (Washington, 1977).
40 For instance, contractually negotiated agreements for self-limitation; on this, see H. Voelzkow, "Organisierte Wirtschaftsinteressen in der Umweltpolitik: Eine Untersuchung über Ordnungspolitische Optionen einer Reorganisation des Verbandswesens," unpublished research paper, Bielefeld, 1985.
41 U. K. Preuss, "Sicherheit durch Recht-Rationalitätsgrenzen eines Konzepts," *Kritische Vierteljahresschrift für Gesetzgebung und Rechtswissenschaft* 3:4 (1988).
42 Cf. W. Streeck, "Staatliche Ordnungspolitik und industrielle Beziehungen..." *Politische Vierteljahresschrift* 9 (1978), as well as F. W. Scharpf, *Sozialdemokratische Krisenpolitik in Europa* (Frankfurt, 1987), pp. 97–117, 242ff.
43 Cf. U. Himmelstrand et al., *Beyond Welfare Capitalism: Issues, Actors and Forces in Societal Change* (London, 1981); R. Meidner and A. Hedberg, *Modell Schweden: Erfahrungen einer Wohlfahrtsgesellschaft* (Frankfurt, 1984).
44 Cf. F. W. Scharpf, "Decision Rules, Decision Styles and Policy Choices," Max Planck Institute for Social Research, Discussion Paper 88/3, Cologne, 1988.

45 This dilemma may explain the harshness of the "Lafontain debate" between German labor and the Social Democratic movement in 1988.

46 C. Offe and H. Wiesenthal, "Two Logics of Collective Action: Theoretical Notes on Social Class and Organizational Form," in Offe, *Disorganized Capitalism* (Cambridge, 1985). For criticism of this view, cf. W. Streeck, "Interest Heterogeneity and Organizing Capacity: Two Class Logics of Collective Action?" in R. M. Czada and A. Windhoff-Heretier (eds), *Political Choice: Institutions, Rules, and the Limits of Rationality* (Boulder, Colo., 1991).

47 For a convincing analysis of the political consequences of the erosive pressure to which this and other institutions are subject, see esp. W. Streeck, "Vielfalt und Interdependenz: Überlegungen zur Rolle von intermediären Organisationen in sichändernden Umwelten," *Kölner Zeitschrift für Soziologie und Sozialpsychologie* 39 (1987).

48 The rational concept of collective actors has been analyzed by H. Wiesenthal with respect to several institutions. Cf. H. Wiesenthal, *Strategie und Illusion: Rationalitätsgrenzen kollektiver Akteure am Beispiel der Arbeitspolitik 1980–1985* (Frankfurt, 1987), esp. pp. 332ff. ("Verzicht auf eine falsche Homogenitätsunterstellung"), as well as his "Ökologischer Konsum – ein Allgemeininteresse ohne Mobilisierungskraft?" unpublished manuscript, Bielefeld, 1988.

PART II

State Theory: Continuities and Reorientation

3

The Theory of the State in Search of its Subject Matter: Observations on Current Debates

Hermann Heller conceptualized the modern, sovereign nation-state as the "externally and internally autonomous unit of authority maintaining its effectiveness with its own means of power, of which the territory and personnel are clearly circumscribed." Heller sees the function of this unit of state power "in the independent organization and activation of cooperation in a territorially defined society founded on the fact that in accordance with historical circumstances, it is necessary for all the contrasting interests in a particular all-encompassing territory to adhere to a common *status vivendi*." This extremely ambitious concept of the state which Heller developed includes in particular "the relative autonomy of the state function" that can only be served "from a perspective that is superordinated to the economy." According to Heller, the task of a theory of the state consists in the attempt "to substantiate the state as an actual uniform center of action among the great number of actual and autonomous, individual or collective centers of action." He answers this question by conceiving of the state as a "sovereign decision-making and acting unit," which is authorized by the subject it rules.[1]

This theory of the state (which was after all conceived during the end phase of the Weimar Republic and emphasized sovereignty, uniformity, and the state's autonomy in respect to societal centers of action) characterizes a point of view from which social and political science have increasingly been dissociating themselves since the end of World War II. In the Federal Republic of Germany, activist and rationalist conceptions of the state[2] experienced a certain, albeit short-lived and theoretically relatively uninfluential, renaissance only in connection with the planning and reform perspectives proclaimed by the administration led by the Social Democrats in the late 1960s and early 1970s. It is peculiar that the subsequent theoretical and normative debate on the state, as well as empirical research in all camps of political theory, very determinately broke away from this tradition.

This by no means applies only to the *neoconservative* or neoliberal political analysis that confronts revived proposals for a "strong" and rationalist etatism with the normative objection that this must amount to both an infringement on freedom and the functional state failures that contribute to the condition of "ungovernability."[3] Efforts to approach the analysis of political processes by means of theories of *pluralism*, which had long dominated the English-language literature, tended also, due to the nature of their basic concepts, to interpret the state not as a sovereign and autonomous unit of action but as the total of reflexes and resultants of particular societal centers of action. The "derived" character of state action was obvious to the multifaceted *Marxist* discussion anyway, even if it was based on different premises, that is, premises established by class theory; accordingly, Marxist theory of the state was essentially developed as "demystification" aimed at reducing the state to zero. *Systems theory* (Luhmann) arrived at analogous results, although it adheres to a different perspective. Its more recent results have contributed to the "disenchantment of the state" (Helmut Willke) and taken great pleasure in taking apart the idea that something like a superordinated, sovereign-ruling authority which is furnished with organizational competencies and global responsibility could possibly exist in "modern," functionally differentiated societies. This idea became even less acceptable because of the belief that state and politics were in reality only one of many other blind, callous, and self-concerned centers of action whose synthesis and cooperation could not be controlled from any conceivable "top" within the global social system.

These findings and positions strikingly agree in their skepticism toward the ability of developed capitalist industrialized societies to influence themselves and their future development by means of rational government planning, control, and intervention. Supporters of this skeptical diagnosis do not at all accept as counterevidence the continual growth of fiscal and personnel resources which the state machinery has been appropriating, and the equally rapid increase of the state's legal, regulatory, and other interventions; on the contrary, and only seemingly paradoxically, these symptoms are taken to confirm the skeptical view. Many of the familiar individual observations and analyses can be summarized in the following patterns of argumentation. The more extensive the state's claims to the right to organize and regulate societal affairs become, and the more the concomitant deployment of resources by the state increases, the more hopeless, at the same time, becomes the claim to (1) sovereign and "binding" as well as (2) "rational" decision-making. For on the one hand, the claim to sovereign, imperative, and obligatory decision-making suffers from the continuous expansion of the subject area in which such decision-making is supposed to take place. The affairs that are to be regulated can only be dealt with if the state *cooperates* with the addressees of the state's orders. Consequently, these addressees have to be granted formal veto power, political bargaining positions, and factual opportunities to obstruct the state's efforts. And on the other hand, and quite independently of this, the state's claim to rational decision-making suffers from the fact that a multiplication of the responsibilities is accompanied by a corresponding increase in instances, authorities, and administrative agents. This results in an internal pluralization and fragmentation of departmental perspectives within the administration, an escalation of the respective rivalries, and, on the whole, an increasing unpredictability of the resulting long-term and "synergetic" effects of individual policies which are nearly impossible to coordinate. Such contradictions between the increase in tasks and the loss of authority and rationality, between increasing assumed responsibilities for societal problems and decreasing regulatory capacities as a consequence of this, are too familiar and ubiquitous to disqualify theoretical generalizations about such paradoxes as an indication of ideological biases of the respective authors. Today, the phrase "decomposition of state power by increase of functions"[4] can be considered an accepted fundamental idea in the evaluation of increased government activity.

Attempts to explain these joint processes of proliferation and shrinkage (which can be observed simultaneously, mutually presuppose one another, and only seem paradoxical) are aided a great deal by the reference, elaborated in Marxist tradition,[5] to the still "liberal" elements in the institutional structure of democratic welfare states. But this is probably not sufficient. It is correct that by protecting and guaranteeing the organization of private property and by making the state in its quality as an interventionist and regulatory state financially depend on the unimpeded reproduction of this economic organization, the state's liberal constitutional organization provides those societal actors whose interests cause the failure of global government strategies with the legal positions that enable them to resist and obstruct "rational" policies. This shows that the state's power is constrained by the very same social and economic mechanism that the state institutionalizes and protects. To maintain the "sovereignty," authority and rationality of government action, these constraints would have to be made permeable, and their continued existence must conversely be paid for with the mentioned losses of authority and rationality.

But these are not the only limits at which the classical project of a global and authoritative statist model fails. From contexts of the state's "cultural" and "socialization" policies (education, crime, media, family, and other "cultural" policy areas, which have recently been the topic of many discussions), it is known that the means (of allotting rights, fiscal resources, and most professional services) available to the state are in effect categorically unsuited to exert regulatory and normalizing influence on societal problems, even though politicians might have recognized them and might have admitted that they are in need of regulation. The intransigence of the structures and social facts that cause the state's policies to fail is not constituted by legal or constitutional guarantees themselves – as is the case with the property relations that are guaranteed by the "capitalist" state. Rather, it must be linked to the "stubbornness" of the traditions, facts, and pathologies of the state's societal "environment." In respect to these (as in the cases of drugs, crime, and many health, family, rehabilitation, poverty, and sex-role problems), any attempt to accomplish anything with the state's traditional means of intervention proves to be a basically inadequate approach, at best useless, sometimes counterproductive.[6]

It seems that it is possible to discern three categories of reasons why the idea of state sovereignty proclaimed by Hermann Heller appears obsolete today. First, it is a matter of the – either institutionally protected "material" or "cultural" – restrictions on the state's regulatory activity, which assert themselves in the societal environment of public policies. Second – and this fact was pointed out in the discussion on positive coordination and "policy coordination" initiated in Germany by Scharpf[7] – it is a matter of the paralyzing internal complexity of highly developed state machineries, whose structure is infiltrated by particularism, symbiotic relationships with individual sectors of the environment, rivalries, manipulations that distort the flow of information, etc. As a result, it is no longer possible to speak, as Heller did, of the state as "a coherent unit of control" in a strict sense. A third set of observable factors giving rise to skeptical evaluations of demands made of the state for autonomy and rationality are the obvious losses of sovereignty that the state is suffering by surrendering strategic policy-making capacities to the "past" and/or to other states or supranational organizations. The first of these two aspects becomes apparent in budget planners' usual complaint about the burden of deficits (accumulated in the past) or legal spending liabilities which shrink the nonallotted portion of the budget available for "active" policies to a trivial remainder. The second aspect, even more important, refers to the exhaustion of the opportunities for nation-states to make plans, which occurred in the course of supranational integration in the economic and military, as well as the legal and sociopolitical spheres, and its requirements for coordination and "harmonization."

In view of these three cumulative sets of factors, it seems as if a reversal has taken place in the long-term development that characterized the evolution of the modern state for centuries, at least in continental Europe: namely, the development that brought about territorial centralization, the effective establishment of a power monopoly, and the political expropriation and subjugation of all secular and ecclesiastical powers inside the state.[8] In contrast to this development (which had been considered dominant and largely irreversible), we observe centrifugal processes and a dispersion of competencies and regulatory authorities. Apparently, important public duties have moved to para-constitutional authorities and procedures, in which the state participates more – if it does at all – in the function of a coordinator or moderator than as a sovereign authority giving orders and exerting power. Formally "private" associations such as trade associations, professional organizations, welfare associations, labor unions together with corporations such as chambers of commerce, and organized science are part of a system of arenas, forums, military-industrial (and also civilian-industrial) complexes and negotiating networks that have soaked up sovereign functions and in this sense "deprived" the state of its functions by making them "societal." With respect to these phenomena, a vast amount of research literature has been developing since the mid-1970s that revolves around terms like neocorporatism, "private governments," refeudalization, "new subsidiarity," etc. These collective actors are bestowed with quasi-sovereign functions (or usurp these functions), and relieve (and thereby deprive) the state of a number of responsibilities, primarily of those belonging to the area of what in the German tradition is known as *Leistungsverwaltung*, or state-organized provision of goods and services.

But even in the area of the "administration of formal rules" (that is, the more traditional area of maintaining law and order, or *Ordnungsverwaltung*), societal institutions and collective actors in many capitalist democracies have successfully opened gaps in the system of the state's power monopoly. These forces include "new social movements" which are pacifist, against nuclear energy, autonomist, regionalist, urbanist, etc. They illustrate the "limits of institutional politics in the modern state," at least for the duration of escalated disputes, and generate the kind of interpretation that (summarizing the finds of a study on a protest movement against an airport construction project in Japan) Apter formulated in this way: "The state itself is no longer an appropriate instrument of modern life and ... its institutions are less and less effective in promoting development, rationality, control and power."[9]

Naturally a broad spectrum of theoretical and politically motivated differences of opinion has existed on the range, the possible reversibility, and finally also the normative evaluation of such centrifugal trends which contribute to the partial dissolution of the state's sovereignty, authority, and rationality. Regarding the state of the debate in the 1980s in West Germany, the prevailing opinion was that of those who, for a number of – however divergent – ideological reasons (namely neoliberal, neoconservative, but also libertarian socialist) and theoretical perspectives (such as systems theory, modernization theory), considered the symptoms just summarized of a decomposition of state power not only as inevitable and irreversible, but also as desirable. As the draft for the 1986 SPD platform showed, Social Democratic theoreticians and policy planners were virtually the only ones to continue to think in terms of a traditional etatist model of public responsibility and state regulation. In doing this, they set themselves off against the ubiquitous proposals for delegation, deregulation, and denationalization, on the one hand, and "autonomist" concepts of self-administration, self-help and decentralization, on the other.

The Social Democrats interpreted expansively the formula that the state ought to serve "a function of preservation, protection and change, which is necessary for society and guarantees its continued existence."[10] As a result, the state ought to be furnished with the fiscal and legal-institutional resources necessary to serve this function. Indeed, it is difficult to imagine how it could be possible to manage pressing sociopolitical, economic, political, ecological, technological, and even international problems and crisis trends, without an institutional machinery (such as the "strong" state) that enables society to exert an effective and rational influence upon itself. Particularly from the perspective of necessary and desirable socioeconomic changes, there is no reliable substitute for the state-mediated mode of society's influence over itself – a circumstance apparently not taken seriously by authors resigned to "evolution" and just registering the decomposition of state power, responding to it with either postmodernist amusement or with anarchoid visions. The new social movements and the political formations that developed from them have frequently, and with good reasons, been remonstrated for the inconsistency inherent in the fact that, on the one hand, they subscribe to antistatist slogans and the fundamentalist critique of the state's "monopoly of force," while on the other hand, they propose large doses of state resources (both fiscal and repressive) to be made available to the causes of desired social change. Consequently, it is no wonder that particularly in the Anglo-Saxon countries (and most clearly in the United States and Great Britain, both of which have undergone the experience of "anti-etatism in power"), there are more and more voices – even on the non-Social-Democratic left – warning of a global and mindless radicalism critical of the state, and trying to reemphasize such self-evident truths as: "The transition from capitalism to socialism is most unlikely to be accomplished without the creation of nationally coordinating, adjudicating, and representative bodies."[11]

Parallel new theoretical approaches in political sociology correspond to these political reorientations, in which the left rediscovered and started to appreciate the potential and promise of "strong" public policies. For example, the editors and authors of an influential anthology with the programmatic title "Bringing the State Back In" argued for an antireductionist research program and a "paradigmatic reorientation." Authors who "have considered states as weighty actors and probed the way in which states affect political and social processes through their policies and their patterned relationship with social groups"[12] are representative of this orientation, which is post-Marxist and postpluralist at the same time. It seems to be equally questionable for normative and theoretical reasons whether the trends of decomposition and dispersion of the state's sovereignty, authority, and rationality that have been observed nearly everywhere will result in a new balance of self-regulatory "coevolution" (Luhmann) of societal subsystems or rather in aggravated risks to stability and to new cleavages within the national (and international) society, and overall to aggravated anarchic and anomic dynamics.

If the second alternative proves the more realistic one (as I think it will), we are caught in a dilemma of "societal guidance" and regulatory policy-making. At first sight, this quandary would only offer the choice between a hopeless, if not counterproductive, revival of traditional statist forms of planning, control, and intervention, and scarcely founded confidence in the forces of spontaneous self-coordination. Given the fact, however, that the restoration of a "strong" and autonomous bureaucratic control of the administrative state appears neither promising nor attractive, and that the liberal/libertarian alternative does not seem to be tolerable either, novel and important questions about the nature and conditions of the implementation of "institutional designs" which provide a way out of this dilemma arise for social and political theory.

From the early 1980s, an intense, theoretically highly ambitious, and ideologically remarkably neutral debate concerning new forms and mechanisms of macrosteering and coordination emerged in the Federal Republic. The focus of this discussion was on questions of the conditions of a simultaneously post-etatist and postliberal conception of sociopolitical "order."

I would like to take up only one thought from this complex and by no means concluded discussion. The diagnosis that there are definite limits to the potential performance and rationality inherent in the state's specific means of intervention (namely, positive law, physical force, and the extraction and redistribution of fiscal resources) focused attention on functional equivalents and possibly more effective alternatives to these means that might accomplish higher standards of regulatory activity and intervention. Comparative studies of such alternative, paragovernmental regulatory mechanisms elucidate the great significance of repertoires of traditions, symbols, institutional patterns, and established routines that are characteristic for individual nations. In other words, what becomes obvious is that countries like Sweden or Austria have resources of historically grown political practices, routines, and nationwide shared assumptions that allow problems to be successfully regulated outside the formal channels of mass democracy and administrative policy implementation – problems which it is hardly possible to regulate in other countries (such as Great Britain) because of the absence of the appropriate traditions and institutional patterns. Although such distinctive institutional practices can be maintained and cultivated in those countries where they exist as the formative heritage of national history, it is not easy to create them deliberately or produce them by means of constitutional policy in countries where they do not exist.

In principle, it is conceivable that the dilemma between the decline of the state's structures of sovereignty and the fact that it is impossible to do without an authority of societal control able to claim "global responsibility" could be solved if the state gave up the (hopeless) attempt to establish itself as the controlling, planning, and regulating pinnacle that claims global responsibility for the entire society. Instead it would have to initiate and steer through paragovernmental procedures for establishing compromises and methods of global control whose function would be to make tolerable the limits of government action (which are insurmountable in complex societies) and to make available alternatives or substitutes able to serve those functions that can no longer be served in an "authoritative" manner. Consequently, the basic idea is to develop the state's policy to "unburden" the state – a policy characterized by the fact that the state would "devolve" institutional structures, procedures, participative conditions and competencies into the society and its associations. Beyond legal supervision and due process, such an "unburdening" of the state would offer the opportunity to do without further activity in those areas where the state has given up its exclusive domain of authoritative decision- and policy-making. This would also avoid the danger that these areas would regress into the anarchy of market processes or of dynamics determined by particular interests. Instead of decreeing and putting through actual rules in an authoritative manner, the state would consequently limit its activity to formally authorizing paragovernmental representative actors and producing such rules by continually balancing through due process and negotiations.

This attractive idea of the state's ordered retreat (which methodically avoids the development of regulatory gaps) behind lines of this sort, which it could anyway only cross by counterproductively and irrationally assuming responsibilities, has attracted great interest in the context of the discussion on corporatism.[13] As a result, interest was renewed – under different premises – in a problem which Social Democrats in the Weimar Republic and Austrian Marxists of the period between the wars (J. Bauer, E. Fraenkel, F. Naphtali) dealt with under catchwords like "economic democracy," "functional democracy," and "collective democracy." However, the chances of such a dialectic turn, which would result in the state's affirmation of its integrative role through abandoning and delegating many of its own responsibilities, seems to depend on three preconditions.

1 Such a governmentally arranged shift in the state's functions would have to be initiated by an extremely "strong" state that has a high degree of authority and rationality; in other words, a state that only has an extremely small structural need for such a solution. Only a state for which the problem was not acute – and vice versa – could solve this problem. On the basis of his insight, which was as desperate as it was great, in 1932 Ernst Fraenkel summarized this connection, which is fundamental for many projects of institutional reform: "If the current Reichstag were able to accomplish a constitutional reform, this constitutional reform would be superfluous. Its necessity results from the fact that it is impossible to have Parliament carry out constitutional reform."[14] The fact that only a "strong" state is able to retreat on its own account also results from the fact that the proper maintenance of the societal negotiation procedures replacing the state's authority

would not only require effective legal supervision but also the permanent and credible threat that in the case of aberrations, rule violations, etc., government organs would be able to step in at any time by deploying their own means of intervention.

2 Second, it is to be expected that the state's formal surrender of its regulatory competence to societal actors will commit these to explicitly and publicly accepting responsibilities that they can assume at most implicitly, informally, and as the secondary result of other declared functions. This would allow the – again only seemingly paradoxical – conclusion that the assignment of public duties to paragovernmental actors would no longer be possible the moment it was *intended* as an explicit assignment of formal competence. For such an assignment would require collective actors to redefine drastically their responsibilities and to solve many ensuing conflicts with (and within) their respective constituencies.

3 Third, due to the distinct differences among the institutional repertoires of the Western European nation-states mentioned above, there is finally the question of whether the culturally and historically determined practices, styles, and routines, on whose efficiency a state-initiated policy of retreat of the state would have to be able to rely, are in fact available or can be activated in all countries. In relation to this problem, the hypothesis seems obvious that these conditions are more likely to exist in relatively small and culturally homogeneous national societies with limited supranational integration than in countries such as Great Britain or Germany.

Notes

1 Hermann Heller, *Staatslehre*, 6th edn (Tübingen, 1983), pp. 142, 230, 222, 224, 260, 278.
2 Renate Mayntz and Fritz W. Scharpf (eds), *Planungsorganisation* (Munich, 1973).
3 Influential examples of this approach include Samuel Huntington, "The United States," in M. Crozier et al., *The Crisis of Democracy* (New York, 1975); Niklas Luhmann, *Politische Theorie im Wohlfahrtsstaat* (Munich and Vienna, 1981). On the topic of ungovernability, see Claus Offe, " 'Unregierbarkeit' – Zur Renaissance konservativer Krisentheorie," in J. Habermas (ed.), *Stichworte zur geistigen Situation der Zeit* (Frankfurt, 1979).
4 Dieter Grimm, "The Modern State: Continental Traditions," in F.-X. Kaufmann, G. Majone and V. Ostrom (eds), *Guidance, Control and Evaluation in the Public Sector* (New York and Berlin, 1986), p. 104.
5 Cf. Bob Jessop, *The Capitalist State* (Oxford, 1982).

6 Jürgen Habermas, *Theorie des kommunikativen Handelns*, vol. 2 (Frankfurt, 1981), pp. 504–47; in English as *The Theory of Communicative Action*, vol. 2 (Cambridge, 1989).

7 Fritz W. Scharpf, *Planung als politischer Prozess* (Frankfurt, 1973); Fritz W. Scharpf, Bernd Reissert and Fritz Schnabel, *Politikverflechtung. Theorie und Empirie des kooperativen Föderalismus in der Bundesrepublik* (Königstein, 1976).

8 Grimm, *The Modern State*; Ernst-Wolfgang Böckenförde, "Die Bedeutung der Unterscheidung von Staat und Gesellschaft im demokratischen Sozialstaat der Gegenwart," in *Staat, Gesellschaft, Freiheit* (Frankfurt, 1976), pp. 185ff.; and Norbert Elias's study on "Sociogenesis of the State," in *Der Prozess der Zivilisation*, vol. 2 (Frankfurt, 1976), in English as *The Civilizing Process* (1-vol. edn, Oxford, 1994).

9 David E. Apter and Nagayo Sawa, *Against the State: Politics and Social Protest in Japan* (Cambridge, 1984), pp. 226ff., 242.

10 Böckenförde, "Die Bedeutung der Unterscheidung von Staat und Gesellschaft," p. 193.

11 B. Frankel, *Beyond the State? Dominant Theories and Socialist Strategies* (London, 1983), pp. 263ff.

12 Theda Skocpol, in Peter B. Evans et al. (eds), *Bringing the State Back In* (Cambridge, 1985), p. 3.

13 Wolfgang Streeck and Philippe Schmitter, "Community, Market, State and Associations?" *European Sociological Review* 1 (1985); on the following, also Claus Offe, "Korporatismus als System nicht-staatlicher Makrosteuerung? Notizen über seine Voraussetzungen und demokratischen Gehalte," *Geschichte und Gesellschaft* 10 (1984).

14 Author's translation from Ernst Fraenkel, "Verfassungsreform und Sozialdemokratie," reprinted in *Zur Soziologie der Klassenjustiz* (Darmstadt, 1968), p. 102.

4

Social-Scientific Aspects of the Regulation–Deregulation Debate

In the name of increased economic efficiency, and in the interests of an expanded freedom of economic action, the political-theoretical demand for, and practice of, deregulation is directed at an alleged excess of state norms, rules, and prescriptions. Deregulation seeks its political justification in an argument which attempts to discredit postwar state regulation by showing it to be ineffective, mistaken, and unsustainable in the light of experience. Since the mid-1970s the debate, conducted mostly by economists but also by political scientists and sociologists, between supporters and opponents of state intervention has resulted in a clear "victory on points" for the latter.

The opponents of state regulation owe their attacking advantage not merely to the strength of the arguments they put forward or the empirical relationships they reveal, but also to the fact that, in Western Europe and North America, there exists a conjuncture of political-ideological, philosophical, and cultural developments which fits well with their position. There are theoretical-ideological affinities between arguments for deregulation and the political positions of neoconservative and market liberal political parties. These are as unmistakable as those between these arguments and "postmodern" cultural phenomena, which on both political and aesthetic planes promote flexibility and an "indeterminate evolution."

In both cases, the possibility of developing binding norms for action is disputed. Barriers, fetters, investment handicaps and other restrictions, which were supposedly rationally justified, are to be set aside, and experiment, mutation, and innovation set free. This methodical derestriction has to be seen not only in the context of economic policy, but also in a cultural-political context. Here, there is an objective derestriction which results from the globalization of competitive relationships, interdependencies, and information flows, and conversely from the growing porosity of national and regional barriers and borders. In this sense there is a relationship of mutual effect between objective losses of autarky and of immunity to global influence on the one hand, and the discouragement of attempts at internal regulation on the other. So the contemporary dilemma of regulative policy may partly be connected with the fact that only relatively well-protected internal realms may be regulated reliably and without consequent harm, while the intensification of competitive relationships and influences on a global scale makes a regulative policy restricted to a national state framework appear unpredictable and without any prospect of success.

The arguments in favour of the state regulation of economic activity arise out of the theory of market failure. This specifies the cases in which markets cannot fulfill their function of providing for free, equal, and efficient transactions, or can do so only with harmful side effects. Thus, for example, markets fail where:

- there are so-called "natural monopolies," in which (as with bridges over rivers) the introduction of competition would lead to an increase in production costs, ruinous forms of competition, or ultimately underproduction;
- external effects appear which are not reflected by the market in the form of price signals; these might be negative effects on a third party not taking part in the transaction; or the parties to the transaction might become victims of distant effects they themselves brought about, albeit at a later date;
- there are so-called "meritorious" goods (for instance, in health care), whose production would certainly benefit all, but for which, due to a typically inadequate steering of preferences, there is insufficient demand, and which the market therefore supplies to an insufficient degree;
- there is an information gap between supplier and consumer, so that in a typical case (as with the products of the pharmaceutical industry) it is impossible for the purchaser to judge a commodity's positive or negative consumer value. Structural asymmetries between market partners can also rest upon basic differences in adaptive capacity; this is typically the case in labor markets. In both cases a formally egalitarian market relationship turns into one of power or dependence.

According to the arguments of advocates of regulative state ntervention, in these and comparable cases the issuing of specific prohibitions and orders valid for particular actors and particular actions is justified and thoroughly compatible with equality and freedom. This intervention takes the form of orders, injunctions, and contractual prohibitions. Through the latter a normative status is attached either to certain basic conditions, which encourage particular actors in particular economic sectors, or to particular product qualities or prices, so that nonlicensed suppliers, or offers forbidden on grounds of price or other criteria, are excluded from individual markets.

The opponents of state regulation have reacted to this with a series of counterarguments. Among the most popular are the arguments that, in practice, state regulation is not restricted to circumstances to which the criteria above apply; that, in addition, these criteria themselves are illegitimately applied and are therefore open to interest-bound interpretations; that even where state regulation is directed unambiguously at cases of natural monopoly, meritorious goods, external effects, and asymmetric distributions of power and information, its results are in effect no better than those produced by the (supposedly suboptimal) allocation dynamic of markets. Therefore state regulation is not an appropriate remedy for market failure.

Furthermore, state regulation not only fails in its intended functions, but also produces undesired results, so that in effect it is only the type, not the level of suboptimality which is affected. Among the negative economic effects of state regulation are included the costs of setting up watchdog authorities and of continuous regulatory control; the undermining of the adaptability and innovative efficiency of regulated branches of the economy; and "exaggerated quality competition" following the prohibition of price competition.[1]

Since the end of the 1970s, above all in the United States and in Margaret Thatcher's Britain, these arguments have given cause and justification for a sometimes drastic reduction in the level of state control and regulation in several economic spheres. Among the by now classic sectors in which a drive for deregulation has gained ground are communication (television, telephone services, etc.); transport (rail, road, and air); parts of the energy sector (oil, gas); parts of the capital market (banks, insurance companies); as well as the "cross-cutting functions" of labor, environmental, and consumer protection.[2]

Deregulation as State Intervention

The advocates of deregulation take it to be empirically established that "the opening up of a market-directed allocation leads to cheaper and better products, increases consumer choice and accelerates the process of innovation."[3] But in arguments of the opponents of regulation, alongside economic objections resting on criteria of efficiency, there is also an unmistakable ideological undertone, a state-critical pathos of "negative freedom." What ought to be resisted, not only in the name of economic rationality, but also in the name of ultimate values such as individual autonomy of action and decision, are the activities of a tutelary, presumptuous, paternalist, technically incompetent, bureaucratic, and arrogant executive power, with its creeping authoritarian intention comprehensively to "shape" the conditions of existence of its citizens.

To be sure, such invocations of a market-liberal pathos of freedom fail to notice that a politics of deregulation, no less than one of regulation, has the character of a massive state "intervention." For both cases involve a decisive change in life situations and market opportunities brought about by public policy. The difference consists only in the fact that this "shaping" is brought about in the first case – that of regulation – through commission, but in the second through express omission. The latter just as much as the former is the work of public policy actors, even if this involves nothing more than the negative decision no longer to regulate the activities and life chances of citizens through "tutelary" prescriptions, prohibitions, price controls and decrees, and to do so instead through the contingent dynamics of market processes. As a consequence, through public policy decisions these dynamics are elevated to the rank of the decisive agent of regulation and as such politically licensed. In this sense, an abstention from a politics of regulation is "politics" nonetheless – as much in its intentions as in its consequences. Only here, the restrictions on freedom which originate in legislative prescription are replaced by those which emerge from the internal dynamics of market and innovation processes.

With respect to the redistribution of incomes, resources and life chances, the consequences of this interventionist policy of regulative renunciation are more decisive than is usually the case with protectionist or redistributive regulative policies oriented to social justice or a social contract – albeit with the opposite results in terms of distribution policy. A further "interventionist" characteristic of the politics of deregulation, which it shares with its opponent, is that it typically relies on policy initiatives in the fields of law, culture, and socialization. With the help of these, the values of "law and order," and "an individualism of property," are to achieve an unchallenged moral hegemony.

An interesting contradiction in the position of the opponents of regulation is revealed here. If their argumentation, based upon the values of dynamic economic efficiency and therewith upon a universal increase in welfare, were actually as compelling as they with unruffled self-assurance claim, they would have grounds to assume that the "failure" of regulation would, as it were, correct itself by virtue of a universal consciousness brought about by economic enlightenment. Nobody who continued to support proposals for regulation would stand a chance of being taken seriously. In fact, however, the project of deregulation is treated as a program which is to be brought about politically. Consciousness emerges not out of economic analysis, but out of political struggle. "The task of the government is to develop a clear will to deregulation and to become aware of the leading role it must assume in the deregulation process. Work in the public sphere may be of the profoundest significance here."[4]

Conversely, deregulation policy aims to discredit the opposing values of social justice, responsibility, and solidarity, and to restrict the room for maneuver of those who represent such values, and disorganize them (above all trade unions, professional bodies, welfare organizations, etc.).

The legislative and political weakening of associations and organized interests, in particular the denunciation of trade unions as "special interest groups" which strive to enrich themselves at the expense of the common good, formed a striking central feature of the internal politics of the Reagan administration in the US and of British Thatcherism.

Deregulation and Political Conflict: Two Interpretations

As we have seen, the advocates of deregulation are thoroughly aware that the freeing-up of market processes which they advocate cannot be accomplished without friction or on the basis of universal agreement, but only through conflict and by means of a struggle for political power. This is hardly surprising given that the politics of deregulation demands sacrifices from more or less precisely defined groups and social categories. Such sacrifices include a loss of job security, income, and housing provision, a drop in the level of transport safety and environmental quality, and effects on other important criteria of living standards, distributive justice, and quality of life. Here those who protest against such losses are by no means primarily those organized

interest associations at whom the continual judgments of the deregulation theorists are directed, but highly diffuse categories of "the
affected," who are less well organized and less well prepared for conflict.

The conflict scenario foreseen by the advocates of deregulation is
one in which there is a common good clearly deducible from economic categories, and threatened by organized interests acting out of
self-seeking and short-sighted motives. Their resistance must be
broken by political means. Only in this way can economic reason
triumph. If we accept this scenario, the question arises of how those
organized interests manage to make the mass of the population blind
to the evidence of economic relationships, and thus to stand in the
way of their collective – and individual – advantage.

No answer will be given here, but an alternative scenario will be presented. For perhaps, as I in fact maintain, the interpretation of the conflict and its parties presented by deregulation theorists is mistaken, or
ideologically distorted, from the outset. The alternative scenario inter-
prets the regulation–deregulation conflict like this. On one side are
those who wish to make possible the unconditional and unscrupulous
dominance of the categories of economic efficiency, and who become
the advocates of a "universalized egoism" (as Marx has it) promoted
by the state. On the other are those political forces, collective actors,
and cultural traditions which do not try to solve the problem of economic efficiency, social justice, and social reciprocity through a one-
dimensional "economic reason," but wish to render it less acute by
means of political compromise and in recognition of multiple value
orientations. In this alternative scenario there is a reversal of the initial
evaluations. Here, the supporters of deregulation are no longer the
shining champions of the common good, but apologists for an unlimited striving for economic growth and efficiency. Their opponents are no
longer the eulogizers of collective harm, but precisely responsible
counsel for an idea of collective utility which has room for more than
the categories of economic rationality. If one accepts this interpretation,
the opposite question arises. How are those proclaiming a "universalized egoism" able to force their opponents on to the defensive to the
extent that has been seen, at least in the USA and Britain in the 1980s?

Although these interpretations are mutually exclusive, both can
claim a certain plausibility on the basis of aspects of economic reality.
The first scenario, which equates economic reason with the common
good and sets itself against the interests of those who wish to enjoy
the benefits of monopoly and protection, gains plausibility through
reference to international relationships of competition and interdependence. These give rise to the strict alternative between maximal

efficiency and innovative dynamism on the one hand, and economic decline on the other – *tertium non datur* (no third way is available). According to this argument, in a globally interconnected system from whose functional context nobody can escape, there is an imperative of increased efficiency which transcends political reason.

Conversely, the advocates of the second scenario believe that they can derive an equally compelling argument for their point of view from the stage reached by industrial capitalist development. Who but the rich societies of the West – which are growing ever richer – could relativize the imperative of economic growth and, through a politics of regulation, judge social development according to decisively noneconomic criteria? Would the resulting loss of economic efficiency not be a price worth paying? And mustn't such a sacrifice be regarded as a blessing in view of the harmful social, cultural, and ecological consequences which have been and will continue to be associated with the dominance of economic criteria of rationality?

Problems of a Social-Scientific Explanation

Such questions already give the second interpretation greater plausibility, because the reference to internationalism and interdependence on which the first relies rests on shaky ground. For the dynamics of international competition, which this interpretation sees as necessitating the unfettering of unregulated market forces, could in principle be shaped in a thoroughgoing fashion by a supranational regulative policy. This would involve either a relative sectioning off of the national economy from the world market, or conversely, internationally agreed and binding norms. The first, like the second, has been worked out theoretically and partly put into practice – under headings such as "autocentric development" or "policy regime." Thus anyone who appeals to the apparently insurmountable givenness of unregulated international competition is not referring to facts, but, under the pretext of doing so, is making an implicit plea for a policy of neglect and unconcern in this highly promising field.

This is not a wholesale denial that the interpretation presented by opponents of regulation has objective grounds. Doubtless there are cases of regulation whose intention and result is little more than to allow certain suppliers to enjoy a monopoly position based on the activities of their interest associations. But where this is the case, and such "distributive coalitions" (Mancur Olson) or "alliances for enrichment" are able to survive, a substantively different type of regulation would be called for, not – and this is the false conclusion drawn by the champions of deregulation – its abolition.

From the point of view of social and political science, once the arguments based on neoclassically inspired "economic reason," and the verdicts pronounced against regulation, have proved inadequate, there arises the question of the societal constellations and developmental tendencies which have helped this economic reason to prevail. In particular, I would like to offer some reflections on the following questions. Under what circumstances do large sections of the population find it politically acceptable to depart from the model of rationality associated with regulation policy despite the losses in welfare, security, and distributive justice associated with it? What are the difficulties faced by the champions of an "active" and ambitious regulatory policy in their attempt to reconquer terrain lost to neoliberalism and to make progress along the traditional path of a social democratic etatism of successful regulatory controls and prohibitions? What alternative strategies are available to a policy of regulative societal steering whose effectiveness and political support have obviously been weakened, but which is nevertheless in a position to avoid a retreat into the passive acceptance of market outcomes and their development?

Legitimation Problems of Regulative Policy

The more heterogeneous and "individualized" social and value structures become, the more an interest in regulation becomes a minority one. The pluralization of these structures produces a corresponding multiplication of the criteria of judgment involved in the question of which social and economic affairs should be regulated according to which standards. It is as if the many regulatory proposals, which, taken by themselves, are always minoritarian, neutralize one another and leave room only for the negative consensus that, since there is no agreement over the objects and contents of regulation, it would be better to renounce regulation altogether.

The theoretical values appealed to in regulative policy appear the less plausible the less they are rooted either in a tradition of "usage and custom" acknowledged by all those affected, or in determinate collective interests shared by broad social categories. This applies, for example, to work-free Sundays; claims about their normality and bindingness can no longer be made by referring to the value of "family life." A large minority of workers does not even live in family units, and the supplementary income to be earned on Sundays leads to a declining interest in work-free weekends even among family members, despite a considerable loss in the value of the consequently nonsynchronized leisure time.

The social-structural basis of collectivism grows weaker, and with it the plausibility of rules for the coding of membership. An indirect index of this "peaceful death of the regular customer" (Wolfgang Streeck) is the exaggerated attempt of political and associational elites to communicate to their bases models of collective identity (such as the slogan of the Social Democrats: "We in North Rhine Westphalia"). Another is the noticeable primitiveness of those proposals of self-categorization in which, with ever greater frequency, appeal is made not to social-structural characteristics but directly to natural and ascriptive ones (such as gender, nation, homeland, ethnic member-ship, or age).

In addition, the "limit values" and rules according to which regula-tive policy can be conducted are often oriented not to examples rest-ing on tradition (for example, the shape of the roofs in an old settlement area, with its valued building material) but to ultimate, mostly preventative statements by technicians and scientists, who recommend these regulative values and often prescribe them by reference to values such as those of security and health. Or these regu-lative and limit values emerge from processes of negotiation involving representatives of economic and professional associations, trade unions and industry-related institutions. As a consequence of this, the suspicion often arises that in the establishment of norms account is being taken not only of a universal interest in security, but of the particular interests of particular groups (such as electricians, or even teachers).

The norms of regulative policies lose their plausibility for two reasons: because of a pluralization of interests and values within the social structure; and because of the "technical" nature of a process of norm formation which does not completely transcend particular interests. And the more this happens, the more they lose their acceptance and "innocence." They are experienced as potential encroachments on independence and decision-making capacities, and as sources of inefficiency, lack of initiative, and inflexibility – and experienced as such not only from the biased point of view of the market-liberal champions of "negative freedom."

This lack of enthusiasm concerns not only public policy and its bureaucratic executors, but also the associative substructure of those trade unions and organizations which are legislatively and adminis-tratively involved in the process of deregulation. To the extent that regulatory goals lack social support and collective plausibility, the associations and trade unions wishing to steel themselves for such goals will themselves be placed under internal stress whenever they try to commit themselves to desirable, universally acceptable and binding norms. The problem of regulation consists above all in holding the members of certain social categories to the standards according to which regulation is to take place.

Debates over shop opening hours prove how difficult it has become, in view of the diverse interest situations of suppliers and consumers, forms and branches of commerce, city and country, to introduce proposals for regulation which would be even halfway enlightened or sustainable, and which would not immediately be suspected of being the expression of minority interests. In several political spheres, especially those of ecology and health, a "naturalistic" substitute for consensus may then be established, derived from a high-dosage rhetoric of *Angst* and the apocalyptic visions associated with it. But where the strong medicine of imagined or very real visions of a physical threat to life has to be applied in order to compel agreement to regulative standards, the acute shortage of other common, genuinely political or moral standards becomes clear.

The Efficiency of Regulative Politics

There are signs that the means of intervention hitherto employed by regulative policy, namely money and law, are becoming unsuitable as providers of order and guarantors of security, and that they are even bringing with them counterproductive consequences. According to the significance of these signs, one can expect that the confidence in the efficiency of the interventionary methods employed by regulative policy is likely to be exhausted. This is true as much for administrators and political elites as for voters and the addressees of norms. Expressed in game-theoretical jargon: if "I," due to a perceptibly weaker binding effect of moral norms, have cause to expect that the regulations issued by the state will not automatically and spontaneously be followed by "everyone else," or that the number of norm violators is not so small that they can be effectively controlled through state supervision or threat of punishment, then "I" will also withdraw my support for regulative policy whenever the following of its norms burdens me with competitive disadvantages. As soon as "I" begin to put into practice the consequences for conduct which follow from this, "everyone else" gets practical confirmation of the negative expectations he or she harbored from the outset, and therewith of the rationality of my action.

This model, of a self-sustaining process of moral erosion, is an appropriate one, if not for a description of reality, then at least for an illumination of the conditions in which regulative policy is carried out. An initial assumption must be that regulative policy's legal rules would have to be meaningful and plausible for administrators and addressees if they were to fulfill their purpose. Formally, as legal orders as such, *and* as norms with a substantive content, they must impinge on "corresponding" dispositions, on a certain degree of prudent willingness to follow them. But that means in turn that neither the state's authority to regulate a particular sphere (a negative case is the liberal-populist slogan "free movement for free citizens") nor the substantive reasonableness of a rule (based on the general assumption that the originator of a norm "will already have given the matter sufficient thought") can be called into question to any significant degree.

However, the emergence of widespread ethical dispositions corresponding to regulative policy is made unlikely by the fact that in many spheres the standards and values of regulative policy can in no way be derived from lifeworld norms or from a repertoire of self-evident good manners. Nor are they based on an explicit political will-formation concerning the standards on which citizens wish to agree in a reasonable and responsible manner. Rather, they rest increasingly on technical-scientific expert knowledge (of nutritionists, labor experts, environmental experts, etc.), and increasingly assume a variable character (according to "the state of science and technology"). This, and the manifest difficulties which experts have in agreeing with one another, undermines confidence in the substantive content of legal regulations.

Formal acknowledgment of such regulations is made less likely when the right of public policy to regulate certain spheres and to encroach on citizens' rights to "negative" freedom is disputed. Regulative norms also lose their plausibility, their recognition as purposeful and meaningful restrictions on action, when there is a large dissimilarity between the activities to be regulated. This can be made clear from the simple example of the regulation of traffic by means of speed limits. A speed limit valid for all and for ever is implausible, because a constant level of road safety obviously requires the observation of certain speed limits only in certain types of traffic. Consequently, a fixed norm can be criticized as a sign of a lack of administrative competence and of a failure to take into account obvious shifts in the amount of regulation required.

Conversely, a government may regulate flexibly, varying speed limits, for example, as in the United States, between day and night, or, as happens frequently in Germany, between wet roads and dry roads, or between cars and lorries. But it is part of the logic of such differentiations, which are concerned to "do justice to circumstances," or to be "comprehensible," that they provoke the additional question of whether further differentiations should not be made according to variables such as season, traffic density, or the technical quality of the braking systems of individual vehicles. But the attempt to address such questions positively would soon run up against barriers to implementation, or indeed to the communicability of ever more differentiated norms. The result would be little more than a command, having the character of a general proposition, concerning the "judicious," "responsible," and "appropriate" observation of speed limits. In view of the variable nature of individual traffic situations and demands for safety, this would appear an inflexible prescription.

Difficulties analogous to those surrounding the establishment of norms arise surrounding the sanctions which are to guarantee their maintenance. These sanctions cannot be increased arbitrarily in money terms because they must remain realistic as "expectations" to norm violators on low incomes or to "enterprises at the limit" – otherwise the loss is greater than the utility. But conversely, this means that all actors above this threshold simultaneously derive a profit to the extent that the threatened, and in given cases executed, sanctions are below their particular "pain threshold." This can be confirmed by the number of luxury limousines to be found among cars which are blatantly illegally parked. Analogously, in commercial and environmental criminal law, better situated businesses can develop a wholly calculating attitude toward sanctions. They profit from the "consideration" which the most poorly situated norm-violators have to make, and can therefore treat certain penalties as cost factors which under certain circumstances they can ignore. There are cases in which, because of the advantages to be gained from it, norm violation becomes "worthwhile." One can assume that not only the deterrent effect, but also the legitimacy of regulative policy suffers from these distribution effects of sanctions.

In his study of the limits of rationality of legal guarantees of security, Preuss has shown that, according to the binary schema of law, everything is permitted which is not expressly forbidden, and that therefore in environmental law "technical limit values ... function as a right to environmental pollution."[5] In this sense, regulative law would explicitly absolve its addressees of reflection on their responsibility for their actions, as long as these remain below the level of limit values, which as a rule are grounded technically, not normatively. And even above this limit, as long as definitions of punishment and the probability of its being carried out are not prohibitive, there is room for a morally neutralized cost calculation. Such a construction clearly serves to separate the level of regulation from "social contexts, assumptions of probability, values and interests and their reflection in a ... social discourse" and to make the "agreement concerning the risk which can be reasonably borne by society" appear renounceable to a greater degree than would be the case with more "societal" forms of self-regulation. "The creation of regulative norms," writes Renate Mayntz, "cannot in principle motivate any conduct which depends upon individual initiative, innovation, and positive engagement."[6]

All this demonstrates that regulative policy, striving to do justice to collective values such as order and security via prescriptions and standardizations of conduct guaranteed by penalties, finds itself in a vicious circle when it comes to execution. Its course is marked by the following stages.

- In order to have a strategic purpose and to be more certain of reaching its target, the power to establish norms must be placed in the hands of experts, and distinguished from norms, usages, and customs already established. The bindingness of and justification for the latter thereby begin to fade and, as a result, actors are absolved of everyday responsibilities.
- However, the regulative norms which are created and given a positive legal form are unable to command recognition as the only ones which are unambiguously valid and binding. For this, in view of the manifold richness of the reality to be regulated, they are too uniform and suffer from an insurmountable lack of complexity.
- The acknowledgment and maintenance of these norms is further undermined by the fact that the issuing of penalties is burdened with obviously regressive distribution effects. The effect of these penalties is more likely to be zero the better placed are those to whom they are issued. Within a given structure of distribution, a greater or smaller number of these will be able to treat a regulative legal order not as a command which they must obey, but as an object of strategic action (that is, as an obstacle which in given cases can be surmounted).
- Finally, in "new" problem situations not foreseen by or provided for in law, a dense network of positive regulative legal norms produces symptoms of "moral underdemand" on the part of the addressees of norms. Citizens' capacities for reflection, innovation, and autonomous self-binding are not exercised, and fail to fulfill their stop-gap function in areas where norms are still absent. At this point there occurs the "tragic" result that positive law, instituted for

the ultimate coordination of action, overstretches itself and, through an overdose, undermines its own authority and order-creating potential. That is, it encourages an awareness of structural short-comings in the execution of policy, an awareness which can only lead to a rational slackening of "my" conformity to norms in antici-pation of the tendency of "everyone else" to deviate from them, as described above.

If, for the reasons mentioned, formal organizations and especi-ally businesses are likely to adopt a strategic-calculative attitude toward the attempts by regulative policy to standardize their conduct, then, whenever the discernible costs and risks suggest that obstruc-tion would be worthwhile commercially, these attempts run aground. The converse is true when the addressees of norms are "natural persons" with everyday habits. The spheres of energy, transport, health, and education policy provide numerous examples of how difficult it is to bring about changes in conduct by exploiting the authority of experts, by means of financial incentives, or by discrimi-nating symbolically or materially against conduct opposed to that desired.

Thus, the use of public rather than private transport, or the forgoing of luxury goods known to be damaging to the environment, can be encouraged via the steering mechanism of regulative policy to a dis-appointingly small degree. It seems that many urgently required means of regulation lie well outside the range of money and law. They can be fashioned in a way which promises success, if they can be fashioned at all, only via a prudent, disciplined, and responsible self-regulation on the part of citizens. At all events, they are not immedi-ately available as a means of regulative policy. Wherever it deals with the everyday practices of natural persons, a policy which is subsidiary rather than "active" is limited to recalling the norms and rules of civilized, collective existence. It will do so by means of information, enlightenment, "moral persuasion," and the exercise of a credible moral social hegemony. But the basis of these norms and rules is not created by policy itself. It can be secured and maintained because their roots lie in the associative structures and cultural traditions of civil society.

Alternatives to Deregulation

Only through a new "regulation of regulation" can one expect the type of institutional solution to problems of effectiveness and legitimacy traditionally bound up with regulation policy which overcomes its functional problems without leading to a "deregulated" version of market socialization. About this "regulation of regulation" there is as little theoretical as there is practical knowledge. Accordingly, a brief mention of the problems which follow from a universally acknowledged "crisis of regulative policy" must remain vague and open-ended. The main difficulty is how to downplay the alternative between regulation and deregulation, nationalization and privatization, and to make institutional arrangements which strengthen the capacity of individual and collective actors in civil society to coordinate with one another by means other than that of market-strategic action, namely in a "reasonable," "solidaristic," or indeed "principled" manner. This can only be achieved by means of institutional innovations such as new and expanded forms of codetermination, self-management, and negotiated equalization of interests, which generate a third position between those of state regulation and the market behavior of private autonomous actors, that is, by means of a framework for fair and responsible self-regulation.

However, the role of democratic institutions and processes of opposition formation will have to be judged more skeptically than is the case in leftist versions of democratic theory, for the very reason that these tend to hypostasize a "will of the people" (or will of the so-called "base") which is given, unified, and rational, and which then must merely be furnished with an improved likelihood of being realized. This suppresses Rousseau's problem, which was that the assumption of rationality does not apply to the will of the people in its "natural" state, but only to the purified version of it arrived at through "education." Skepticism is also in order here because the left tradition has consistently, and to its disadvantage, managed to ignore the view worked out by Max Weber that the expression of the will of the people (or of a class) presupposes a growth of bureaucratic structures as much as it produces them, and that as a consequence the principle of democracy is burdened with a tendency toward self-negation.

The distinction proposed by Guy Kirsch, between "ex ante rules" and "ad hoc rules," seems to offer an initial resource for the institutional reconstruction of regulative policy practices. Ex ante rules involve standardizations of a cultural, legal, and institutional type which abstract from any given situation. Ad hoc rules are defined by the fact that they emerge from the very situations to which they apply. They are "developed and further developed in the course of interaction ... [and] are the result of the societal intercourse which they [should] form and order."[7] To be sure, this way out of the paradoxes of regulative policy would be far more promising if (in accordance with the definition of ex ante rules) it were not the content of the rules which were established ex ante, but the mode in which these rules are to emerge "ad hoc."

The decisive question is: how can it be established in advance that in the process of "ad hoc" norm formation all relevant and competent interests legitimately claiming to be "affected" are acknowledged and given a voice in such a way that particular power interests are safely neutralized? The problem thereby shifts to that of the appropriate procedures for doing justice to this universalistic criterion. Neither the public discourse of all individual citizens, nor the closed arena of corporatist associations, which in negotiations are accorded the privilege of free collective bargaining, can provide a plausible or realistic model for such procedures. Perhaps there will even have to be a general renunciation of the ambition to arrive at a theoretical outline of the process of norm formation which lies between these poles and is fitting for all times and all cases. "Correctly" established procedures would then be replaced by a culture of experimental innovation and the continual evaluation of procedure according to its fairness. This would then have to be paid for with a certain loss of that procedure's rigidity and predictability.

A further useful building block for an institutional reconstruction of regulation could also be derived from an idea of Pierre Rosanvallon.[8] From this perspective, the demand for regulative provision and intervention arises out of insufficient attention on the part of actors to the external and long-term effects of their actions. As a consequence, the demand for regulation can be reduced if it proves possible to increase this attention and "capacity for foresight" within civil society. The simple formula reads: societal prevention instead of state prevention ("reducing the need for state intervention"). The latter would not thereby completely lose its function, as the supporters of deregulation foresee, but would, so to speak, be sent to the substitute's bench. There it would serve as an index of the self-regulatory capacity of civil society and its institutions, a capacity which would still be insufficient; or, much more, it would play the role of demanding that this gap be closed.

The utopian content of this idea lies in the implied "dedifferentiation" of formal organizations, and in an implied increase in their secondary function, that of attending (on their own initiative, not at the state's behest) not only to organizational goals but also to the external effects to which their own actions give rise. For them to be able to do this, it would be necessary in the first place that these effects became recognizable through the development of appropriate organizational organs of perception ("creating greater visibility for the social"). In addition, the moral capacity of organizational members to deal with the perceived consequences of their own actions responsibly and with solidarity would have to be appealed to, developed and exploited to the full ("reinstating mutual support as a function of society"). The result of both would be that multidimensional relevance structures would come into play "at the coal face" (in enterprises, schools, universities, local authorities, communal bodies, families, associations, etc.). They would be recognized in the perception of reality as well as in the decision-making of those involved. To the degree that such an expansion of cognitive and moral horizons is achieved, regulative policy can be replaced gradually by societal self-regulation, and at the same time, the consequences of deregulation can be avoided.

Notes

1 R. Kroker, *Deregulierung und Entbürokratisierung* (Cologne, 1985).
2 L. W. Weiss and M. W. Klass (eds), *Regulatory Reform: What Actually Happened* (Boston, 1986); R. Soltwedel et al., *Die Deregulierungsdebatte in der Bundesrepublik* (Tübingen, 1986).
3 Soltwedel et al., *Die Deregulierungsdebatte*, p. 285.
4 Ibid.
5 U. K. Preuss, "Sicherheit durch Recht – Rationalitätsgrenzen eines Konzeptes," *Kritische Vierteljahresschrift für Gesetzgebung und Rechtswissenschaft* (1989), p. 10.
6 R. Mayntz, "Politische Steuerung und gesellschaftliche Steuerungsprobleme – Anmerkungen zu einem theoretischen Paradigma," in T. Ellwein et al. (eds), *Jahrbuch zur Staats- und Verwaltungswissenschaft*, vol. 1 (Baden-Baden, 1987), p. 98.
7 G. Kirsch, "Die Deregulierungsdebatte. Anmerkungen zu einem bonierten Streit," in T. Schmid (ed.), *Entstaatlichung. Neue Perspektiven auf das Gemeinwesen* (Berlin, 1988), pp. 38ff.
8 P. Rosanvallon, "The Decline of Civil Society Visibility," in J. Keane (ed.), *Civil Society and the State* (London, 1988).

5

Constitutional Policy in Search of the "Will of the People"

In a quite specific sense, there is no alternative to liberal democracy today: there are no theoretical alternatives worthy of attention that would serve to justify collectively binding decisions made via the agency of the empirical will of the citizens. Needless to say, this does not exclude practices by states and political associations that endeavor to survive without a theoretical form of justification that can be taken seriously and, in extreme cases, rely on mobilizing ethnic and chauvinist support or the tactics of gang warfare. As soon as we start talking about legitimating justifications, however, then there is indeed no alternative to the "will of the people" as the final agency justifying political rule. The law admittedly defines at any given point in time the scope of democratic decision-making. But such law is itself "positive," that is, it is in turn subject to democratic legislative decisions. The economy also places limitations on democratic decisions. It is impossible in the long term to decide politically to spend more than the tax base created by economic activity yields. And, of course, physical laws cannot be decided or simply annulled democratically. Yet, within these broad limits, politics is generated by democratic sovereignty and can only expect to be obeyed if it refers to this origin.

There is, in other words, "no alternative" to liberal democracy. I do not mean this in the sense that there are alternatives still in existence but which have been rejected as less worthy of being considered valid when compared with liberal democracy, as based on universal, free, and equal adult suffrage. Instead, the opposite is the case: such an alternative *no longer* exists in modern societies. Democracy, therefore, does not resemble an elected constitutional form (that could consequently be changed by election), but rather an ineluctable fact. Alternatives to liberal democracy, irrespective of whether they have their foundations in a dynasty, a theocracy, a particular philosophy of history, or in natural law, simply no longer come into consideration factually, especially after the events of 1989 and the breakdown of state socialism. No one would be prepared to take them seriously. Modern societies are condemned to rely solely on the "will of the people" as it ensues from equal and free rights of participation when it comes to the basis for justifying themselves, that is, to the final agency of and impetus for collectively binding decisions.

Democracy has changed from being a virtue we should adhere to and has become a fact that we have to get by with. This does not preclude, above all in the process of European integration, that the "final agency" for justification, namely the "will of the people," is filtered through so many interim stages that the people themselves are hardly able to recognize the results of their will in the double sense of the word. It is, I believe, above all the prospect of a foreseeably deficient democracy in an integrated Europe that has prompted the political elites in Germany today to start thinking of compensatory aids.

The only, albeit extensive, opportunities that still exist for institutionally shaping the political process focus on three issues: first, *who* should participate in the formation of the will of the people (that is, enjoy full political civil rights); secondly, *how* should the will of the people be formed; and, thirdly, *what* objects may and should it extend to. The following discussion will concentrate on the second issue.

A perception of these tasks of shaping the political process is highly important because the remaining justificatory basis for political action – that is, precisely the will of the people – exhibits three problematic features: it is *fictitious, fallible,* and *seducible.*

(1) The will of the people is initially *fictitious* because it cannot be conceived of as an entity which can be consulted at any moment, as can the holy book of religions of revelation. Nor is it something from which we can glean, if necessary with the assistance of authorized scholars (or pollsters?), binding instructions as to the right path to pursue with political decisions. Instead, we must assume that no "will of the people" exists on most themes at most times. What exist are the factual, temporal, and socially differentiated preferences of citizens. In other words, some citizens want this or that decision, so opt for one thing, others opt for another, and, moreover, they want one thing today, another tomorrow. Furthermore, most people are undecided anyway whether they actually want something with regard to most matters at most times, because the *attentive energy* which the normal

citizen can devote to political matters is far too limited, and citizens, rationally enough, do not have a great deal of *confidence* that it is worthwhile investing more energy in the first place.[1] It would be thus be pure chance if the confusion of voices expressing individual opinions and preferences, even those colored and predefined by associations and party politics, were to meet even the most modest of criteria for *objective logical consistency, intrinsic concurrence,*[2] and *temporal constancy.* And these are precisely the features which we impute to someone when we believe that he or she has a "will," and a well-considered, stabilized, informed will at that, and therefore one that is worthy of consideration and recognition.

Our ideas on that domain of everyday life which is subject to our direct control and is much closer to us are much clearer and more robust: for example, on healthy nutrition, correct education, or satisfying working conditions. In the field of politics there are at best views that are widely shared yet remain so vague that no decisions can be derived from them, views that we term "our political culture" and which cover civil rights and duties, the relationship between citizens and between citizens and the organs of state rule, views on law and morality, on nations and the world community, etc. The only "will" which we can assume exists among the people of a sovereign nation-state takes a reflective form, namely the will that uniform and autonomous will formation should come about.

To impute a political "will" to "the" people in the first place, of the sort that occurs in the usual talk of "popular will" or "the will of the voters," is thus a turn of phrase which amounts to using a metaphor that is as sublime as it is risky. In this context we should bear in mind the essentially uncontroversial fact that the "will" of the people is an *artefact* of those institutional procedures which we ostensibly only use to *measure* precisely that will. The will of the people *does not exist* prior to these procedures and independent of them, but instead *arises* in them. The will of the people has the character of an answer;[3] and what is important, then, is the question which is put in order to come up with the answer, and the procedure used to arrive at it.

(2) What arises in these procedures and what is then represented by the people and by the political elites as the "will of the people" is decidedly *fallible,* just as, of course, the will of those in political office or invested with political authority is fallible. The question is thus whether, given irreversible *democratic* conditions, fallibility or erroneousness are even meaningful criteria, because, and this is by definition the case in liberal democracies, where there is no truth and correctness that serves as the basis of political decisions, there can also

be no errors or false decisions. Or at least not as long as the political decisions do not go against *constitutional law* with regard to the procedures by which they must be reached, that is, are recognized to be impermissible and therefore without effect.

I will, however, show that political decisions which depend on the will of the people can also be wrong even in instances where they are permissible under constitutional law and no objections to them have been forthcoming. This is, in short, the case when a decision once made appears *retrospectively* to be not only a decision we should *regret* (for instance, because the impact it was expected to have did not ensue, since our original knowledge of the state of affairs was inadequate), but one which we should actually *deplore*. We must *regret* earlier decisions if we are dissatisfied with their results now but can at least say in their favor that we could not have taken a better decision at the time, given our knowledge and intentions then. We should *deplore* a decision, however, where this justification does *not* apply, for example, in the case of cities we once designed to facilitate the flow of traffic. Here, in retrospect it becomes clear that "we," that is, the totality of active citizens, *could* or *should* have morally and cognitively known better at the time and should with foresight have taken into account the disastrous consequences the decision now faces us with. Therefore, by extension, we should have decided differently and better. If these conditions are given, then it is justified to speak of a false or erroneous "will of the people." These conditions are all the more likely to exist the more current decisions are likely to extend into the future. And the more this is the case, the longer is the path of impact along which as a rule we are tied into the irreversible but possibly regrettable consequences of decisions. They were decisions which, at the time when we took them, all too easily caused us to give in to the temptation to prefer short-term advantages at the cost of long-term but foreseeable damage impact.

(3) The fact that the will of the people can be seduced has, essentially, only to do with a subordinate case of its fallibility. Let us assume that, as stated above, the popular will is first formed in the process by which it is measured, and outside that process at best dons the shadowy form of unconnected and fluctuating elements of will. This being the case, with regard to the *social construction of the will of the people*[4] by the media, the political parties, associations, and educational institutions, great effort must be made to ensure that the dissemination of information and attention is "undistorted" and "balanced" in a sense that is hard to define and even harder to create norms for. The interested manner in which such institutions and collective actors

appeal to fears, prejudices, passions, interests, and hopes may, on the one hand, improve the ability of citizens to make rational decisions. It may, on the other, mislead them, by which I mean that decisions result which, in the sense explained above, are retrospectively to be considered "false." To the extent that the latter is the case, we can speak of the will of the people having been "seduced" or "misled." The corresponding dangers clearly grow to the degree that citizens depend in the process of will formation on premade decisions for their orientation. This is the case to an exceptional degree in all areas of politics today. The sheer complexity of things renders us veritable illiterates on most public matters, because all of us, whether mere citizens or holders of offices or authority, will never get far with our own experiences and ability to judge. We are correspondingly dependent on the questions for which decisions are to be made being prepared in advance in a manner we can trust, and on the alternatives, including the foreseeable consequences, being fairly and sincerely presented to us. The enormous amount of help we need before being able to judge creates correspondingly great opportunities for abuse on the part of those (regularly interested) parties on whom we rely for help.

In this context we must in particular warn against the widespread and false assumption that procedures which focus less on electing representatives and more on a direct democratic poll of opinion, such as popular initiatives, petitions for referendums, and the referendums themselves, ipso facto *inevitably* generate more *authentic* results than do the usual procedures of a representative democracy, specifically periodic elections to legislative bodies. This assumption is usually based on the notion that such a result is forthcoming because such popular procedures are *not* mediated via the institutionalized competition of the political parties. And it is false not only because of the limited ability we all have to judge matters, but also because popular initiatives and petitions for referendums can, certainly at the federal level, clearly only be organized by the political parties. To this extent, what would be involved would merely be twofold competition between the parties under the simple pretext of suspending or correcting them. Thanks to the pollsters who are constantly monitoring the political opinions of the population, government policy is consistently to a great extent in line with the population's preferences on important matters. Given that the political elites are already acquainted with these opinions, where they are conveyed through the referendum-like functions of political opinion polling, and given that they have cause to heed them, it is not exactly obvious why an additional channel of communication, namely referendums etc., should lead to the government being made aware of additional contents. Oppositional political preferences which have even the remotest chance of achieving a quorum have turned up on the pollsters' x-ray screens long before they have had a chance to crystallize into suggestions or proposed bills. To this extent the political elites again have the upper hand when it comes to the preemptive dispersal and pacification of popular initiatives.

Against the background of these deliberations we can now go on to take rough stock of the relative capacity of representative procedures as opposed to procedures involving direct democratic votes on issues where it comes to measuring and concomitantly creating the will of the people.

In the long history of incisive literature on the subject, numerous flattering assumptions have been made about the qualities of *legislative representative bodies*, specifically with regard to their rationality, reasonableness, maturity, knowledge of the material, impartiality, collective intelligence, and capacity for judgment. To remain realistic, among these notions – and they all speak in favor of parliamentary decision-making procedures possessing an intrinsic rationality – only two can be upheld.

First of all, unlike popular assemblies or the collection of signatures on petitions, parliaments are subject to the "law of reencounter." Every participant in the parliamentary body or its committees must expect to be continually subject to the scrutiny of all the other participants with regard to all the statements he or she makes, and to be assessed on credibility, knowledge of the material, sincerity, consistency, and dedication.[5] Those who say something tomorrow that contradicts what they said today, or have opinions outside the building which differ from those expressed inside it, or do not know their documented facts are likely at the very least to expose themselves to mild forms of disapproval, and anticipation of this is likely, as a rule, to function as a discipline and ensure that a minimum of seriousness is exhibited.

Secondly, compared with assemblies or referendums, committees have the advantage of creating a more fruitful communicative situation: not only can you say yes or no, but you can also operate using the dimension of time (earlier versus later), introduce new objects into the negotiation (this way or that way), facilitate compromises by offering exchanges (if you forgo this, I'll forgo that, "log-rolling," etc.). These two advantages must, however, be weighed against the disadvantages that stem from the fact that all acts are embedded in strategies intended to maintain power and coalitions, are influenced by a consideration of the constant election campaign fought out in parliament and the interests of the individual members of the parliament in ensuring that their chances of reelection are not impaired.

Forms of the legislature based on *plebiscites* are characterized by advantages and disadvantages that offset each other. The underlying totality of citizens can only answer given questions with yes or no, and when answering (or at least we cannot preclude this happening) are subject to moods and emotions specific to that moment in time. The latter can, moreover, be controlled by a third party directing their attention. The "nascent need for regulation in the people," which a typical petition speaks of with moving sensitivity, might just as easily have been *teased into birth* by strategic parties. Conversely, to their credit, citizens directly involved in legislation are clearly relatively free of an innate desire to maintain power – if not necessarily free of an interest in acquiring power. Thus, in the case of potential forms of legislation by the people, we should exclude all such matters (such as fiscal laws)[6] where we can reasonably expect that worries about the size of their disposable income may tempt many citizens to attribute less importance to the state provision of infrastructure and collective goods than they otherwise would, or would want to.

On the other hand, a broad consensus among international scholars in the areas of theories of democracy and political sociology expressly confirms the assumption that the democratic political system has failings. These could lead to lower acceptance of its institutions and to the latter ceasing to be able to function in an integrative, binding, and legitimizing manner. This could perhaps be alleviated by involving citizens to a greater degree in various ways. But we must warn here against innovations that adhere to the logic of *exchange* and are introduced with great haste and little reason. For example, those made with the gesture: We, the politicians, are granting you, the citizens, great rights to participate and take the initiative. We expect in return that in future you show greater respect toward the agencies of politics and the administrators thereof. For it is neither certain that the "political caste" does indeed forfeit overall control with the introduction of such innovations, nor can we assume that, should it do so, the citizens would really honour the concessions granted it in the manner expected. To oversimplify, the problem at hand can be portrayed in terms of two points.

1 Large political organizations, above all, political parties, but also trade unions and other associations, have lost much of their function as a point of orientation for their members and for the public as a whole. In view of the complexity of the decisions they have to make and the plurality of values and interests that have to be taken into account in the process, the actors shaping our political life are

themselves dwindling in stature. They leave behind them a vacuum of moral and political leadership and are therefore suspected of essentially acting as an opportunistic cartel exercising patronage and endeavoring to stay in power.

2 The ongoing process of individualization and differentiation within society is drying out the ground which was once fertile for major political communities that functioned as points of orientation and as the seedbed of solidarity. Instead, it promotes the confined and oscillating formation of political preferences. Each trend fosters the other: the talk is of the "gradual death of a steady political clientele," of increasing apathy and cynicism on the one hand, and of a dearth of ideas and a lack of clear profile among the political parties, on the other. The latter have substantially lost the ability to mobilize their clientele behind them and therefore cling to state and, above all, financial guarantees for their survival, pursuing a strategy of cartel formation to the detriment of potential third parties.

Now one could bemoan these trends or "realistically" accept them. What is probably not a bone of contention is the fact that taken together the effect of the two trends leads to a decay in society's *political resources*, that is, to a devaluation of the institutional means with which society can purposively influence its own development and subject this to control. At the same time, the overall trend improves the chances of those on the political market who use populist "direct sales" to callously sell anything on the political market which is likely to find a ready buyer. And they do so by appealing to innate resentment or an individual instinct for greater wealth.

The introduction of citizens' initiatives, petitions for referendums, referendums themselves, and consultational and definitive polling of or votes by citizens is by no means the only way of enhancing the opportunities for citizens to help shape politics. Two other levels of reinvigorating institutions may possibly serve the same goal far more effectively. The first is to open up the system of political institutions to a far greater extent to the *discursive processes of the political public sphere*, processes that establish the norms in the first place; and the second is the internal *democratization of political parties* and possibly also of associations. After all, democratization can be effected not only from "below" through forms of participation involving plebiscites, but also "internally" (participatory rights in political parties) and "externally" (via public opinion). It appears conceivable that if clear successes can be scored at these two levels, the option being debated of augmenting the representative system by means of elements of direct democratic involvement of the electorate could probably be dispensed with altogether. Furthermore, in this light, the possibility of augmenting political will formation by means of direct democratic participation is in reality a relatively meagre basis for improvement. And it is a basis that political elites currently enjoy chiseling away at, in part because thus they can seem to offer decisive concessions without actually doing so. It allows them in the main still to exercise the right to formulate the issues and only then ask the people to take a decision on them. In fact, under certain conditions they would also gain the welcome opportunity to shirk their responsibility for tricky issues where decisions have to be made, particularly international issues, by leaving the task of decision-making in these cases to the purported original agency of the "will of the people" as expressed by plebiscite.

Stronger public discourse It was a striking feature of political developments in the Federal Republic of Germany in the 1970s and 1980s that new initiatives, ideas, and moral criteria for assessing the quality of domestic and foreign policy first saw the light of day not in the political parties and the large trade unions and associations, but in institutions that were located on the relative periphery of the political system. I include in this category churches, universities, the media, the free professions, citizens' initiatives, social movements, and also individual members of the artistic professions, such as film-makers, musicians, and writers. With at times great and enduring success and with the velvet power of convincing political and moral arguments, they (the women's movement, the peace movement, the environmental movement, Third World groups) brought the political leadership under pressure to take certain problems into account. Indeed, they forced them to deal legislatively with matters and conflicts hitherto left by the wayside and to develop such legislation further. If a branch of the press gives several hundred respectable women the opportunity to confess publicly that they have had abortions, then at one fell swoop this creates a keener awareness of the moral and political-legal relations between men and women, between church and state, between women and fetuses, between law and the free professions than could any popular initiative with its encouragingly high quorum. Such formations, and some of them were very loosely organized, were able to exercise such functions all the more convincingly because they did *not* have as their goal participation in formal decision-making by winning a majority to their cause, etc., but instead wished to sharpen the capacity of the mass of the population and their political elites for judgment on such issues. They contributed more, or so I would claim, to increasing the political resources of the population of the Federal Republic of Germany than could realistically be expected from the proposals for changes to the constitution to usher in direct democratic processes. It bears remembering that the aforementioned forms of political action were successful not because of innovations in procedural law, but by dint of the fact that their deliberations and conclusions were convincing,[7] and because of the process of osmosis, as it were, whereby new value standards and sensitivities gradually filter through into legislative (as well as executive and juridical) decision-making.

Needless to say, we must concede that this assertion, even if it were to be universally accepted, does not address the issue of current thoughts on reforming the constitution by introducing innovations that allow for direct decisions by the electorate. Or rather it does not to the extent that the vitality of the democratic public sphere and something which I would like to call its moral and political creativity are hardly affected by (constitutional) legislation, or at least not in a positive sense. The legal system can, of course, to a certain degree assist the critical creativity of the noninstitutional processes of the democratic public sphere in two ways. It can ensure that executive processes are as transparent as possible. And it can forgo imposing police or legal sanctions on unconventional and at times clearly "disruptive" forms of expression of political protest, thereby discouraging them.

Some occasionally argue that the historical process of the collapse of the command economies in Eastern Europe in general, and of the system of rulership in the German Democratic Republic in particular, give compelling moral cause to take into account those types of will formation which exerted the main momentum in the peaceful revolutions of Eastern Europe, with a view to changes to the constitution, and in order to emulate them. This being the case, we are more likely when studying events in Eastern Europe to come across the factor of a diffuse public sphere made up of dissidents and their form of "antipolitics," to use a phrase of György Conrad and Vaclev Havel, than across practices of "popular legislation," or even calls for such. It is this practice of laying siege[8] to the powers of the state in a morally sensitive manner, such as to question its norms by means of "flows of communication not permeated by power," which would thus be what we should emulate if we seriously wish to learn from the civil movements in Central and Eastern Europe.

Democratization of political parties This is the other level at which the political resources of citizens can be enhanced without any introduction of controversial elements of plebiscite-based activity whatsoever. It involves opening up the parties, and by extension parliament, both socially and in terms of issues. To my mind, one problematic fundamental aspect of our political system is the fact that less than 5 percent of the enfranchised population, namely the active citizens who are members of political parties, decide among themselves during elections which persons are put up for election and what factual alternatives the parties stand for. Incidentally, one consequence of this party monopoly is that the social composition of the political elite (the "political caste," as a popular label would have it, which is currently enjoying a quite troublingly successful career in Germany) deviates sharply in all relevant dimensions (and certainly not just in terms of gender) from the composition of the population it represents. There are numerous conceivable ways of alleviating the situation, starting with the participation of nonmembers in party will formation and personnel policy, through new forms of party financing up to the use of quotas (and not just based on gender) to a greater extent than has hitherto been the case. But even such proposals remain tied to the level of legislation on parties and elections and are therefore only mentioned here because I wish to show that there are means of augmenting the political resources available to citizens which are more simple and/or more effective than merely giving them rights in the legislative process via plebiscites.

This leads me to three conclusions. First, there is only a need for action on the "direct democracy" front if the belief is that the decay of political resources, which we should indeed take seriously, cannot be combated by other means. I have in mind here means such as revitalizing the democratic public sphere – and retuning the receptors in parliaments and governments that home in on it – or the democratizing reform of parties and associations and opening them up to new members and issues. The conceivable effect of direct democratic elements does not offset the omission of action on these two other fronts.

Secondly, if the representative system of the German constitution, over and above any more or less uncontroversial one-off referendum on constitutional matters is to be supplemented by plebiscite-related elements for continual use, the aim cannot be to make the enhanced political rights thus enjoyed by citizens a routine procedure of collective decision-making. An enhancement of this sort resembles both the impact of the "right to strike" on policy on the distribution of wealth (an impact which is more pervasive than the fact of there being strikes now and again) and the function of nuclear weapons in defence policy (which, after all, depends on their *never being used*, but always being ready for deployment). In like manner, the main success of direct democratic procedures empowering citizens can be seen to be the sheer fact that they are always there as a possible means of action for citizens to use. In a favorable scenario, the fact that they are there would cause the political elites to find careful arguments to support their legislative actions, or failures to legislate, in order to avoid the potential of such unpleasant surprises as the Danish referendum on membership of the European Union. And, conversely, the mere presence of plebiscite-related, democratic forms of participation might help to overcome the conception citizens have that they are at the mercy of political elites. (Irrespective of whether it is cynical or merely convenient, it can in any event be exploited by populists.) The healthy impact of plebiscite-related procedures would not lie in their actual use, but in their mere existence.[9] Which is why the procedural instrument must be designed in such a way that it neither tempts people to use it without thinking, nor presents insurmountable obstacles to its being used.

Thirdly, the mere possibility of a plebiscite-related procedure being available would, in the case of a series of legislative themes, immediately trigger latent wishes and provoke passions that would *in all probability* and with great *damage potential* stand in the way of well-considered decisions. When assessing the impact of technology we understand "risk" as the mathematical product of the probability of the scenario happening and the damage intensity this would have (and then are well advised to minimize the probability of the damage occurring and also proceed according to the *maximin* rule: "ensure that the worst possible scenario is as little bad as possible"). A similar procedure can be adopted with the "political technology" of legislation by the people. A *negative catalog* should be drawn up of issues on which decisions must be made in which the values of *both* must be regarded as relatively high (probability of an "ill-considered" decision and the damage impact of the same). The issues involved are ones in which citizens' direct interests are so strongly affected either favorably or unfavorably that it is not possible to rely on their due ability to distance themselves from these issues when weighing them up. Fiscal law would be an example I have already mentioned: to subject fiscal law to plebiscites would be like granting a free license that categorically privileged the income interests of the majority vis-à-vis the claims to welfare state support by the minority. Another example would be issues involving the physical integrity of persons. Certainly, under the immediate impression of spectacular acts of criminal violence, a plebiscite would lead to the introduction of the death penalty, just as clearly as the impression of civil wars in the Third (or "Second") World would result in a vote against out-of-area peace-keeping military operations. Minority rights can also swiftly be threatened in contexts that it is easy to imagine. In all these cases, the partiality of private interests and passions can be so overpowering that it would be exceptionally dangerous to assume counterfactually that legislation based on the direct involvement of the electorate would be sufficiently open to principles and to considerations of the common good and the long-term consequences of decisions. The concept of an enlightened will of the people also undoubtedly includes that will mustering sufficient power to subject itself to "autopaternalistic" reservations, and thus to forgo the opportunity to make itself heard in the legislative process on *all* issues at *all* times.

Notes

1 The classic argument, put forward by A. Downs in *An Economic Theory of Democracy* (New York, 1957) runs: given that it is exceptionally improbable that precisely *my* vote "counts" in a decisive manner, it is not worth the effort to ensure that I am well informed and have formed a well-reasoned opinion. And since this is true of everyone and everyone thinks this way, everyone puts less effort into nurturing and using the available political resources and rights. And, one could conclude, this is a state of affairs the administrators of the business of politics in parties, associations, and parliaments are quite content with.

2 The criterion of "concurrence with oneself" refers to the difficult state that all adults are presumably familiar with, namely, when we want something while at the same time not seriously wanting to want it. We, as it were, observe in ourselves a will we "actually" do not want to have – and this is undoubtedly not just an experience known to drug addicts.

3 Cf. Ernst W. Böckenförde, *Demokratie und Repräsentation. Zur Kritik der heutigen Demokratiediskussion* (Hanover, 1983). Böckenförde draws on the classical approach put forward by Erich Kaufmann in his "Zur Problematik des Volkswillen," in Kaufmann, *Gesammelte Schriften*, vol. 3 (Göttingen, 1960, originally published in 1931).

4 Cf. the recent monograph by Danilo Zolo, *Democracy and Complexity: A Realist Approach* (Cambridge, 1992).

5 Cf. Giovanni Sartori, "Selbstzerstörung der Demokratie? Mehrheitsentscheidungen und Entscheidungen von Gremien," in Bernd Guggenberger and Claus Offe (eds), *An den Grenzen der Mehrheitsdemokratie. Politik und Soziologie der Mehrheitsregel* (Opladen, 1984).

6 Cf. the skeptical findings on direct democratic participation in legislation in California in Rudolf Billerbock, *Plebiszitäre Demokratie in der Praxis* (Berlin, 1989), and Thomas Kupka, "Plebiszitäre Gesetzgebungsformen in den USA," *Kritische Justiz* 4 (1990).

7 "Deliberation" is a notion used frequently in political theory in recent times to describe the critical potential of a public sphere not tied to the yoke of political institutions. See James S. Fishkin, *Democracy and Deliberation* (New Haven, 1991); Bernard Manin, "On legitimacy and Deliberation," *Political Theory* 15 (1987); and Claus Offe and Ulrich K. Preuss, "Democratic Institutions and Moral Resources," in David Held (ed.), *Political Theory Today* (Cambridge, 1991).

8 Cf. Jürgen Habermas, "Volkssouveränität als Verfahren. Ein normativer Begriff der Öffentlichkeit," in Habermas, *Der Moderne – ein unvollendetes Projekt. Philosophisch-politische Aufsätze 1977–1990* (Leipzig, 1991).

9 This is also the view advanced by Tilman Evers, one of the theoretically well informed advocates of opening the German constitutional system up to forms of plebiscites, in his essay "Volkssouveränität im Verfahren. Zur Verfassungsdiskussion über direkte Demokratie," *Aus Politik und Zeitgeschichte* (31 May, 1991), pp. 3–15.

PART III

The Politics of Social Welfare

6

State Action and Structures of Collective Will Formation: Elements of a Social-Scientific Theory of the State

The Problem of Explanation: Theoretical and Practical Weaknesses of Etatist Activism

Since the mid-1970s doubts about the efficiency of the state have dominated the political as well as the social-scientific scene. These doubts can be explained by a series of social, political, and theoretical changes which have taken place both in Western Europe and beyond it in all the OECD countries. These changes appear to have resulted in the dramatic loss in the reputation and credibility of the idea of a welfare state which is "active" internally and externally sovereign, democratic and capable of reform, a welfare state, moreover, in which society crystallizes into an "effective unity" (H. Heller) and as such achieves control over the effects of its actions. In the first place, I would like to recall some of the developments and changes which can be held responsible for what, in retrospect, appears to have been a turning point in the development of the Western democracies, or at least in prevailing thinking about the opportunities for, and responsibilities which fall to, public policy.

Like other raw material crises, the so-called oil crisis of Autumn 1973 and the resulting increase in oil prices at the end of the 1970s helped to define more clearly the limits of action of nation-states. At no time in the postwar period has there been a conjuncture characterized by such a sharp asymmetry between the possibility of influencing external causes and the weight of internal consequences. Until that point it had been the norm that external causes emanating from the international system and threatening serious consequences within states could be dealt with by military means (as with Suez in 1956) or through trade policy, or at least that their effects on internal growth and employment, and on the credibility of the state's interventionary activity, could be warded off sufficiently to ensure that no serious damage would result.

Viewed from the perspective of national state sovereignty, the crises in the world economy of the mid-1970s represent a caesura, whose characteristic feature is a new constellation of inaccessibly distant causes and possibly grievous consequences, consequences whose limits are hard to specify. The divergence between the horizon of events by which states are passively affected (namely, the world market) and the horizon of those events which they can still actively control and direct (namely their own internal affairs) is by no means an isolated case resulting from the oil-price shock. Japan's development into a leading economic and technological power, the entry of authoritarian, low-wage developing countries into world markets for high-tech goods, the effects of the Third World debt crisis and of the United States's dramatic budget and trade deficits have all heightened this discrepancy.

The difference between what *affects* individual states and what those states *can achieve as* individual states exists in relation to markets for goods and capital as well as to those for oil and other raw materials. Current long-term threats to ecological balance and to human living conditions ("the hole in the ozone layer," the pollution of the Rhine, the state of the Brazilian rainforests, Chernobyl, etc.) correspond to the same structural pattern, which has led to the nation-state's *regulatory competence* retreating hopelessly into the background in the face of a supranational *state of nature* made up of technical, economic, military, and ecological interdependencies and long-range effects.

The outlook is no better when we attempt to assess the condition of the *internal* sovereignty of the state in developed industrial democracies. Perhaps it is not too far-fetched to outline this development in a simple dialectical phase model. Its first phase consists in the cumulative acquisition by the state of responsibilities for comprehensive and long-term provision, driven forward by competition between national political parties. They include, in particular, responsibilities for full employment, growth, exchange rate stability, an external trade balance, and comprehensive social security. They include, too, responsibilities which these presuppose, namely for a continuity in the level of qualification of capital (through science and technology policy) and of labor (through policies in professional and further education). Both are supplemented by collective infrastructural investment in the fields of transport, communication, energy, health, and urban and regional development.

Then, in a second phase, there occurs a break with this trend toward a mounting up of the state's responsibilities. Within the institutional framework of a *steering state* (which must secure to itself the material means with which to carry out this ambitious catalog of responsibilities by creaming them off from an economic process steered by the market) and a *capitalist economic system* (in which investment and employment decisions are made by private entrepreneurs free from public control and oriented to individual profit), public policy *cannot* have at its disposal all the powers and resources it *would have to* have in order successfully to bear the burden of the responsibilities it had taken on. This is true even under crisis conditions (or under those of relatively mild turbulence). The state finds itself confronted here with the apparent task of solving a series of n equations with $n + m$ variables. In practical terms this constellation results in an increase in the veto powers and opportunities for obstruction of those individual and collective actors whose cooperation on the one hand *is indispensable*, but on the other hand *cannot be enforced*. Because their bargaining position is at once to their advantage *and* likely to undermine the achievement of political goals, they can increase the price the state must pay should it wish to secure their cooperation. This statement of the problem is by no means peculiar to Marxist theories of the capitalist state.[1] It has been made by neoconservative political theory on the basis of similar intellectual resources.[2] Central to this theory is the idea of a tradeoff between the state's *authority* and its *functions*[3] (its promised achievements). Its practical application is a warning that the state may be strained by and overloaded with its responsibilities, responsibilities which it can take on only at the price of self-inflicted harm to its decision-making authority, and with the consequence of its becoming over-indebted (in a literal as well as a figurative sense). The upshot of this analysis is that emergent steering deficits can be identified not only in the external relationship between nation-state and world market, but in the internal relationship between the state and its "internal environment," civil society.

Finally, in a third phase, some lessons are drawn from these experiences of disappointment. The result is a professedly "realistic" reduction in the scope of the state's steering claims, competences, and responsibilities, and of the agenda of what can and should be the object of public policy.[4]

That such a restrictive redefinition of the agenda and level of ambition of state action did occur at the end of the 1970s and beginning of the 1980s is not disputed, even by those who do not wish to adopt immediately such handy global formulas as "the end of the century of social democracy" (Ralf Dahrendorf). Over the following ten years, in the leading Western European countries, social democratic or socialist-led governments and center-left coalitions were replaced by liberal and conservative forces. This remarkably homogeneous trend was followed for a short electoral period (1979–82) even in Sweden's classic social-democratic political system. Its result has been that the active interventionism of the parties of the left, with its pretension to direct investment, to guarantee full employment, and to develop further the social state, global steering, and supranational Keynesianism, in short, the idea of an active, preventative and positively coordinated policy, has evidently exhausted itself.[5] And it has meant that today the remnants of a social democratic hegemony are to be found only at the northern and southern edges of Western Europe, and even then in the form of weak and brittle versions of it.

The reasons for this are not merely respective shifts in voting patterns, but also the political-theoretical discrediting of certain economic policy doctrines (such as all "left" variants of Keynesianism) and of the universal and long undisputed assumption that the responsibility exercised by the state for the living standards and quality of life of its citizens would ultimately converge with their actual needs and wants. At all events, at the end of the 1970s and beginning of the 1980s the theoreticians of the left found themselves confronted with the uncomfortable realization that (1) those "commanding heights" of the state from which, according to the old socialist idea, a society's mode of production and of life were to be transformed had been undermined and leveled off; and (2) a majority mandate for a social reformist etatist program could be achieved virtually nowhere – and this under precisely the crisis conditions for which this program took itself to be, so to speak, ready, and with which it assumed it was especially able to deal.

Conversely, the retreat into which reformist etatism saw itself forced on a broad front – in "public policy" as well as in "politics" – gave marked impetus to a wide variety of neoliberal, neoconservative, populist, and postmodern theories of the state and politics. In the social sciences, two particular variants of these uncommonly timely doctrines of state-theoretical resignation have gained attention and influence. On the one hand, systems-theoretical sociology announced that the concept of steering itself, as well as that of the individual or collective actor as a "subject" of steering, was to be renounced. On the other, there is the neo-utilitarian theory of order represented by the "New Political Economy" (NPE). Here I will confine myself to a few remarks on the second of these influential theoretical developments.

Determination of the Tasks of the State through Utilitarian Calculation?

The NPE provides critical as well as constructive arguments in answer to the question of which social functions and activities should be assigned to which sector – state, market, or private household – in such a way that a maximum of collective utility ("welfare") is produced. It begins with an individualistic definition of utility, whose consequence is that the only thing which counts as utility is that which is evaluated as such by individuals on the basis of free decision, and confirmed by them in conduct through corresponding dispositions over their property ("revealed preferences"). In this way the utilitarian theory of order has identified a wealth of suboptimalities and steering pathologies with which the majority of state activities, above all ambitious social security programs and the provision of collective goods, are apparently burdened. Among these are rationality deficits, state and professional paternalism, vicious circles, administrative inefficiencies, indiscriminate manipulation of needs, perverse stimuli, collective self-harm, free-rider phenomena, negative externalities, and a series of further examples of the irrationalities inherent in a system of state steering which has apparently hypertrophied. According to the NPE, checking and decisively reducing the scope of this system is imperative in the interests of maximum welfare.

It cannot be my task here to assess, even in outline, the results of a neo-utilitarian state theory whose argumentation is often distinguished by surprising insight, shrewd deductions, and a high degree of formal elegance. Instead, I would like to explore two implications which this approach has for political theory: (1) the relationship between the categories of "right" and "utility" which underpins it; and (2) the relationship which is thereby established between the rationality of action and an overarching authoritarian-technocratic "system rationality" or "metarationality" (P. Herder-Dornreich).

(1) For discussion of the first point, appeal can be made to the distinction between "nomocratic" and "teleocratic" argumentation strategies. Nomocratic strategies relate present actions to the past, and ask in which pregiven rights (that is, rights established in the past and currently valid) action in the present is grounded. Conversely,

teleocratic strategies relate action in the present to the future, and ask through which purposes and consequences it can be justified. The problem with the utilitarian theory of order is that it does not present itself with this alternative. Rather, it makes a doctrinal decision in advance in favor of a teleocratic strategy. As a result, rights come into play neither from the point of view of whether they accord with nature, with religious tradition, or with moral principles, nor from the point of view of whether they are "just" or substantively and formally reasonable, and can exercise a rationally groundable binding influence on action in the present (even where this entails a partial sacrifice of welfare gains which might otherwise be possible). Rather, they come into play from the opposite point of view, that of an economics of rights and institutions to which one-sided priority is given. This point of view asks whether institutions should be accepted or reformed within the instrumental perspective of their contribution to the maximization of "welfare."

However, this one-sided problematic deprives the New Political Economy of the success for which it strives, deprives it of a rational, scientifically persuasive foundation for, or critique of, institutions. For it is by no means clear that actors prefer certain institutions *solely* on "teleocratic" grounds, that is, because of their expected contributions to welfare. It could also be the case that institutions are preferred (or in cases of evident suboptimality, tolerated to a considerable degree) because they embody ideas of justice and collective identity. The stronger version of this objection, which I take to be sustainable, runs: Institutions always emerge and are transformed in contexts in which "nomocratic" and "teleocratic" elements are inextricably linked; they synthesize criteria of validity and of purposiveness; and just for this reason they cannot be criticized or legitimated solely and one-sidedly from the point of view of the latter. And the mixture of "nomocratic" and "teleocratic" points of view (one could say, in Weberian terms, of value-rational and purposive-rational orientations) which emerges in a concrete historical context is the result of a social, political, and cultural process of identity and will formation.

(2) The New Political Economy systematically neglects this many-sided foundation for institutions, treating them as if they were nothing more than welfare-maximizing machines. Therefore, it is compelled to substitute for a *recognition of the validity* of institutions, for which it cannot conceptually provide, the right, based on economic expertise, to identify theoretically and put into practice "correct," that is, welfare-maximizing, institutions.[6] Thus, for example, it rules out of court (what are identified as) institutional "inefficiencies" such as

rights of trade union amalgamation, human rights, social state guarantees, or if necessary democratic elections, all in the name of a universal increase in welfare. This necessary consequence of the New Political Economy's intellectual perspective makes it clear that its methodological neglect of valid rights, and of the nonutilitarian basis of their validity, that is, its one-sided fixation with purposiveness, deprives it of every argument against openly authoritarian,[7] indeed terroristic, uses of its theory of order.[8]

Determination of the Tasks of the State through Processes of Political Legitimation

The impressive international boom which the neo-utilitarian theory of "public choice," or "rational choice," is currently enjoying must, as I say, be seen against the background of the real disappointments met in the mid-1970s by the ambitions for an active reformism. The goal of full employment, as a matter for which the state is responsible, serves to illustrate the connection between political theory and reality. Under circumstances which effectively prevent the state from carrying out the responsibility it asserts for full employment, and in which the blame is put on that very assertion, an economic theory showing that full employment cannot come about through public policy, but only through *abstinence* from it and through deregulation of the labor market, provides – according to the psychological mechanism of "sour grapes" – a welcome relief. In other policy spheres too, such as education, the New Political Economy's welfare-theoretical analyses fulfill the palliative function of explaining how a reduction in the state's organizational responsibility leads to a gradual increase in welfare. But while they provide aids for dealing with disappointment, they do not provide compulsive arguments which would really explain the process through which the field of the state's tasks is to be restricted.

So far we have established that the spheres of state competence and responsibility have shrunk, and mentioned as candidates for an explanation of this process: first, social and economic changes, such as the growing autonomy of the state's internal and external environment; second, loss of confidence in and credibility of the etatist social-democratic model; third, the scientific-political success of neo-utilitarian theories. I do not believe that any of these explanations are convincing, least of all the third. The fact that unfavorable circumstances, such as interdependencies conditioned by the world market or distant effects, can make the business of "public policy" more difficult is not a compelling reason – and not one which is equally effective everywhere! – for a paradigm shift in the understanding of what public policy means. And pointing to certain fluctuations in voting behavior or changes in the climate of public opinion itself is not enough: they demand an explanation before they can be accepted as being one.

It seems to me that an important condition for an explanation of the phenomenon which interests us, the increasing practice of a doctrine of state-theoretical resignation,[9] is that we conceptualize the agenda of state action and the range of material resources and confidence entrusted to the state by society for the carrying out of its tasks as themselves the result of a political – or if it is one will, metapolitical – process.

Here, as a counterposition to economic determinism (be it Marxist or neoclassical) of a positive or normative type, I would like to propose and defend a point of view which initially leaves open, "voluntaristically," the definition of the state's activity and tasks. Hence the tasks of the state would be the totality of what, within the framework of existing political institutions, the bearers of social and political will formation *wish and expect* the tasks of the state to be. In other words, it is not "facts" or scientific theories which determine whether an existing conception of the tasks of the state, or of the power mechanisms which the state ought to have at its disposal, should be retained or allowed to lapse. Rather, this is the result of a conflict between organized social forces and voluntary associations, which support one (more ambitious) or another ("minimalist") conception of state activity. The range and content of the concept of the state are the product of a conflict between interpretations of social policy and political culture defended and put into practice by citizens and their voluntary associations as bearers of political will formation. My thesis is thus: the range of activity which the concept of the state (as the sum of its tasks and powers of intervention) substantively implies depends on the relative capacity for mobilization, organization, and conflict, and on the "politics of interpretation" of collective actors within "civil society."

For clarification of this thesis we can refer to the Swedish example, from which it can be concluded that a high degree of social class and group organization, and a high degree of centralization of such organizations, stands in a reciprocal relationship with an extensive capacity for state intervention and regulation.

In what follows I would like to examine in more detail four related hypotheses, without being able to provide more than a plausible basis for their proof.

1 The state's robustness and immunity to crisis depend neither on empirical events and developments in its national and international

environment, nor on the scientific plausibility of theoretical doctrines. They are far more directly dependent on conflictual processes of sociopolitical interpretation and will formation, whose result is "the social construction of state power."

2 These processes of interpretation and will formation regarding the content of the concept of the state will lead to the construction of a "strong" state when – according to the model of "organized capitalism" – their bearers are large, strong, secure, wide-ranging, and centralized organizations, formally organized hegemonial "blocs," and corporate collective actors, and when they are worked out via conflict between these actors.

3 These organized processes of will formation ("politics") result in demands, in definitions of progress, and support potentials which bring a wide range of "issues" on to the public policy agenda, and which demand from, or permit to, the executive a high degree of interventionary competence, regardless of the "color" of a particular government. But on the level of "policy" too, that is, in the formulation and carrying out of political-administrative intervention, a robust associative substructure is decisive for the success and structural durability of the state's interventionary competence. This is because formally organized and centralized collective actors are more sensitive and "responsive" to the specific means of intervention employed by public policy – money, law, information – than is to be expected when weak, pluralistic, or fragmented political actors dominate the state's field of action, or when the development of formal associations has not taken place or cannot take place for structural reasons.

4 For reasons mentioned in (2) and (3), on the input ("politics") as well as the output ("policy") side, a positive correlation is to be expected between the strength and robustness of the state, and the strength (that is, capacity for organization and mobilization) of its associative substructure of "political estates." However, the capacity for organization and conflict of collective actors active on the level of the associative substructure of the state depends for its part on social-structural changes in the division of social labor and in social stratification, on processes of cultural change ("individualization"), and on divisions occasioned by particular types of political issues. In accordance with the hypothesis of "disorganized capitalism" defended here,[10] the structural, cultural, and political tendencies mentioned work toward the replacement of a relatively solid system of large sociopolitical organizations by an amorphous multiplicity of groups and actors organized on a populist or syndicalist basis. This is at the very least unfavorable to the emergence and maintenance of an ambitious theory and practice of state intervention and regulation.

Collective Action and its Social-Structural Conditions: Premises of "Active" Policy

In accordance with the hypothetical framework sketched here, a positive relationship can be expected between, on the one hand, the strength and interventionary competence of the executive as the "sovereign" collective actor, and on the other, the capacity for organization and action of intermediate social organizations. But still more interesting than an exploration of this relationship, whose attendant problems of operationalization and data-gathering we cannot even begin to confront here, is a question which follows directly from it. What are the possible explanations for that weakening of intermediate collective actors which, according to our hypothesis, the state's lack of interventionary and steering competence would bring with it? Here I would like to present just a brief overview of the hypothesis and assumptions which the social-scientific literature has to offer on this second question of *the causes of weakened "associability" in industrially developed capitalist democracies.*

(1) For a number of years, a standard topos of empirical and theoretical research into social structure has been the finding (and its interpretation) that "modern" social structures tend toward the dissolution of large-scale uniformities of social position and social mileu, and the replacement of these by atomized, pluralized, and rapidly changing social and cultural formations ill-suited to association. The sociological analysis of social structure through the construction of types and an empirically supported presentation of normal forms, normal biographies, and normal processes proves increasingly difficult and risky. The conceptual building blocks of such types (class, occupation, self-employment versus wage labor, country versus city, family, religion, etc.) become blurred, and their suitability for synthesis into type constructs is increasingly called into question. The sociological problem seems to be that the probability of a correlation between an individual's biography and social situation is becoming indeterminate and variable. Drawing a conclusion about income level from profession, about profession from education, about voting behavior from confession and church membership, and about family forms and modes of upbringing, consumer behavior, political orientation or membership of voluntary associations from all of these variables, becomes risky, and statistically supportable generalizations become correspondingly difficult.

That would be trifling were it simply a problem for sociologists, who in the face of it nevertheless retain the possibility of bringing to bear an entire apparatus of observational and analytical techniques. But to problems *sociologists* have of type formation there correspond problems of *social* coding confronting every individual who, in the classification and sociocultural placing of relevant others (work colleagues, members of the opposite sex and of other generations, friends from club, association or party, neighbors, etc.), is forever and increasingly faced with unfamiliar experiences and surprises. For these "others" do not fit preconceived expectations and stereotypical perceptions, or they turn up in contexts where they are not expected. Added to this is an involuntary or achieved mobility which multiplies this problem of orientation.

The result of this structural situation, or so it is widely assumed, is a reflexive pluralism. The consequence of this is that it must appear advisable to everyone to make the average number of experiences shared with others as low as is feasible, to raise thresholds in a defensive or privatizing attitude, and in general, with no concern for their generalizability or groundable claims to validity, to wander about in the postmodern market of fashions and opinions, styles and techniques, chances and choices. To the extent that such descriptions, widespread in social science and philosophy, literature and film, are accurate, one can conclude that opportunities of large social groups or categories for binding, organized collective action will be dramatically reduced, that, so to speak, the structural presuppositions of associative mass formation will deteriorate.

(2) Wolfgang Streeck has penetratingly described how collective actors such as churches, trade unions, professional associations, and also political parties typically respond to decreasingly favorable opportunities for collective action with a search for a way out of their organizational dilemma, a search which sooner or later leads them to seek organizational assistance and resources provided by the state, or the institutional subsidies which are now widely available for forms of collective action which, under the circumstances described, cannot, or can no longer, support themselves. The best-known example through which to appreciate this is the German debate over the funding of political parties. But conversely, just as the principle of "external" state support for forms of association unable to support themselves appears defensible and even desirable from a functional point of view, or on grounds of social justice, so one cannot ignore the dialectic in which artificial respiration via state subsidies weakens rather than strengthens associative energies within "civil society." In the first place, as political parties and other organs of collective will formation and interest representation are turned into state bodies, an image can

arise of "detached," "encrusted," or "congealed" "elite cartels." This then serves as an excuse or reason for groupings of populist reaction and moralistic crusades with their unavoidable organizational and substantive primitiveness. In the second place, in accordance with the principle that what the state has given it can take back again, the absorption of associational life by the state gives rise to the opportunity and the temptation deliberately and selectively to attack individual bearers of sociopolitical will formation and interest representation.

(3) In view of the current constellation of nation-states and global forces, and of current social problems, it is not wholly mistaken to speak of an erosion of political programs and visions able to mobilize widespread support. In conditions of a "new obscurity" and because of a lack of basic clarity and distinctiveness, political-theoretical formations such as "socialism," "conservatism," or "liberalism" can contribute neither to the organization and orientation of action nor to a descriptive coding of the universe of forces, demands, and problem solutions. In this sense, perhaps the thesis put forward by Daniel Bell in the subtitle to his well-known book of 1960 (*The End of Ideology*) is correct, albeit for a different period: we could speak of "an exhaustion of political ideas in the 1980s." As proof of this one would have to add the increasing popularity in the 1980s of "partial" or "syncretic" political theories.

Measured against the classical standard of *complete* and *consistent* political theory, the shortcomings of their current representatives are obvious. Since the seventeenth century, classical political theories have been distinguished by their demonstration of the principles according to which the rational interests of numerous individuals result in a just and peaceful order, which all can acknowledge as such and without coercion, and which is thereby stable. Instead of this, the formal similarity which exists between Western European social democracy, Eastern European party communism, Anglo-Saxon economic liberalism, and the politically significant new social movements is that, in a state of more or less open perplexity, they attempt to synthesize or achieve a precarious balance between entirely heterogeneous principles of political and social order. And they do so without the projected patchwork of political order having the slightest claim to be what Marx thought he already saw before him in the Paris commune: *the* "political form at last discovered [under which to work out the economic emancipation of labor]."[11]

Instead of that, both in theory and in practice, either definitions of institutional forms of social life are cross-bred (be it in the "mixed economy" of welfare state and market, or in the Eastern European synthesis of command economy and political democracy), or classical political theoretical constructions, such as allowing the category of individual interest to expand into that of a universal order, are simply smuggled in. This is done by economic liberals, who cannot show how a stable and just aggregate state is supposed to emerge from the dynamics of sanctified business interests, and by green fundamentalists, who certainly have before them a vision of a stable and just order (at least of the relationship between nature and society) but who are in no position to show why the mass of the population ought to take an interest in it.

(4) A direct result of these political theoretical shortcomings is the absence of political institutions and constitutional arrangements with the qualities exhibited by what March and Olsen call "appropriate institutions."[12] These are distinguished by the fact that they exercise a unique obligation effect, only created by institutions which are above the suspicion of being strategically exploitable or burdened with internal political bias. In Germany at least, such immunity to what the authors call the "consequentialist" suspicion of illegitimate interest-political bias is not attributed either to political parties, parliamentary bodies, the media, the bureaucracy, or to organized science. Rather, in science, politics, and journalism, there is a widespread fear that under modern, or postmodern, social-structural conditions, it is not possible for those institutions which would be up to the task of supporting a modern equivalent of republican virtue through their obligation effect, and of activating unexploited moral capacities and cooperative willingness, to have their credibility either reactivated or "reinvented."[13]

The Dilemma of State Intervention in Unorganized Fields of Action

According to the hypothetical framework introduced above, there is a positive relationship between strong associability and the steering capacity of the state. This is so not only on the "input side" of the political process, where it requires a dense network of stable alliances and hegemonial bloc formations within "civil society," but also on its "output side," where state steering is directed at stable, organized, reliable, and addressable partners in its social environment. At the same time, these partners function as relay stations for state intervention, and can do so because, as formal organizations, they on the one hand show an interest in their own continued existence, and on the other understand the "language" of financial, legal, and informational signals through which public policy is "communicated."

However, in the Western European states in latter years there has occurred a unique and underresearched phenomenon which contrasts with public policy in the 1950s and 1960s. This is the prevalence of issues and explicitly thematized steering problems in which public policy is addressed not to *constituted collective actors*, but directly to the *everyday life praxis of individuals* and the material circumstances of social bodies which are informally or poorly organized. The prevalence of the distinct steering problems of social systems which are not formally organized makes it difficult for the state to rely on the intermediary understanding and positive reaction of associations in society when implementing its policy strategies and programs. Thus the impression is given that the state is incapable of steering, or that conditions in its problem environment are irremediable.

When public policy entails a change in the conditions of action of regional bodies, individual industrial concerns or banks, welfare associations, trade unions, or medical bodies (that is, formally organized bodies), an algorithm of reactions might be worked out and built into a conception of rational policy. But a comparable degree of certainty is hardly to be expected when policy has to influence the conduct of individuals in a politically desirable way with respect to the environment, transport, health, education, neighborhood, consumption, crime, or reproduction. Yet it is precisely those steering problems involving relatively diffuse actors who are difficult to address collectively and whose behavior is hard to predict which seem to be increasing in number and significance. They belong to the category of political fields in which state bodies have to deal with the life practice of individuals, and beyond that possibly with collectivities such as self-help groups, citizens' initiatives, social movements, and more or less closed milieus and scenes, all of them with a low degree of formal organization. In all these cases, "pedagogic" intervention (F. X. Kaufmann) presents itself as a solution, as is demonstrated by the proliferation of special curricula offered by schools.

If the distinction made here, between steering problems involving organized addressees and partners and those where the problem environment is unorganized, can be drawn relatively sharply, and if my impression is correct that there has been a decisive relative growth in the second category within the spatiotemporal boundaries discussed, then the question arises as to possible explanations for such a restriction in the range of objects of state steering. Here I would like to contrast two, without deciding between or judging them.

A more "strategic" type of explanation could appeal to the fact that the conservative political right, and the leftist and libertarian politics of small parties and new social movements, have for very different reasons, but in a formally similar way, pushed into the foreground a broad agenda of "soft" quality-of-life and lifestyle issues. These contrast with issues such as those of "living standards" and their internal and external security. Thus the period since the mid-1970s has seen a conjuncture of socialization, cultural and, if one may say so, "moral" political issues for which, as far as I am aware, the 1950s and 1960s offer no parallel. Among these are themes of family and sexual morality, law and order, penal policy, the work ethic, and the duties of citizens; they extend on the one hand to the defence of national and ethnic identity, and on the other to questions of the morality of gender relationships, conduct toward the environment, relationships with the Second and Third World, and responsibility toward future generations. In order to explain this it does not seem too far-fetched to assume that here, too, we are dealing with a strategic calculation on the part of political elites or counterelites, and that when the prospects for success in the field of "old" policies of growth, security, and distribution appear limited, they attempt to "change trains," from a more corporatist program to one with a more expressive-moralizing style.

This would not be wholly incompatible with the second, more "objectively" oriented explanatory approach. Its point of departure is the phenomena of disorganization and social pathology which become policy issues of the type referred to, and which lie so "deep" that they remain out of reach of the established methods of steering and collective action. From this perspective the next step is to refer to very real problems which are by no means artificially "inferred," but which are pregnant with consequences, and a potential threat to social integration. These manifest themselves on a collective level in the sphere of attitudes to health, socialization, and deviance, in ways of coping with adolescent crises and rites of passage, and in the interaction between ascriptively defined social categories (above all those of gender, age, ethnic membership, and health).

Notes

1 A. Przeworski and I. Wallerstein, "Structural Dependence of the State on Capital," *American Political Science Review* 82 (1988).
2 S. Huntington, "The United States," in M. Crozier et al. (eds), *The Crisis of Democracy* (New York, 1975).
3 See N. Luhmann, *Politische Theorie im Wohlfahrtsstaat* (Munich and Vienna, 1981).

4 The three phases could be supplemented, speculatively, by a fourth, which would consist in a renewed expansion of the public policy agenda. A reason for this, and in general for a cyclical expansion and contraction, would be an assumed crisis of "understeering" occurring at the end of the third phase.

5 Thus one of the main speakers at the 1988 annual party conference of the SPD in Münster, Oskar Lafontaine, confirmed that the economic premises of a "national taxation sovereignty" no longer existed, but, symptomatically, gave no thought to whether and how such a sovereignty might be restored.

6 As, for example, the current Chilean constitution institutionalizes in an authoritarian way the viewpoint, derived from the Chicago School, that under no circumstances should the Chilean state own and manage economic enterprises.

7 Compare the publications of L. Mead, *Beyond Entitlement: The Social Obligations of Citizenship* (New York and London, 1986), and C. Murray, *Losing Ground: America's Social Policy 1950–1980* (New York, 1984), which have enjoyed success in the United States.

8 It is to be noted in the interests of completeness that the same point of view, with opposite signs attached, could be brought to bear against attempts within jurisprudence to establish the content and limits of state activity through a one-sided exaggeration of the "nomocratic" perspective and by means of dogmatic forms of argumentation.

9 The research group "Tasks of the State," which in 1988–9 worked at the centre for interdisciplinary research at the University of Bielefeld, and under whose auspices the author presented some of these ideas as lectures, began with a conference whose title was as stimulating as it was symptomatic: "Dissolution of the Concept of the State?"

10 Compare here S. Lash and J. Urry, *The End of Organized Capitalism* (Cambridge, 1987); C. Offe, *Disorganized Capitalism* (Cambridge, 1985); as well as W. Streeck, "Vielfalt und Interdependenz. Uberlegungen zur Rolle von intermediären Organisationen in sich ändernden Umwelten," *Kölner Zeitschrift für Soziologie und Sozialpsychologie* 39 (1987).

11 K. Marx, "The Civil War in France," in Karl Marx and Friedrich Engels, *Collected Works*, vol. 22 (London, 1986), p. 334.

12 J. G. March and J. P. Olsen, *Rediscovering Institutions: The Organizational Basis of Politics* (New York, 1989), ch. 9.

13 Compare C. Offe and U. Preuss, "Can Democratic Institutions Make 'Efficient' Use of Moral Resources?" in D. Held (ed.), *Political Theory Today* (Cambridge, 1990).

7

Beyond the Labor Market: Reflections on a New Definition of "Domestic" Welfare Production

WITH ROLF G. HEINZE

Structural Bottlenecks in Welfare Production

A characteristic social-structural feature of the postwar history of the Western European industrial societies – at least until the mid-1970s, when an unprecedentedly long period of prosperity came to an end – was that the extent of formal wage labor mediated by the labor market absolutely and relatively increased, and expanded at the expense of sectors and forms of labor which had yet to be modernized.[1] To be sure, the time devoted to paid employment *per labor unit* dropped due to various reductions in working hours, but this effect was more than compensated for, above all by a growth in part-time work. The result was a net growth in the time devoted to paid labor *per household*. Thus households are increasingly integrated into the labor market in order to satisfy their need for monetary income.

The consequence and at the same time the presupposition of this increasing "commodification" of labor is that many goods and products which were hitherto produced by independent domestic labor are now obtained by the expenditure of monetary income on appropriate markets for goods and services, or from national and local governmental institutions. We can characterize this as a twofold coupling of household to market. Our interest here is in some unintended and less obvious consequences of this coupling, and in the problems which result from it. These will include such phenomena as:

- an extensive deskilling of household members with respect to the capacities, knowledge, and motivation required when the satisfaction of needs takes place through independent labor and self-provision outside, or relatively far away from, the market;
- a gradual transformation of the domestic sphere into a sphere of consumption largely freed from productive functions;
- a corresponding alteration in household structures, with an important role being played by the fact that economic stimuli to the formation of "larger" household units lose their importance, and in particular the "extended family household" loses its positive economic function as the predominant form of domestic life.

However, such tendencies toward a long-term social "modernization" of the private household run up against two countertrends which have clearly emerged since the mid-1970s. On the one hand, the continuing and persistent employment crisis places limits on the opportunities for earning income on the labor market. On the other, the spending power of the private household, which is thereby reduced, encounters an increase in the price of services relative to that of goods. For both these reasons a countermovement emerges whose objective tendency, at least, is to make the satisfaction of needs through domestic self-provision and "self-service" increasingly attractive and economically rational. On the one hand, "time" as a resource is increasingly available for such activities (due to the decreasing labor time to lifetime ratio resulting from the continuing employment crisis). On the other, an effect on economic motivation would presumably result from the comparative advantages of self-provision in the context of a relative increase in the prices of just those services which have a "domestic" character.

Another factor working toward a requalification of the domestic sphere could be the fact that "domestic time" is increasingly taken account of in the rationalization strategies of those offering public and private services, and is treated by them as an unpaid-for factor of production.

In business and industry, the supply of half-finished products from which one can assemble the finished one at home is increasing (for example in furniture and electrical goods). DIY stores selling a wide range of materials and tools are experiencing a boom. Mention could also be made of traditional domestic tailoring and knitting. Were the use of solar panelling and heating pumps to spread in future, they would make possible a higher level of self-provision of domestic energy supplies. Independent labor features strongly in the construction of family housing. In commerce, self-service has become self-evident. The same goes for public transport. This applies not only to self-service in the purchase of tickets for urban transportation or the replacement of porters at stations or airports by trolleys, but above all to the use of one's own car. In bodily hygiene and in cleaning, automatic washing machines and new washing powders have halted the expansion of large launderettes, and new products have made shaving and haircare easier in the home. A swimming pool at home replaces visits to the public baths. In tourism, self-service restaurants, holiday homes and camping sites feature strongly. Progress in the electronics industry has allowed record or cassette players, radio or video to replace visits to theatre, cinema, or concert.[2]

Gershuny,[3] who believes that the upshot of these trends is a gain in the significance of independent production within the household, sums them up with the concept of a "self-service economy." He thereby distances himself from the vision of a "postindustrial" service economy (Daniel Bell). According to Gershuny, the growing "tertiary" needs of consumers are being satisfied less through enterprise in the service sector, whose consequence would be an increase in employment, than through a combination of capital goods (mainly labor-saving domestic appliances) and individual work in the household. Without going into the social policy implications of a "domestic economy" (such as the privatization and isolation which accompanies it), we wish to illustrate briefly, with some data, how far the average West German household has developed into a sphere of capital- and technology-intensive production. Here, the fixed capital value of its consumer goods and commodities is greater than the average investment costs for one industrial workplace.[4] Thus, in 1983 the average four-person household of middle-income employees contained a multitude of consumer durables (such as washing machines, cookers, fridges, etc.). The list shows the percentages of such households possessing selected consumer goods in that year.[5]

Car	87.9
Telephone	90.4
Colour television	85.1
Video recorder	10.6
Camera	94.7
Motor/Sailing boat	1.8
Fridge	82.1
Fridge-freezer	21.7
Freezer	69.5
Dishwasher	33.2
Washing machine	76.1

| Vacuum cleaner | 98.2 |
| Electric mixer | 92.4 |

In addition to cost factors, there are *qualitative* considerations which suggest that some branches of welfare production are shifting back into the sphere of domestic self-provision. These considerations include not only the qualitative superiority of domestically prepared food over ready meals, but also the notable quality disadvantages and deficits in the realm of psychosocial, educational, and care services, deficits which are largely bound up with the bureaucratic-professional form in which these services are provided.

However, against the temporal, financial, and qualitative reasons for a *reactivation* of domestic self-provision there are also counterforces. Some of the structural changes which the household has undergone in the past stand in the way of such a "trend reversal." One could say that the household has become part of a process of modernization, or commercialization, and that a way out of this process, toward greater self-provision, is prevented by a series of obstacles. These include, chiefly, the absence of a cultural or motivational basis for self-provision, the completely dequalified nature of domestic independent labor, that is, the decline in the "human capital" it requires, and a decrease in the size of the private household. Indeed, there is a significant difference between the older forms of domestic self-provision and independent labor (for example in the growing, conservation, and preparation of food) and the newer forms of self-service. The basis for the first type of activity was plans, resources, knowledge, and skills *peculiar* to the household, whereas in the second case, only the simplest tasks of household members are taken into account by suppliers *external* to it, and appealed to by them in order to cut their own costs (an example here is the self-assembly of low-cost furniture). One reason for the decline in independently planned labor of the first type is the decreasing size of the average household. Its "small format" character is accompanied by dramatic negative economies of scale, making self-provision on a larger scale "no longer worthwhile."

While around 44% of households at the turn of the century still contained five or more members, in 1982 in the Federal Republic of Germany the figure was only 8%. A comparison of household sizes in 1925 and 1970 reveals the following characteristic changes:

- the proportion of single-person households rose from 6.7% to 25.1% (the largest proportion of this group being widowed or divorced people over 40);
- the number of two- or three-person households rose by 17.3%;

– the number of "large households" (five or more members) fell by 20.6%.

The proportion of single-person households continued to grow: in 1984 it already stood at 31%, and in 1985 in certain big cities (such as Hamburg) 40% of households were already made up of people living alone. In 1982 in the Federal Republic 7.9 million lived alone. These are not just older people, but to an increasing extent those in middle age, who have either lived alone for some time or who do so following divorce or separation (including here the death of a partner).

The proportion of two-person households also increased: in 1982 28.7% fell into this category. Furthermore, at that time only 17.7% of households had three members (in 1950 23%) and only 14.4% had four.[6] This trend toward smaller households and the reduction of the household to the nuclear family is starkly illustrated by the fact that the proportion of households containing members of more than two generations shrank to less than 5%.

The household's limited production potential, caused by its unfavorable "size of enterprise structure," is brought out not only by diminishing family size and change in family structure; it is also demonstrated in the family's growing *instability*. One index of this is the divorce rate (annual divorces per 10,000 marriages). Between 1965 and 1982 this doubled from 39.2 to 78.4. In 1984 there were 364,000 marriages and 130,000 divorces. In 1960 the figures were 500,000 marriages and 50,000 divorces. An Austrian study of family demography suggested that more than 30% of all marriages which had taken place in the immediately preceding years would end in divorce.[7] The number of "incomplete" families, occasioned by a greater number of divorces, is increasing: in 1982 the proportion was 11.4% as against 7.7% in 1970. In total, in 1982, there were almost one million single mothers or fathers with one or more children under 18.

Parallel to the growing instability of the family, which, if opinion polls conducted among young people are to be believed, has had hardly any effect on the attraction of the family as a way of life,[8] nonmarital shared households and communes have expanded. According to the Emnid Institute, in the mid-1980s there were over one million shared households whose members were not married, four times as many as in 1975. By contrast with the traditional family household, these households may well reveal an even higher rate of membership fluctuation.

Taken as a whole these data reveal a constellation of problems which we have called the "modernization trap." Traditional forms of independent labor and domestic self-provision are suppressed by, on the one hand, the link between private household and labor market, which became ever closer during the prosperous postwar period of growth and full employment, and, on the other hand, by markets for goods and services. Households become dependent on an external relationship to goods and services. In turn, the object of those is an extensive rationalization of domestic labor (in cleaning, food preparation, and caring) and the transformation of what was once "domestic time" (above all for female household members) into economically "productive time" (possibly in part-time employment). However, under conditions of mass unemployment, this dynamic circle in which household and goods and labour markets are integrated through reciprocal stimulation comes to a standstill. In these circumstances, from a cost-cutting point of view, or from that of how one disposes of one's time, or from that of the quality of goods and services, it *would be* rational for households to "switch back" to forms of independent labor or self-provision. But, apart from the numerous examples of *externally* organized "self-service," this option is largely closed to them because of the circumstances outlined above, which are a result of a structural and cultural process of household modernization.

Natural Adaptation Processes

In response to this contradictory relationship between the rationality of increased self-provision and a structurally limited capacity to make use of it, a large number of partial solutions has emerged. These lie in the grey area between market/state and household. However, in many of these more or less "informal" arrangements suboptimalities can be identified, be it with respect to the cost and quality of goods and services, or to negative collective consequences. To begin with, we will examine a few of these arrangements and identify the provision deficits (that is, deficits in collective goods) which accompany them.

Do-it-yourself activities This is certainly the most important form of domestic self-provision, and it has been stimulated by a wealth of products developed specifically for this purpose. According to some estimates, in the Federal Republic of Germany in 1985 DM 30 billion was spent on tools, building materials, machinery, carpentry materials, etc., while the figure at the beginning of the 1960s was not even a tenth of this. Construction and DIY markets can be found in all larger regions and cities, with warehouses and DIY centers experiencing a growing boom. In 1983, approximately 12.7 million people in the Federal Republic of Germany regularly engaged in do-it-yourself activities; in addition, approximately 11 million did so occasionally.

That made a total of 23.7 million spending a significant part of their leisure time on handicraft work in the domestic sphere – 3.84 million spent more than a hundred hours a year on "crafts." Although this group has since become differentiated and encompassed new groups, a profile of the typical active home craftsperson can be established. He is male, aged between 40 and 60, relatively well qualified (a specialist or an office worker), has a middle income, owns or is building his own home, and has a large household with two or three children.[9]

The DIY movement is not merely a temporary wave of fashion; its expansion has deep-lying causes. Alongside a shortening of working hours in the postwar decades, which first created the temporal conditions for this type of work, there has been a significant change in attitudes toward paid and independent labor. For a growing number of DIYers, work for income appears to have lost more than its quantitative significance, and at the same time the willingness to undertake domestic renovation or self-help in the building of one's own home has increased. Welfare surveys of 1980 and 1984 established that handicraft work as well as routine domestic tasks were performed largely as self-provision.

A considerable number of households carry out work which demands craft skills. In 1984, for example, 62% of households replied that they normally wallpapered their homes themselves. By no means all of the remaining households employed a firm. This was true of only 24% of households; 17% received help from relatives, neighbors, or friends. Another sphere of independent labor is housebuilding. In 1980 30% of private households claimed to have built the basic shell of the house largely by themselves, and 37% had undertaken its interior fitting.[10]

Apart from the need to "at some time make something oneself," this development is encouraged by the considerable increase in the price of services offered on the market. The costs of work done by professional craftspeople have increased to such an extent that many have no alternative but to become craftspeople themselves.

However, more recently the boom in DIY appears to have declined. Several firms have registered a loss in turnover as a result of falling disposable incomes, the construction of fewer new houses, and the relative durability of equipment. In the DIY sector the period of double-figure growth rates (in the 1970s) may be over. But according to some estimates the real growth rates will still be 3–4% a year, as DIY activities are increasingly concentrated on the improvement of existing fittings and furnishings and on home comforts.

But the efficiency of this arrangement is limited by the fact that the capital costs of the procurement of equipment (either in an absolute sense of per unit of output) is for many households too high, or cannot compete with the unit costs of externally provided services. The space required for DIY activities, which in typical domestic conditions can be a problem, also has a limiting effect. A further limit may be a lack of the required knowledge and skills, resulting in a lower standard of provision. This can have a negative impact on collective interests, such as the interest in security (as for example, when vehicle repairs are carried out incompetently). The predominantly "less than professional" nature of the tools contributes here to the inferior quality of the goods and services for which they are used.

A feature of DIY activity is that the desired independence of household from market is not supported through resources peculiar to the household, but is secured through markets for the appropriate tools and materials: one must buy something in order *not* to have to buy something else. And this condition ties DIY to structures of *income* distribution. In addition, it remains bound to knowledge and skills which households are able to supply on the basis of their members' *professionally* developed stocks of knowledge, competence, motivation, and contacts. Only if the requisite knowledge and skills are supplied in an organized way (for instance, by technical colleges) can the efficiency of DIY arrangements in certain spheres (such as repairs) be extended further. And there is now an enormous demand for appropriate courses and learning opportunities. Alongside the factors of income, space, and qualifications already mentioned, a further condition for the economic rationality of self-provision may be that the time devoted to it be evaluated not solely as "labor time," but at least partly as time devoted to a hobby and as an opportunity for "productive fulfillment of self." The disadvantageous cost–benefit relationship manifesting itself in small household size, underuse of tools, and correspondingly high capital costs per unit is frequently compensated for in this way.

Work in the black economy This is a limit case of normal wage labor, characterized by the fact that labor costs are not burdened with taxes and social security contributions, and that the corresponding savings are shared between the supplier of labor power and its beneficiary. Accordingly, the market for illegal labor will be the larger the sharper is the separation between *wages* and labor *costs* on account of labor's being legally burdened with taxes and contributions. It will also be the larger the more restricted are earning opportunities of a formal-legal type. In fact, work in the black economy is limited as a rule to that which is available intermittently, in construction, repairs, and maintenance. It is performed by various population groups. Many are merely pursuing a second job in their leisure time, others are employed wholly "illegally" (that is, illegally hired laborers, those unemployed or reported sick). A report published in 1983 by the International Labor Office in Geneva speaks of 10 percent of employees in the industrialized countries being employed in the black economy. In the Federal Republic of Germany, too, the supply of illegal (mostly foreign) labor power continued to grow in the 1980s. An estimated 300,000 positions were filled by means of this "modern slave trade."

Work in the black economy finds a particular center of gravity in artisanal trades, although empirical estimates of its scope are not as yet readily available.[11] To be sure, work done "underground" is offered on an individual basis and provided through personal contacts, but it is nevertheless in large part paid labor whose basis is the motivation to earn an income. It remains bound thereby to the operating principles of a market economy, differing from the official economy only in the way it lies outside tax and social insurance legislation. For this reason Pahl and Wallace include illegal work for money in the category of wage labor.

> Wage labor can be registered or not, protected or not, and the social relationships of wage laborers can to a greater or lesser degree be modified or moderated through the action of the state. We claim that where wages and salaries are exchanged for work, the character of the work remains at its core the same, regardless of whether it is formally designated in national statistics or not. This sphere can include small enterprises with their particular relations of production, which have their own nonregistered, hidden aspects or "shadows."[12]

In the schema proposed by Pahl and Wallace, the second sphere encompasses work which meets household needs, and the production and consumption of goods and services by household members, and finally there is a third sphere, of further interest here, which

> encompasses all those activities performed by members of other households, regardless of whether or not they are relatives. On the whole, the point of this work is not payment, or if it is, the payment does not follow strictly market principles. It is more likely that goods and services are exchanged according to norms of reciprocity, which in particular areas can be especially binding and effective. But once again our interest here is in these activities as a whole, regardless of the motivational structures and type of compulsion under which the work is done. Work is defined here by the specific social relationships and local contexts within which it occurs.[13]

This eminently sensible sociological distinction makes clear how mistaken it can be to classify as part of a *single* sector, such as the "informal" or "shadow" economy, all those productive activities standing outside tax and social security legislation, be they those of the household, self-help groups, or illegally hired labor. Illegal work is a prominent issue in politics and the media because, on the one hand, there has been a considerable increase in the losses of public enterprises, and on the other hand, politically influential groupings (middle-class associations and the politicians linked with them) make noises about the "dangers" of a shadow economy. According to relevant reports,[14] in the Federal Republic of Germany in 1984 the shadow economy had a turnover of DM 150 billion (as against 100 billion in 1980). The resulting loss in tax revenue amounted to around DM 50 billion in 1984, and the loss in social insurance contributions around DM 30 billion. That corresponds to a million job vacancies, and it is often argued that, in the interests of the middle class and employment policy generally, such vacancies could and should be filled by "legal employees."

However, despite measures to stem the tide of illegal work, a significant reduction in its scope is hardly to be expected. Rather, it is a reaction to the functional shortcomings of the formal economy, and – especially when there is a chronic surplus of labor – has negative and positive effects on the interests of all parties, whether employers, employees, or consumers. "Illegally" employed *workers* seek an income which supplements transfer, insurance, or market income, and which their market position or qualifications prevent them from seeking on the regular labor market. They pay for it with a loss in the security of wage, job, and benefits which is a feature of regular working conditions. *Households* taking on illegal labor exploit price advantages for the work concerned – and pay for it with uncertainty over quality and guarantees. *Employers* who take on illegal labor gain the advantage of substantially lower wage bills and above all labor costs – and pay for it, sometimes completely, through punishment in case of discovery. The *collective* consequences of illegal work are, on the one hand, the generation of income which would not otherwise be generated and the satisfaction of needs which would not otherwise be satisfied, but, on the other hand, "collective self-harm" to the economy, which can range from shortfalls in public revenues from taxes and contributions, through a deterioration in the social situation of "marginal" groups of workers, to loss of markets for middle-class suppliers of labor.

For all that, it remains the case that, sociologically, illegal work is a form of adaptation *within* the context of a distribution of work and income mediated by the *market*. But our interest here is in precisely those factors which lead, or can lead, to a transgression of the boundaries of this sphere. In this sense our concern is with perspectives which suggest that the adaptation mechanism of "illegal" work or employment actually runs up against such boundaries, and that it cannot compensate adequately for the employment crisis. For the limited fields to which it applies and the unequal access to it – it is often necessary to have knowledge, relations, contacts, etc., to enter a market rendered invisible by its illegality – are arguments against "work in the black economy" as a system for the satisfaction of needs. An empirical study from Great Britain also shows that it is precisely the unemployed who lack opportunities in the "market for illegal work," and who, being cut off from the labor market and the resources supplied by it, are less able to do informal work in the home than those who are in work.[15] A similar line is taken by Jessen et al., who conducted a study of informal work done by industrial workers outside the enterprise.

> Material and social dependence on wage labor in an enterprise is also decisive for the role in provision played by work outside the enterprise. This connection between formal and informal labor consists above all in the simple fact that informal work, too, requires resources: material (space, equipment, machinery, raw materials), social (personal networks and contacts), and technical and moral qualifications (skills, work discipline). Under given social conditions, for industrial workers these resources are largely dependent on one's position in the formal economy. A wage income makes possible the procurement of the means of production for highly valued informal work. Professional qualifications are frequently put to use outside the enterprise. The social network of those employed in enterprises is usually superior in qualifications and information to neighborhood groups and relatives. Finally, access to the enterprise opens up a broad potential in materials, equipment, and machinery.[16]

Neighborhood assistance and self-help As a result of the fall in average household size, the instability of its composition, and indeed, its increasing spatial mobility, a limited potential for organized "inter-household" neighborhood assistance is to be expected. Where such forms of self-help exist, they mostly involve small-scale, discontinuous, and sporadic forms of need satisfaction, whose functioning also requires a considerable degree of "trust." For the consumer of the service in question (for example, caring), this will be trust in the service's quality and in its having no negative effect on the intimate sphere of domestic life. The supplier must be confident of adequate compensation in the form of money or services in kind, or in the helping relationship's being honored for its own sake.

All this demonstrates that spontaneous forms of neighborhood assistance are largely sporadic, small in scale, have a limited range of objects, and are threatened by instabilities arising out of the high value placed on the intimacy and anonymity of private life. In view of the demands for mobility, only a few households are able to develop continuous and reliable reciprocal relationships, although a growing demand for assistance activities is likely. Neighborhood assistance may be concentrated in social services such as childcare, and care of the sick, the ill, the elderly, or the handicapped. Families with several children are more tightly bound to neighborhood networks; and women and children are in general the essential "supports" of neighborhood assistance.[17]

Nevertheless, the extent of neighborhood assistance lags decisively behind help from *relatives*, as welfare surveys from 1980 and 1984 suggest.

> Care for the ill and handicapped, as well as childcare, are undertaken mainly by relatives, with neighbors and friends playing only a secondary role. Other tasks are exchanged among neighbors only in exceptional cases. Evidently they are confined to "emergency aid" in matters of everyday life. The type and frequency of help given depends above all on appropriate skills and specialized knowledge. In general, older respondents offer less assistance, especially to friends or in extensive handicraft work, though they clearly help with childcare, care for the sick, and with personal problems. Auto repairs and building work are done mostly by qualified workers, and as a rule provided through contact networks whose roots lie not in the domestic sphere or neighborhood but in relationships with colleagues. Once again, this indicates that part of the assistance network embraces services which require very specific qualifications. On average, handicraft work is done three times as much by men as by women, childcare and care of the sick twice as much by women as by men.[18]

The extent of neighborhood assistance may thus be limited to relatively homogeneous and immobile working-class and middle-class neighborhoods. Moreover, it is clear that private assistance networks among neighbors, friends, colleagues, and relatives are limited by the fact that guarantees of assistance are bound in many cases to expectations of reciprocity. In a survey conducted in 1984 among 2,084 selected heads of household on the subject of the voluntary and informal activities of household members, emphasis was given to the importance of informal work for one's standard of living, but nevertheless clear limits were placed on "natural" forms of neighborhood assistance and voluntary work. Some of the more important results were that:

– voluntary work was mentioned in only 8% of cases, in particular by well-qualified heads of household with property and a high income;

- mutual assistance in shopping trips was given frequently in only 5% of cases;
- 15% of respondents referred to an exchange of services (without gifts), with professionally employed household heads mentioning stronger exchange relationships;
- work done free of charge by a third party occurred "regularly" in only 8% of cases, "occasionally" in 13%;
- the main reason given for providing one's own services was that those on the market were too expensive, and that one's own knowledge and skills ought to be available to a third party;
- active neighborhood assistance was given for money in only 9% of cases. The resulting income was described as essential in only 19% of these.[19]

Although this is not the only investigation to have established that informal social networks have a limited potential and that they are therefore in no position to provide a substitute for public sector services, recent years have witnessed a renaissance in voluntary work. With the rediscovery of self-help, and the renewed career of the concept of "subsidiarity,"[20] voluntary work is experiencing a boom. Even official government statements stress citizens' self-help and neighborhood assistance. These are energetically supported by activities, hearings, and conferences taking place across the country, so that it is not wholly incorrect to claim that the concept of "voluntary work" is "an essential element of a state rationalization strategy which binds together a crisis-induced ideological production, on the one hand, with the creation of a willingness to take on work (unpaid work), on the other."[21]

An argument which may be essential to the political rediscovery of informal social activities (from neighborhood assistance through voluntary work to self-help groups) is that they are likely to reduce costs to the public purse, especially that of local authorities. Yet it remains questionable whether the mobilization of honorary assistance has met with tangible success, so that welfare organizations, in which the greater part of voluntary work is undertaken, have been complaining for years about a decline in participation.[22] The following characteristics of the situation give particular cause for skepticism about the efficiency of voluntary and self-help activity. The first, illustrated by the data in table 7.1, is that the declared *interest* in and (albeit conditional) *readiness* for voluntarily undertaken social assistance is significantly greater than the *extent* of the activities which actually occur. To be sure, this discrepancy warrants neither the "pessimistic" conclusion that the interests expressed were "not genuine," nor the "optimistic" one that there exists an unexploited potential of non-professional assistance. A far more realistic interpretation seems to be that modern social structures lack the forms of association and accumulations of tradition to provide the framework to make it possible to activate and direct an assistance potential which is obviously lying fallow, while at the same time avoiding the danger that it will dry up from too much tutelage and regimentation.

Table 7.1 Actual and potential readiness for voluntary social participation according to education and age group (%)

	16–39		40–54		55–64		64+		Total	
	(a)[a]	(p)[b]	(a)	(p)	(a)	(p)	(a)	(p)	(a)	(p)
Middle school (no apprenticeship)	9	34	7	27	6	17	4	9	6	21
Middle school (apprenticeship)	11	38	12	29	11	18	6	11	10	28
'O' levels	13	40	17	30	14	29	11	11	13	33
'A' levels/University	22	48	27	39	14	31	18	14	22	42
Total	13	39	13	29	10	20	6	10	11	29

[a]The column marked (a) ("actual") designates the percentage of *positive* answers to the question: "In the social sphere there are honorary activities or forms of secondary employment which cannot be treated directly as professional activity, for example, care services, cooperation in associations, care of toddlers or schoolchildren. Are you from time to time engaged in such secondary jobs?"
[b]The column marked "p" (potential) designates the additional percentage who gave a *negative* answer to the first question but said "yes" or "sometimes" to the supplementary question: "Would you be interested in activity of this sort?"

Source: Infratest INIFES Special Survey, "Citizen and Social State," 1981.

The second, as table 7.1 makes equally clear, is that the realized as well as the unexploited potential for assistance is extraordinarily unevenly distributed between ages and types of qualification. Indeed, this is so in the (apparently) paradoxical sense that the interest and readiness is greatest among those groups who can be described as – by age and qualifications – relatively well situated in the labor market, and therefore likely to express a less than average willingness *themselves* to assume responsibility for the assistance they offer or say they are prepared to offer. This suggests that the surveys could be revealing a "middle-class altruism" which, because of the demands on time made by formal wage labor, is extremely difficult to organize and put into a practical form.

Thirdly, the crucial problem of finding an appropriate organizational form in which potential assistance can be taken up is brought out by experience with existing self-help institutions. They reveal themselves to be temporally, objectively, and socially limited in equal measure. From a temporal point of view there arises the notorious problem of lack of continuity or reliability;[23] objectively, they suffer from the fact that the quality and appropriateness of the services offered cannot be guaranteed or checked;[24] and in view of the social distribution and accessibility of informally supplied services, it is likely that the restrictions and barriers which are an oft-lamented feature even of formally supplied services will occur to a greater degree.

This short overview shows that in the intermediate realm between market, state, and household, there occurs a whole series of adaptive reactions and more or less spontaneous forms of need satisfaction. But it shows, too, that there are shortcomings and functional limitations which are related to restrictions in the responsibilities they can objectively bear, to their independence from social presuppositions, to the quality of what they provide, and to harmful side-effects and temporal instabilities. Beyond this, the shortcomings of systems which develop *between* market, state, and household become clear when one recalls how small is that proportion of household "productive" functions (preparation and conservation of food, cleaning, caring, raising children, etc.) which can be transferred to such "intermediate arrangements." Therefore, in most of these fields, the private household remains tied to the alternative between strict self-provision, on the one hand, and an external relationship to the market (or to public services provided by the state) on the other.

The Three "Pure" Steering Principles of Need Satisfaction

Inquiry into the normative criteria referred to by the various forms of welfare production and need satisfaction reveals that there are three types of demands, at least within the horizon of the normative repertoire and valid criteria of legitimacy of "modern" societies. These are demands for *reciprocity, freedom,* and *equality.* Taken by itself, each of these relative values has a close affinity to a known steering principle which maximizes it, albeit often at the expense of harm to, or insufficient consideration of, the other relative values. These relationships can be briefly summarized.

Collective ("solidary") arrangements for welfare production maximize the relative value of reciprocity wherever and so long as they function, but do little for those of freedom and equality. Reciprocity here means the absence of relationships of exploitation or deception, at least according to prevailing understandings of interaction and their attendant expectations. A characteristic of "collective" social forms is that they do not require formalized rights and duties or monetarized relations of equivalence between members, and that instead of this, through the validity of shared norms, symbols, and identities, they secure members' confidence that every contribution they make to the welfare of the community will be paid for sooner or later by reciprocal contributions from others, without the need for monetary or authoritative regulation.

An important structural feature of such communities is that they have no temporal limitation: it is assumed that the interactional relationship and therewith the opportunity for reciprocation will persist for an indeterminate period, so that no member is able to accept the services of others while withholding his or her own contribution until a calculable endpoint, and thereby exploiting the community. The moral obligation to contribute something to the community need not be supported by an expectation that those who do so will *themselves* enjoy the fruits of reciprocal contributions. The moral claim to contributions which reciprocate one's own contributions and sacrifices may well be directed at future third parties (such as a grandchild). This mechanism of solidarity through expectations of continuity, of which nationhood and marriage furnish examples, functions not merely prospectively but also retrospectively, and thereby in a manner which is self-stabilizing. If through confidence in future reciprocation one has "saved" a certain amount of "credit" in the form of one's own contributions to the community, it will be irrational to leave it – and the more irrational the longer one stays away – since the prospect of receiving this credit back exists only *within* the community.

Of course, this does not mean that in national, marital, or other communities, exploitation and lack of reciprocity do not *objectively* occur, and that all recompenses are always paid. It simply means that such communities exist only as far as their members' *subjective confidence* in the long-term reciprocity of contributions stretches. This trust makes guarantees of equivalence unnecessary, and allows one's own contribution to appear as a "gift," "sacrifice," or "endowment" which has no strings attached and whose granting binds and obliges the beneficiary all the more strongly. Thus, as long as this trust exists, it would be irrational to insist on a scheduled equivalence of action and counteraction (as in markets) or to sanction the rights and duties of members through formal rules. In political philosophy (Rousseau) and more recent sociological articles,[25] it is frequently implied that such mechanisms for the satisfaction of needs, which rest on solidarity and reciprocal moral obligation, are found in small and not very complex social formations. Yet they do seem to have been successfully appealed to in large social movements (the labor movement), social security systems (the "contract of generations"), and especially by nations waging war (with their call to "die for their country").

But to the extent that communities rest on and also generate such expectations of reciprocity, they are decidedly unsuited to the realization of the values of freedom and egalitarian universalism. Communitarian arrangements conflict with the value of freedom insofar as they normatively rule out the "exit" option, and appear economically more irrational the longer they persist. Communities cannot be universalist and egalitarian as long as the normative basis of their internal reciprocity is a particularistic definition of membership and collective identity, and an antithetical relationship between the community and its environment.

Market arrangements reveal analogous strengths and weaknesses. A characteristic feature of market relationships is the way they are tied to a point in time. With respect to the future they stand under a general discontinuity proviso: every seller must take into account the fact that the buyer may shop elsewhere the next time, and only by orienting themselves to this eventuality in the long run will sellers gain "loyal" customers. Something similar is true for the past: trade with others does not require a shared identity or common life history. Its unique abstraction from past and future means that the market is the only medium which, in the form of the *world* market, can provide for long-term global relationships between actors.

This abstraction also extends to norms of authority or community. The feeling of one of the parties that he or she has been exploited or cheated by a market exchange can remain a matter of indifference to the other party as long as the conditions of unequal exchange, and therewith the defrauded party's compulsion to submit to them, persist. The parties may withdraw at any time – if they can, that is, if they come across more favorable opportunities to satisfy their needs elsewhere. This extreme "unbrotherliness" of market relationships, with its meagre normative presuppositions, ensures the highest degree of formal freedom, but at the same time exhibits an oft-noted downside – it leads to the erosion of communitarian relationships and has a "desolidarizing" effect. The market's inherent mode of functioning is just as harmful to universalistic and egalitarian values. At best, markets ensure equality of opportunity, not of result. Moreover, the strict ties which markets have to a point in time, and their exclusive use of money as a medium of exchange, give rise to numerous unevenly distributed social costs which cannot be expressed in monetary terms, and to unseen burdens on the future.

The strength of *state* forms of need satisfaction consists in their generalizability, that is, in their ability to establish, and maintain in the long term, the same life conditions and premises of action for all the state's citizens in numerous spheres. Such wide-ranging functions and highly specific universalizations are the decisive characteristic not just of the modern welfare state, but also of the bureaucratic constitutional state of the nineteenth century. Their intention, at least, is to generate a cumulatively increasing degree of reliability, predictability, and (social as well as military) security.

The collision between a state, which as provider universalizes and standardizes, and the claims of individual freedom has traditionally been seen to lie in the fact that the state, which is financed by taxes and contributions and intervenes regulatively in market processes, reduces the volume of economic values which can be put to use in markets, as well as the freedom of economic subjects to dispose over these values. A more recent critique, aimed specifically at conditions in modern welfare states and losses of freedom occurring therein, concerns the increasing control and surveillance, institutional tutelage, and legalized heteronomy of the social state's clients. Less familiar is the conflict between social state universalism and *communitarian* reciprocity. This conflict, so the argument goes, is one in which comprehensive provision and legal regulation by the state tends to level off those particularistic collective identities which once served as the foundation for communitarian forms of welfare provision. Furthermore, it is feared that the development of a state system of provision and distribution may rob small networks of family, extended family, neighborhood, and communal solidarity of the chance to establish themselves. For it creates a climate in which everyone supposes that other people's needs for welfare provision and assistance will somehow already have been met by the state.

The result of this brief and schematic review of the three classical steering principles (community, market, and state) is that while each of them promotes a particular relative value (reciprocity, freedom, equality), because of their mode of functioning they tend to harm, sometimes permanently, the relative values which they do *not* promote. From a practical point of view this means two things. First, that each recommendation of "more market" (or more community, or more state) amounts to a proposal to take one step forward and two steps back. Such a procedure would only be rational if, contrary to the premises introduced above, the equal rank of the three values could be called into question and the sacrifice of the negatively affected values be assumed to have some grounds. Secondly, if this path is deemed undesirable, a solution seems to be possible only by means of a complex *combination* of the three "simple" steering principles. This would rule out the maximization of one relative value at the expense of the others.

New Sources of Welfare Production through a Combination of Steering Principles?

We have shown how labor market and employment crises, as well as bottlenecks and gaps in the state's provision of welfare, generate a structural need for new sources of welfare production (in the first section); that the formation of "spontaneous" structures and reciprocal arrangements is by no means sufficient to meet this need (in the second section); and finally, in the light of the analysis in the third section, that simply redirecting an increasingly inadequate market and state provision toward domestic self-provision gives rise to serious losses in freedom and equality (where the latter includes stability and reliability over time). A similar normative critique of the attempt to solve these problems through the "informal economy" and household self-provision has been articulated with particular vehemence by social-scientific and political feminism. This critique is very convincing when directed – empirically as well as normatively – at proposals in which the *private (family) household* of today, with its size, resources and typical needs, is to take on an important additional responsibility for self-provision, and to fill gaps in that of market or state.

However, in view of the problems outlined in the first section and the qualitative shortcomings of the "spontaneous" solutions and stop-gap measures outlined in the second, there is no reason, under the assumption that this critique is justified, simply to abandon the search for constructive and innovative solutions to the problem of the private household's (empirically and normatively, quantitatively and qualitatively) insufficient capacity for self-provision. The continuing, indeed increasing, urgency of this problem is further indicated by a wealth of social and sociopolitical reform proposals which – often under the ambiguous slogan "from welfare state to welfare society" – implicitly or explicitly assume that opportunities do exist today for a greater utilization of domestic, voluntary, solidary, and honorary forms of activity.

Thus, in the labor market and social policy debates which have taken place in West Germany, both on a political and scholarly level, three phases are clearly identifiable. In the first, attention is paid to a comparatively narrow steering realm in which *incomes*, second jobs, and production costs are distributed and redistributed through social policy and fiscal measures. In the second, the horizon is expanded to include the redistribution of employment *opportunities*, mainly through policy measures concerning working hours. In the third, debate is no longer merely about patterns of income distribution or of the distribution of employment opportunities, but concerns the distribution of "useful *work*," of which, as the feminist critique again makes abundantly clear, formal employment represents only a part. It could be said that, at least in Germany and also in such different countries as the USA, France, Britain and Italy, the social policy debate has reached this "third round." And in view of justifiable doubts about whether a return to "full employment" is realistic (or desirable), theoretical and practical interest in a redistribution of formal employment and informal "useful activity" (that is, activity unrelated to and not remunerated via the market) is unlikely to fade.

In response to quantitative and qualitative problems besetting wage labor, such as the uncertain employment situation and relations of domination and working conditions in enterprises and state bodies, numerous practical proposals and theoretical arguments of an "alternative economic" type have been developed. These derive from ideas of cooperation, traditions of "municipal socialism," and visions of a "new autonomy," and they share the goal of guaranteed secure employment under working conditions which are qualitatively acceptable, oriented to the quality and specific value of the work concerned, and democratic. It could be said that "alternative economic" measures of this type lead to a "domestication" of labor in the enterprise, as the characteristically "modern" division between work and domestic spheres gives way to a reintegration into the enterprise of social relations typical of the household (solidarity and reciprocity, the coexistence of production and consumption functions). In this way, at least according to the advocates of an "alternative economy," the enterprise becomes a social site where existing relationships of formal domination and market exchange are supplemented and relativized.

However, the proposal for an "alternative economy" is only one of two possible applications of this logic of reintegration. As well as a "domestication" of the enterprise, an "industrialization" of the household may be possible. This is confirmed by some of the findings reported in the mid-1980s by the Oldenburg project[26] and the Sheppey Island study.[27] According to these studies, the capacity of private households to provide themselves with goods and services depends essentially on whether – through members employed in enterprises – they have access to knowledge, skills, capital goods, materials, and cooperative relationships. It is precisely those households whose stable integration into the formal economy renders them least urgently in need of welfare who are most well-equipped for self-provision.

The unemployed or marginally employed are badly placed with respect to *both* formal employment and self-provision.

Below, on the basis of ideas presented so far, and by following the model of an "industrialization of the domestic sphere," we present an institutional model which we call a *"cooperation circle."* Our purpose is to expose this model to theoretical and normative-political critique, and to generate or provoke further preparatory work so that it can be tested in practice and empirically evaluated (for example, through a program of experiments with accompanying research). The criterion of efficiency of cooperation circles should be that they enhance the qualitative and quantitative self-provision of private households *without* undermining the norms of reciprocity, freedom, or equality (or stability over time), or bringing them into conflict with one another.

We argued earlier that one of the main problems households face in providing themselves with goods and services is the smallness of the household itself. From an economic point of view, the modern (predominantly one-person) household suffers from "diseconomies of scale." This structural disincentive to self-provision then makes it appear rational for the household to act almost exclusively as a consumption unit; to draw its goods and services from external markets or benefit offices; and, for the rest, to strive to maximize its capacity for consumption by increasing its members' income. This economic disadvantage of small household size has two main causes. First, the procurement of domestic capital goods (freezers, DIY equipment, etc.) is frequently not worthwhile, because they would not be used often enough, and thus the unit costs of self-made products would be too high. Secondly, analogous bottlenecks emerge on the human capital side, where small households rule out opportunities for specialization, and where the formal acquisition of knowledge and skills is, for reasons already mentioned, worthwhile primarily for the purpose of consumerist self-fulfillment (in pottery, music, etc.), not self-provision.

Now this central economic problem, the inefficiency of small private households, could perhaps be overcome by an increase in scale, or the introduction of a system of links *between* households. Examples of this include forms of neighborhood assistance resting on stable expectations of reciprocity, and the institutional collectivization of certain capital goods (such as washing machines) for shared use by several households. More ambitious variants of the first are initiatives and clubs for the care of small children, school pupils, and old people. A version of the second was the well-known housebuilding projects in "Red Vienna" in the 1920s in which the responsibilities of individual households for provision were minimized and for the most part pooled in collective institutions near to residential areas.

Both proposed solutions to the problem of size, the *communitarian* and the *institutional*, have weaknesses. Communitarian organizational forms have an extraordinarily high demand for "confidence in reciprocity" among members, and are therefore vulnerable unless that confidence is constantly regenerated through their motivation and perceptions. By contrast, institutional collectivization largely forgoes "communitarian" need satisfaction, and instead, through formal rules (fees, regulations and timetables of use, etc.), confers a normative status on a standard product for individual use. But in this way the product tends to meet only minimal standards of quality, and – as with the tension between compulsory and private insurance – to offer the better placed members of the circle of its consumers a way out into (generally) higher quality "private" provision, that is, provision confined to the individual household.

Because of these difficulties our model of a "cooperation circle" proposes that the collectivization of provision be organized neither in a communitarian nor in an administrative manner, but in the form of a *market*, albeit with two provisos. First, that the exchange of services should take place not through the medium of money, but through *service vouchers* valid only among members and only for the purpose of trade in services between a locally delimited number of households. Secondly, that the coming into being and maintenance of a market of this type, with nonconvertible currency, should be *publicly subsidized*, not financially, but through the provision of rooms, equipment, payments in kind, and human capital. This would have the advantage of freeing such collective arrangements from presuppositions of solidarity and reciprocity, since they are only partially effective and always arbitrary. On the other hand, it would avoid a schematic and standardized solution with its qualitative shortcomings. In other words, the motivation to contribute and provide services would in this way be related neither to the indeterminate prospect that those who currently benefit from the assistance they receive will at some time reciprocate, nor to the circumstance that (in the meantime) there is nothing "better" which one can do, but to the *rational calculation* of the most efficient possible satisfaction of need.

At the same time, such an interhousehold market for goods and services would be decoupled from the regular market by the fact that payment would be in vouchers rather than money. The point of their introduction would be that services could only be drawn *from* other households on the basis of previous services *to* other households (not on the basis of income), and that the means of exchange would prevent processes of accumulation and relationships of exploitation. With the vouchers one receives one can do nothing but spend them in turn on the services of others. In this connection, in order to stimulate continual transactions and avoid hoarding, the idea of a temporally limited value of vouchers would be adopted. For example, it may be decided that the vouchers lose their value after three months. A further difference from the regular market mediated by money would be the fact that no free price formation could take place and that only the "total" value of vouchers could be spent or received. In practice one could imagine that, on the basis of annually reviewed agreements, two or at most three classes of goods and services would be defined (divided, for example, into cleaning and transport services; payments in kind and repairs; and personal services such as health care). An hour's work would then be valued at one, two, or three units of value.

A likely structural advantage of such an arrangement would be that it allows and stimulates specialization, and that appropriate capital investments for domestic self-provision now begin to be worthwhile. As we suggested, the latter might be strengthened by the public sector's taking on the costs of this type of cooperation circle. All these advantages rest on the fact that between the two currently available alternatives – self-provision in the individual household and external provision through market and state – a third option would be introduced, combining solidary, market, and administrative-subsidiary forms of provision. At the same time, free access to, or withdrawal from, this cooperative system would keep the level of transaction costs within strict limits: each interaction takes place solely on the basis of free association and an "individual economic" estimation of utility. Compulsory consumption or dictation of demand by interested suppliers is excluded. If such a cooperation circle were constructed on a small scale – say of between 100 and 500 neighboring households – the costs of information and transport would not be substantial. There would be no immanent need or reason for the emergence of a distinctive associational form or for an administrative apparatus for the allocation and supervision of tasks or the adjudication of disputes.

Despite these probable advantages (which, because of their range and presuppositions, are relatively easy to test empirically), a series of difficulties and problems are to be expected, and we would like to conclude with these. In the first place, problems may emerge in the *constitution* of such a cooperation circle: a "starting capital" of relationships of trust between neighbors must be available if such an arrangement is to develop. One can, however, imagine that favorable conditions for this might be created by the exemplary effects of existing projects, the prospect of public subsidies, advertising, and local political mobilization.

Furthermore, under certain circumstances it is likely that potential participants will express a very distinct preference for either *external* provision or *individual* domestic provision, and, in the name of values such as anonymity and the protection of the private sphere, treat all intermediate forms, of which our model is one, with mistrust and suspicion. Information about the scope and intensity of such anticooperative reservations can only be gleaned through empirical research, making it possible to assess the potential for change.

Finally, it seems likely that groups of suppliers from the formal economy would mount vehement protests and counterinitiatives as soon as interhousehold cooperative relationships began to invade a noteworthy part of their markets. Economic and social policy objections of this type are also likely to be raised by retail and craft associations, as well as trade unions and professional bodies. Here, the relative strengths of the conflicting interests, their strategies, and their legitimations would provide a worthwhile field of empirical research.

Notes

1 See B. Lutz, *Der kurze Traum immerwährender Prosperität* (Frankfurt and New York, 1984).
2 J. Skolka, "Der autonome Sektor der Wirtschaft," in H. Seidel and H. Kramer (eds), *Die österreichische Wirtschaft in den achtziger Jahren – Überlegungen zu den Entwicklungstendenzen* (Stuttgart, 1983), p. 88. See also B. Joerges "Konsumarbeit – Zur Soziologie und Ökologie des 'informellen Sektors,' " in J. Matthhes (ed.), *Krise der Arbeitsgesellschaft? Verhandlungen des 21. Deutschen Soziologentages in Bamberg, 1982* (Frankfurt and New York, 1983), p. 249; M. Garhammer, "Erwerbslosigkeit und Erwerbsarbeit im Kontext der sozialen Arbeitsteilung: Deskription zentraler Entwicklungslinien für die Bundesrepublik 1973–1983 und einige Hypothesen zur Entstehung der Erwerbslosigkeit auf der Grundlage einer differenzierten Sichtweise der Erwerbsarbeit als einer Form innerhalb der sozialen Teilung der Arbeit," Diss., Universität Erlangen-Nürnberg, 1985, p. 320.
3 J. Gershuny, *After Industrial Society: The Emerging Self-Service Economy* (London, 1978).
4 See also Joerges, "Konsumarbeit."
5 Statistisches Bundesamt (ed.), *Datenreport 1985. Zahlen und Fakten über die Bundesrepublik Deutschland* (Bonn, 1985), p. 13.
6 On these data see R. von Schweitzer and H. Pross, *Die Familienhaushalte im wirtschaftlichen und sozialen Wandel* (Göttingen, 1976), p. 21; W. Kordmann, "Produktionsverhältnisse und Haushaltsstruktur. Eine historisch-soziologische Studie," MS, University of Mannheim (VASMA project), 1984; J. Schumacher and R. Vollmer, "Differenzierungs- und Entdifferenzierungsprozesse im Familiensystem," in K. O. Hondrich (ed.), *Soziale Differenzierung* (Frankfurt and New York, 1982); Statistisches Bundesamt, *Datenreport 1985; Die Zeit*, 25 Oct 1985; and "Die Familie in der

Bundesrepublik Deutschland," Federal Center for Political Education, Bonn, 1985.

7 See W. Lutz, "Hieraten, Scheidungen und Kinderzahl," *Demographische Informationen* (Vienna) 5 (1985), p. 3.

8 See, among others, R. Vollmer, "Die soziale Gravitation von Familie und Beruf," in K. O. Hondrich and R. Vollmer (eds), *Bedürfnisse im Wandel* (Opladen, 1983).

9 Data of the Institut für Freizeit-Wirtschaft, as reported in *Marketing Journal* 5 (1985), p. 493.

10 Statistisches Bundesamt, *Datenreport 1985*, p. 437. See also W. Glatzer, "Haushaltsproduktion," in W. Glatzer and W. Zapf (eds), *Lebensqualität in der Bundesrepublik* (Frankfurt and New York, 1984), and the contributors to S. Burgdorff (ed.), *Wirtschaft im Untergrund* (Reinbeck, 1983), and J. Skolka (ed.), *Die andere Wirtschaft. Schwarzarbeit und Do-it-yourself in Österreich* (Vienna, 1984).

11 See the contributions in K. Gretschmann, R. G. Heinze and B. Mettelseifen (eds), *Schattenwirtschaft. Wirtschafts- und sozialwissenschaftliche Aspekte, internationale Erfahrungen* (Göttingen, 1984), and the empirical data in Skolka, *Die andere Wirtschaft*.

12 R. E. Pahl and C. Wallace, "Arbeitsstrategien von Haushalten in Zeiten wirtschaftlicher Rezession," in J. Krämer and R. Neef (eds), *Krise und Konflikt in der Grossstadt im entwickelten Kapitalismus* (Basle, 1985), p. 341.

13 Ibid.; see also R. E. Pahl, *Divisions of Labour* (Oxford, 1984).

14 J. Grünbeck, "Schattenwirtschaft mit kräftigem Wachstum," MS, Bonn, 1985.

15 See Pahl, *Divisions of Labour*.

16 J. Jessen, W. Siebel, C. Siebel-Rebell, U.-J. Walther and I. Weyrather, "Mythos informeller Ökonomie," *Leviathan* 13.3 (1985), p. 415.

17 See T. Bargel, R. Fauser and J. W. Mundt, "Soziotope und Infrastruktur – Lokalität als Bezug einer Sozialpolitik für das Kind," and K.-P. Strohmeier, "Soziale Räume und die Umweltbeziehungen von Grossstadtfamilien," both in J. W. Mundt (ed.), *Grundlagen lokaler Sozialpolitik* (Basle, 1983); H. A. Schubert, *Soziologie stadtischer Wohnquartier* (Frankfurt and New York, 1977).

18 Statistisches Bundesamt, *Datenreport 1985*, p. 485; see also T. Olk and R. G. Heinze, "Selbsthilfe im Sozialsektor. Perspektiven der informellen und freiwilligen Produktion sozialer Dienstleistungen," in T. Olk and H.-U. Otto (eds), *Gesellschaftliche Perspektiven der Sozialarbeit 4. Lokale Sozialpolitik und Selbsthilfe* (Darmstadt, 1985).

19 H. Schulz-Borck and J. Cecora, "Zur informellen Tätigkeit von Mitgliedern privater Haushalte," *Hauswirtschaft und Wissenschaft* 33:3 (1985); see also the empirical results in C. Badelt, *Politische Ökonomie der Freiwilligenarbeit* (Frankfurt and New York, 1985), who points out the special significance of voluntary work in the provision of social services.

20 See the contributions in R. G. Heinze (ed.), *Neue Subsidiarität – Leitidee für eine zukünftige Sozialpolitik?* (Opladen, 1986).

21 H.-J. Kondratowitz, "Motivation als Staatsaufgabe," in F. Ortmann and C. Sachsse (eds), *Arbeitsmarkt, Sozialpolitik, Selbsthilfe: Perspektiven einer neuen Sozialstaatlichkeit* (Kassel, 1985), p. 113; see also G. Backes, "Ehrenamtliche Dienst in der Sozialpolitik – Folgen für Frauen," *WSI Mitteilungen* 38 (H. 7) (1985); I. Ostner, "Haushaltsproduktion heute.

Implikationen eines Konzepts und seine Realisierung," in F. Fürstenberg, P. Herder-Dornreich and H. Klages (eds), *Selbsthilfe als Ordnungspolitische Aufgabe* (Baden-Baden, 1984); R. Süssmuth, "Ehrenamtliche Tätigkeit als Ausweg aus der Krise von Sozialstaat und Arbeitsmarkt?" *Katholische Akademie Schwerte, Arbeitsgesellschaft im Wandel* (Schwerte, 1984).

22 R. G. Heinze, "Verbandlichung der Sozialpolitik? Zur neuen Diskussion des Subsidiaritätsprinzips," in J. Krüger and E. Pankoke (eds), *Kommunale Sozialpolitik* (Munich and Vienna, 1985).

23 See Badelt, *Politische Ökonomie der Freiwilligenarbeit*, p. 232.

24 See Ostner, "Haushaltsproduktion heute," p. 150.

25 See, for instance, F. Hegner, "Solidarity and Hierarchy: Institutional Arrangements for the Coordination of Actions," in F. X. Kaufmann, G. Majone and V. Ostrom (eds), *Guidance, Control and Evaluation in the Public Sector* (Berlin and New York, 1986), p. 422.

26 Jessen et al., "Mythos informeller Ökonomie."

27 Pahl and Wallace, "Arbeitsstrategien."

8

Democracy Against the Welfare State?

Within any modern state, citizens are structurally related to state authority in three basic ways. Citizens are collectively the sovereign *creators* of state authority, they are potentially *threatened* by state-organized force and coercion, and they are *dependent* on the services and provisions organized by the state. The notion of citizenship within liberal-democratic welfare states involves all three aspects: citizens are (1) the ultimate source of the collective political will, in the formation of which they are called on to participate in a variety of institutional ways; they are also (2) the "subjects" against whom this will can be enforced and whose civil rights and liberties impose – by constituting an autonomous sphere of "private" social, cultural, and economic action – limits upon the state's authority; and finally they are (3) clients who depend on state-provided services, programs, and collective goods for securing their material, social, and cultural means of survival and well-being in society. It is readily evident that these three components of the concept of citizenship have their ideological roots, respectively, in the political theories of liberalism, democracy, and the welfare state.

These theories – and the corresponding dimensions of the concept of citizenship – can clearly be located on an evolutionary axis that represents the development of the "modern" state. In such a rough historical sequence – as suggested in a famous essay by T. H. Marshall[1] among others – first came the "liberal" solution of the problem of state authority as a threat to life, property, and cultural/religious identity. The institutional response to this problem has been the constitutional legal guarantee of freedom and liberty, which made certain spheres of existence and activity exempt from state control. This is the *liberal* component of the modern state, the formal limitation of its power, and the exemption of market interaction and other "private" pursuits from state control. It is a set of institutional devices that organizes a protective framework ("rule of law"). This protective arrangement is intended (and often seen) to counterbalance effectively the threatening administrative, fiscal, military, and ideological means of control that the modern state has accumulated.

Second, because the modern state does not have a universally recognized "metasocial" mandate from which its legitimacy can be derived, it turns to the "people" as its ultimate source of authority. This is the "voice" principle, institutionally embodied in the rules and procedures of *democratic* government and representation. The most important of these are the universal right to vote, competing political parties, general elections, majority rule, and so on.

Finally, the citizens depend on the state due to the loss *both* of feudal forms of paternalistic "welfare" *and* of individual economic autarky. "Insecurity" and the structural incapacity of maintaining the necessary preconditions of the existence of civil society as a whole are no longer a purely military problem (to be taken care of by the apparatus of the "warfare state"), but also become increasingly a recognized condition of virtually all civilian actors within the civilian life of civil society. They come to depend on a great variety of economic and social policies the institutional framework of which is today known as the *interventionist welfare state*. Thus the three components of the model state–citizenship relation in the West can be said to be the *rule of law, representative democracy,* and provisions for "civilian security" through the *welfare state*.

The problem I want to introduce is familiar from much of the literature on the state in general and on the welfare state in particular. It is centered on the question of the stability and viability of a political system made up of these three institutional components. Two extreme perspectives can be distinguished. One emphasizes harmony, compatibility, even evolutionary mutual reinforcement among the three, while the opposite perspective emphasizes strains, stresses, contradictions, and incompatibilities. It must remain a theoretical, and ultimately an empirical, question, which of these perspectives is valid, and for what reasons, in what respects, and under what conditions.

The global problem of potential inherent tensions within this ensemble of three institutional components can conveniently be broken down into three subproblems. These concern the viability of *partial* syntheses, namely those of (1) the liberal and democratic components, (2) the liberal and welfare state (or, in the somewhat more specific German terminology, *Rechtsstaat* versus *Sozialstaat*), and (3) the democratic and welfare state components. As far as the first of these compatibility questions is concerned, which shall remain entirely outside the scope of the present essay, there exists a large tradition of political theorizing and an equally broad body of litera- ture that is often skeptical and critical in its findings and of which the works of Wolfe, Macpherson, and Levine[2] are well-known, if hetero- geneous, examples. The second compatibility problem, that of the "fit" of liberal and welfare state institutional elements, is a favorite of the (neo)conservative political discourse and will be briefly discussed in a moment. The third set of subproblems is relatively the most neglected one in the theoretical literature. It is this subproblem to which most of the present discussion will address itself.

Liberalism and the Welfare State

In the early 1980s, much of the dominant discourse of the problems and future developments of the welfare state focused on the alleged antagonism between the collective civilian security aspect of the state (that is, the *welfare* state) and the *liberal* aspects of the state (that is, its guarantee of private property, of contractual market relations, and hence of a capitalist economy). This discourse, in which the philo- sophical and political perspectives of the neoconservative and liberal right prevail, postulates that the welfare state has become too heavy a burden on the economy, whose growth potential and competitiveness are consequently seen to suffer from the excessive costs and rigidities imposed on the market by state-organized welfare and social security provisions. On the other side, these theories, predictions, and alarmist speculations are countered by arguments and programmatic views by the democratic left, unions, and Western European social democratic and socialist parties and governments. The *tableau* within which this debate is framed is schematically represented by the matrix (figure 8.1 overleaf), which categorizes supposed causal links between the liberal principle of a market economy (ME) and the welfare state (WS). The propositions of the neoconservative critique are summarized in cell 4 of the schema.

Controversial as all of the propositions within the four cells of this schema are, they are at least explicit components of a well-established and fairly conventional economic, legal, and political debate. The only new (or perhaps very old?) argument within a broad discourse that emphasizes the long-term incompatibility between the welfare state and a liberal market society is perhaps the proposition, put forward in

causal link	supportive	antagonistic
ME → WS	expanding private sector economy generates tax base for "growth dividend" out of which welfare state transfers and services can be financed	labor-saving technical change, capital flight, domestic demand gap, etc., undermine prospects for long-term full employment on which WS is premised
		1 2
		3 4
WS → ME	provision of skills, health, peaceful industrial relations, "built-in" demand stabilizers, etc., generate necessary input for ME and support its further expansion	excessive tax burden; crowding out effect of state budget deficit; WS as disincentive to invest, employ, and work; WS as cause of labor market rigidities and "immoralist" attitudes

Figure 8.1 Conceptualizations of the interaction between market economy and the welfare state

a number of publications, that the damage that the welfare state inflicts on the liberal order is not so much of an immediately *economic* but of a *moral* nature. According to its proponents, the "fiscal crisis" and "economic inefficiency" crisis of the welfare state are mediated through a moral one. Focusing on the highly developed Dutch welfare state, one author, for instance, argues that due to its abstract formal-legal modus operandi, the modern welfare state has cut itself loose from the moral resources, common values, and potentialities for solidarity within civil society, thereby rendering these resources useless and the adherence to solidary commitments worthless. This critique of the welfare state condemns its destructive impact on the moral fiber of society and, by virtue of *this* effect, also on its economic efficiency and productivity. The author gives the following illustration of the demoralizing effect and hence the "immoralist" nature of state welfare:

> After a fund-raising event for a charitable goal, members of a voluntary organization are able to present the money personally to the recipients of their benefaction, whereas the recipients of welfare state benefaction remain anonymous members in a bureaucratic system, receive their cheques by mail, while the money of the system has been collected by a gigantic tax system. This welfare package does not require any commitment or initiative, nor can any moral energy be invested in it. Nobody bears any responsibility, nobody is accountable, nobody needs to show

loyalty ... to this abstract system [which, according to this view, is characterized by an] in-built lack of moral principles [and an elective affinity] between the welfare state and the immoralist ethos.[3]

Leaving aside its alarmist undertones, there are a number of potentially valid points on which this argument can be based. These include:

1 The self-augmenting dynamic of demands on the welfare state, as more and better organized groups of clients and claimants are formed, as they voice demands in competition with each other, and as new issues are included in the agenda, a self-propelling process of "rising expectations" is set into motion that implies a shift from the prevention of poverty to the universal guarantee of status. As a consequence, the welfare state "does no longer guarantee *minimal* standards of welfare and well-being, but is counted upon as the provider of maximum standards of welfare."[4]

2 The liberal principle of the rule of law and, more generally, the protection and recognition of the private sphere of economic and family life prevent the welfare state from transgressing, except in marginal cases, the limits of formal-legal entitlements and thus distribute benefits according to principles of attributed need and/or demonstrable desert. This also makes it infeasible to make the receipt of benefits conditional on any kind of moral obligation to which recipients would have to conform. This situation involves an easily exaggerated potential for " 'moral hazard' and 'free-riding' that ... are typical for 'common-pool problems.' "[5]

3 As makers of social policy are forced to take into account the imperatives of the capitalist economy, welfare state programs tend to be "reactive" rather than "active," or "differentiated" rather than "integrated"[6] except under the most favorable of institutional and economic circumstances (of which the Swedish welfare state is often considered to be the prime example). That is to say, the liberal nature of the economy prevents social policies from achieving the degree of comprehensive rationality and effective implementation that would make it immune from the corrosive impact of economic change, fiscal crises, and business cycle fluctuations.[7] The very constraints that govern the formation of social policies render them highly vulnerable to changes of economic and fiscal parameters.

To the extent that these observations are valid, they are likely to lead to the cumulative frustration with the welfare state of client and claimant groups (due to point 1), of taxpayers and voters (point 2), and eventually of political elites themselves (point 3). The conflict between liberal and welfare state principles is emphasized not only by economic liberals, but also by humanistic libertarians who have grown increasingly sensitive to the alienating, decapacitating, and depersonalizing effects that the welfare state and its legal-bureaucratic or professional modes of distribution, treatment, and surveillance can have on communities and individual "lifeworlds."[8]

The (partial) validity of these liberal and libertarian arguments, however, does not enhance the plausibility of the solutions typically proposed to overcome the conflict between liberal and welfare state principles. For the assumption that the structural "demoralization" of the welfare state can be overcome by some government-sponsored strategy of "remoralization" is as simplistic as it is questionable in terms of its ethical plausibility. Yet it is exactly this "remoralization" strategy for a postliberal welfare state that has been proposed, along remarkably similar lines, by Mead[9] for the United States and by Spieker[10] for West Germany. Mead criticizes the American welfare state for its "permissiveness," by which he means its failure to impose binding "civic obligations" on the recipients of its benefits and services. By *civic* obligations he means such civic duties as accepting (hard and low-paid) work, supporting one's family, respecting the rights of others, and acquiring through formal education the basic skills that are required for literacy and employability.[11] Taken together, these civic virtues make up what Mead calls the competent or "functioning citizen," whose creation he envisages as a function of a new style of social policy that would operate with educational means and outright punishments to shape citizens after this model. "Government must persuade people to blame themselves"; the poor must be obligated to accept "employment as a duty."[12]

The "authoritative" – or authoritarian – paternalism that forms the basis of this proposal is justified by the fact that what is demanded from the welfare clientele is nothing but one set of traditionally American virtues. Thus "being" American justifies these state-enforced moral requirements of "civic obligation." A similar shift from legal entitlement to moral desert is proposed by Spieker, this time not on the basis of national culture but of Catholic doctrine. According to this author, the welfare state has nurtured a "hedonistic" and "parasitical" conduct of life,[13] against which not only work- and family-related virtues but also an attitude of "friendship toward the state"[14] must be restored and enforced. Such proposals "resolve" the tension between the liberal and the welfare components by abolishing both of them, certainly the former. They proclaim a state-sanctioned and state-enforced set of moral standards and virtues, although it is evidently beyond the powers of any *"modern"* state to form a unity of moral will even on the elite level, to say nothing of imposing it "authoritatively" on the mass level. Moreover, such proposals do not recognize the contradiction that what they theoretically (though counterfactually) claim to be a *universal*, generally recognized set of virtues would turn in practice into a specific and highly *selective* disciplinary device directed against clients and recipients of benefits; for none of these authors has ever proposed state punishment for family breakup or failures to comply with the work ethic in *middle* income social categories. Finally, proponents of plans for a "remoralization" of the welfare state remain silent about the obvious problem of what should happen to those who *fail* as "functioning citizens," that is, the "undeserving" poor. While these unsettled questions deprive the "remoralization" approach of much of its intellectual interest, they do not necessarily interfere with its latent political function, which is to undermine whatever norms of trust and solidarity have remained intact, to label the poor and other welfare recipients as morally unworthy and undeserving, and thus to absolve political elites (and taxpayers in general) from *their* moral obligations toward the recipients of welfare benefits and services by blaming them for failures to live up to their presumed moral obligations.

To some extent, the left-libertarian critique of the welfare state is the inverse image of the neoconservative "remoralization" approach. What the latter calls for as a remedy, the former criticizes as a pervasive component of already existing state practices. The alienating, depersonalizing, and morally destructive impact of bureaucratic and professional intervention into the lifeworld of clients is viewed with growing alarm and suspicion, while no reasonably realistic vision of a communal, solidary, "convivial," and nonalienating alternative to the welfare state has yet emerged very clearly.[15] All that can be stated is the deep ambiguity of state power, which, according to Habermas, is a "perhaps indispensable, but not truly innocent" instrument for taking care of society's welfare problem.[16]

Democracy and the Welfare State

Let us now turn to relationships and tensions that exist between the democratic and the welfare components of the modern capitalist state. Consider some hypothetical links between these two structural elements.

Concerning these two structural variables, much of the conventional wisdom converges on the intuitively highly plausible assumption

causal link	supportive	antagonistic
PD→ WS	universal franchise strengthens political power of wage-dependent majority of citizens; collective interest of wage workers in welfare state; electoral "power of numbers" outbalances economic power of property	welfare backlash; individualism; authoritarian anti-welfare state populism; new particularistic tendencies (tax revolt, institutional racism, etc.)
	1	2
	3	4
WS→ PD	convergent pattern of party competition; reduction of intensity of political conflict; political integration of entire electorate; "end of ideology"; structural vanishing of political radicalism, which might lead to antidemocratic challenges	corporatist deformation of PD; marginalization of groups, interests, and cleavages not served by WS; rise of new forms of noninstitutional political conflict

Figure 8.2 Conceptualizations of the interaction between political democracy (PD) and the welfare state (WS)

that capitalist democracies tend to generate political forces supporting welfare state developments (figure 8.2, cell 1) *and* that, unless these forces are defeated by a combination of economic crisis and authoritarian political regime changes, welfare states will then generate positive repercussions on democratic political institutions for the kind of reasons indicated in cell 3. These two assumptions seem to capture the essentials of the mainstream of postwar social-democratic theory in Europe. The welfare state is, in the words of Richard Titmuss, a set of "manifestations, first, of society's will to survive as an organic whole and, secondly, of the expressed wish of all the people to assist the survival of some people,"[17] and political democracy is the institutional means by which this manifestation and expression of will is made possible. At the same time, political democracy is seen as a powerful means of forcing political elites and ruling-class political representatives to accept welfare state arrangements. "Elite fear of social conflict, and ultimately revolution, was the catalyst in explaining social policy making in interwar Britain."[18] Underlying this optimistic assumption is (1) a model of *rational collective action through democratic politics*, and (2) a model of self-stabilizing and *self-reinforcing institutional dynamics*. The twin assumption is that rational actors in a democracy will join a pro-welfare-state majority and that, once the welfare state institutions are established, they become increasingly immune to challenges. As it is the central claim in the theoretical discussion that follows that both of these assumptions are in need of basic revision, let me elaborate each of them in more detail.

(1) The key figure within the collective rational action assumption is the property-less male wage laborer, employed full-time for most of his adult life, whose material subsistence and that of his family depend on a continuous stream of contractual income. He shares these features with a large number of fellow workers who, taken together, constitute the vast majority of the economically active population. Like them, he is exposed to risks partly inherent in the dynamics of the capitalist mode of production. These wage workers also share some common cultural patterns, such as a certain productivist discipline, a sense of solidarity, and the perception of being involved in some fundamental social conflict that divides labor and capital. This overarching sense of solidarity and conflict manifests itself in certain political and economic forms of participation and association, experienced as the only available means of promoting their collective interests in income maintenance and social security, in adequate working conditions, in continuous full employment and the prevention of poverty, and in the redistribution of income and economic control. This configuration of conditions and orientations can be described summarily as *labor-centered collectivist statism.*

Moreover, this policy package of social security plus full employment, plus health, education, and housing, plus some poverty-related social assistance is something that could appeal to rational actors *outside* the working class as well, and eventually to all well-intentioned citizens, that is, except for a small minority of the most narrow-minded and selfish ones. This is so for three interrelated reasons suggested by Therborn,[19] all of which have to do with the nature of the welfare state as a provider of public goods. First, any rational voter is supposed, according to this line of argument, to support (and be prepared to make disposable income sacrifices for) the welfare state as it helps to *avoid* collective *"evils,"* ranging from street crime to the spread of contagious diseases to economic recession to disruptive political conflict. Second, support of the welfare state can be seen as an *investment* in a positive public good, such as the development of human resources, labor productivity, and so on. Finally, support for the welfare state can be perceived as the fulfillment of altruist *social obligations* and hence of normative preconditions of legitimacy and justice. With all these class-related, interest-related, and normative considerations to rely on, why should such support fail to be forth-coming in a democratic polity?

(2) The corollary assumption is one of institutional self-reproduction, inertia, and irreversibility that would immunize welfare states, once entrenched, from challenges and basic revisions. This assumption, which appears rather heroic today, can still be based on the following set of arguments. Within an established welfare state, none of the competing political parties can attempt to abandon the welfare state accord, and this is increasingly the case the broader the range of *individual* goods (such as income) provided by the welfare state and the greater the proportion of the population that benefits from these goods. Furthermore, large-scale and complex programs (such as the various branches of social security of West European welfare states) tend to commit political elites to their continuation, especially if major corporate collective actors are involved in social policy formation and implementation, an arrangement that would serve as a "muffling effect of social policy"[20] and discourage protest. Finally, centripetal elite politics and the constraining power of existing programs, budgets, and legislations not only interact with each other, but also condition favorable developments of public opinion and mass ideological orientations.[21] Along the line of this "institutional inertia" argument, the welfare state can be expected to breed its own sources of political support, partly via the broadening self-interest of individuals and groups who receive such benefits as inflation-proof pensions, and partly via the mechanism of ideological accommodation. What emerges from this brief elaboration of the "institutional inertia" assumption is a reassuring picture of interlocking virtuous circles, which, taken together, amount to a giant negative feedback mechanism of the welfare state in operation. Note that all of the component arguments – concerning both the "rational collective action" and the "institutional inertia" assumptions – are based on the presumption of rational action by individuals, classes, parties, unions, elites, voters, and clients of the welfare state.

This overall picture, however – associated with social democratic political theory – is hopelessly antiquated if we look at Western European welfare states and their foreseeable futures in the mid-1980s. In none of these states has a constitutional change taken place that even comes close to the abolition of democratic procedures and institutions. Yet both the situation itself as well as its perception and interpretation on elite and mass levels have changed in dramatic and unanticipated ways. This new divergence between democratic politics and social policies is so pervasive that it cannot be accounted for in terms of transient deviations from a long-term trajectory. It must be understood, or so the core thesis of this chapter suggests, to be reflective of structural changes and new situations in which rational political actors (individual and collective) find themselves. The mutually supportive relationship of mass democracy and welfare stateness (as depicted in cells 1 and 3 of figure 8.2) no longer amounts to a convincing hypothesis. To the contrary, there are many indications, as well as meaningful theoretical assumptions and conjectures, that lead us to expect that democratic mass politics will *not* work in the direction of a reliable defense (to say nothing about the further expansion) of the welfare state.

The dependent variable that thus needs to be explained is the stagnation and partial decomposition of welfare states in Western European democracies since the mid-1970s. There can be little controversy about the phenomenon itself, although the overall picture – including national variations – is hard to capture by a few indicators, especially because economic conditions, institutional structures, and cultural traditions in these countries produce a great deal of variation. I suggest the following list of indicators that produce a fairly uniform picture of what has been happening since the mid-1970s.

1 There has been a continuous and sometimes rather dramatic series of electoral losses and defeats of social democratic and socialist parties, that is, the traditional hegemonic forces of pro-welfare-state political interests and alliances. In fact, by 1986 social democratic-led governments were pushed back to the northern and southern margins of Europe – in sharp contrast to the situation in the late 1970s and early 1980s. On the level of public opinion as measured by longitudinal and comparative analysis of survey data, it has been observed that "in general, the direction of the change has been to the favor of anti-welfare state views."[22] Differences within scholarly interpretation do not concern the direction of this change, but the extent to which it has occurred, with only a few authors finding reasons to believe that the population "in general [is] either satisfied with provision or supports more expenditures."[23]

2 There has been marked and often abrupt discontinuity in the development of the *absolute* level of welfare state expenditures, leading either to stagnation or slow decline of budgets, in contrast to a continuous rise of expenditures during virtually the entire period since World War II. One careful study of these fiscal and expenditure developments found that "cuts are on the political agenda in a way which would have been unthinkable a generation ago."[24] Even a country relatively unaffected by the mid-1980s by changes in growth rates and governments, namely West Germany, showed a sharp

decline in the proportion of social policy legislation implying increases in benefits or coverage.[25]

3 There has been an even more dramatic decline of welfare state transfers and services *relative* to the level of need that is itself caused by unemployment and demographic as well as sectoral economic changes. As a consequence, for instance, a growing rate of unemployment coincides with stagnating unemployment insurance budgets, leading either to a deterioration of benefit entitlements and/or to increased exclusiveness of entitlements of the unemployed.

4 The growing gap between (what used to be recognized as) need and actually provided benefits has not led to large-scale and/or militant conflict in defense of the welfare state and its continued expansion. To the contrary, patterns of political conflict have shifted in three directions. One is the mainly unpromising phenomenon of militant, sectoral, local and regional strikes, and sometimes riots, such as occurred in the British mining and printing industries, and in poverty-stricken communities. Another is the sometimes dramatic electoral defection of the core working class to liberal-conservative political forces, implying a strong sign of political support for anti-welfare-state cuts and legislation even among those who belong to the classes and social categories in whose name the ideals and ideologies of state-provided welfare have traditionally been advocated. Finally, a further shift has centered on problems (such as the rights of citizens, the environmental question, feminist and peace issues) that are absent from the welfare state's agenda and that are now being carried out by nonclass social movements.[26]

5 Parallel to these changes of policy and politics, there are strong indications that the *egalitarian-collectivist* component of its theoretical heritage is receding in significance, while *libertarian, anti-etatist*, and *communitarian* ideals and projects become increasingly dominant on the political left. It is exactly at the moment of severe challenges and defeats that major forces within the political left seem to abandon what has been the left's central project, namely, a collectivist-etatist version of industrialism. This shift in the left's own ideological orientation is well captured by Przeworski and Wallerstein when they write:

> The predicament [of the left] is political: historical experience indicates that governments cannot be trusted with precisely those alternatives that would make a difference, those that require large doses of state intervention. The dilemma of the Left is that the only way to improve material conditions of workers and poor people under capitalism is through rather massive state intervention, and the state does not seem to be a reliable mechanism of intervention. The patient is sick, the drugs are available, but the doctor is a hack.[27]

On a more analytical level, Habermas has raised the problem that the welfare state, after having reconciled to some extent the tension between the capitalist economy and the democratic polity, is now confronting a dual problem as a consequence of which it is deprived of the mobilizing potential of its utopian vision: on the one side, it is met with distrust by core working-class and upwardly mobile social categories who defect from collectivist ideas, and on the other, by those who, while recognizing the welfare state's accomplishment of a measure of social justice, are aware of its built-in contradiction between state power and lifeworld, or between the welfare state's method and its goal.[28] Taken together, these two sources of growing frustration and disappointment would force the defenders of the welfare state to reformulate their political vision in quite fundamental ways.

Rethinking the Macro-Sociology of the Welfare State

Largely in line with the hypotheses contained in the left-hand columns of figures 8.1 and 8.2, recent comparative historical research has found that the rise of the welfare state has been correlated with such variables as economic growth, democratic political mass participation and bureaucratic centralization, and the rise of collectivist tendencies in dominant ideologies and public opinion.[29] What is missing in this analytical design is the role of individual actors and their style of rational responses. Structures do not *directly* translate into outcomes and developments; they do so by virtue of the responses, interpretations, memories and expectations, beliefs and preferences of actors who *mediate* the link between structure and outcome. The recent resurgence of methodological individualist approaches in the social sciences has helped to remind us of this missing link within much of the macro-sociological research tradition.

The *social validity* of propositions concerning the correlation of, say, the democratic form of government and the welfare-stateness of the polity stands, as it were, on *two* legs, one being the testable correspondence of the proposition with *facts* and *events* in the outside world, the other being the way in which *actors* are constituted and rationally motivated to *accept* the proposition as a cognitive premise and as a guide to a particular mode of action, so as to consider it credible in itself and to adopt it as a belief – often with the consequence that the proposition is *then* validated as an empirical truth due to the operation of a self-fulfilling interpretation loop.

There is, of course, a third type of validity of beliefs that is diametrically opposed to the second one. Its basis is neither empirically demonstrated *truth* nor strategically selected interpretation guided by *interest*, but *trust* in the validity of such norms as reciprocity, solidarity, or justice. According to this type, belief formation follows normative conceptions of the respective segment of reality conceptions that are, as long as they prevail, counterfactual and infallible and, therefore, immune from empirical refutation and/or strategic selection. The structural conditions that can give rise to such normative foundations of validity attribution are probably the opposite of those underlying our second type: the firmly established collective identities, homogeneity, immobility, and continuity that Rousseau described as the precondition of a viable "volonté générale."

Depending on which of these criteria of "social validity" of such propositions we concentrate on, the task of the social scientist in testing, confirming, or criticizing such claims differs considerably. For instance – and most important in the present context – how do we deal with politically consequential beliefs of the second type, which are "real in their consequences" but, at least initially, unsupported by empirical fact? Their social validity results, as we have seen, not from their cognitive adequacy but from their interest-dependent individual attractiveness as a political project under conditions of high uncertainty, and thus from strategic considerations. In such cases, both the reference to facts (that is, type 1 beliefs) and to norms (that is, type 3 beliefs) fail. Strategically selected and adopted beliefs, being based on interest, defy critical assessments of their irrationality, which are based on either truth or norms.

As a way out of this dilemma, it seems to me that we must return to the level of empirical analysis – this time, however, not of the *facts* to which the propositions in question refer, but to the *actors* and their individual reasons for *accepting* these propositions as valid. In this perspective, the correspondence that would become the focus of critical attention is *not* the correspondence between facts and propositions. Neither would it be the correspondence between values and political projects. Rather it would be the correspondence between certain types of social actors and the parameters of choice given within their situation of action, on the one side, and their rational motivation to adopt certain interpretive patterns about the world, on the other. It is this latter approach to the analysis of the welfare state – an approach that could perhaps be described as a combination of structural, phenomenological, and rational choice approaches – whose contours I want to explore further.

Returning to our two matrices and the propositions that are schematically represented by them, the question is no longer "Who is right?" but rather "Which types of structural changes, perceptions, and specific uncertainties make it rational for various categories of actors to adopt, and to act on the basis of, either of the conflicting interpretive perspectives?"

Rationality, Trust, and Welfare

The case of the liberal-conservative democratic attack on the welfare state is easily reconstructed in terms of rational choice theory. As we know from Olson's theory of collective action, there is no natural reason for a public good to be produced even if it could be shown to be in the interest of each individual member of a (large) collectivity. For rather than contributing to the production of the public good, the more desirable option to the rational individual is to let everyone else pay for the good while the individual takes a "free ride" on the efforts of others without contributing herself or himself. As long as the benefits from the goods cannot be limited to those who have actually contributed to its production, free-riding is a rational strategy from the point of view of the individual utility maximizer. This is so for three reasons: first, because one's own contribution to the good would be so small as to make no real difference (in a "large" group) for the continued production of the good. Second, because the good is in fact available as a "public" good, that is, free of charge to its individual consumers. Third, because individual actors may have reasons, according to their perception of the propensities and inclinations of other actors, for suspecting that the latter will fail to cooperate in the relevant future, which would render the original actor's position that of the "sucker." As a combined consequence, and as everyone waits for the others to contribute to the good, the good, although collectively beneficial, will not be produced.

This well-known paradox serves as the backdrop for the analysis of cases where collective goods *are* actually produced. In such cases, the question must be asked: What makes the members of the group act so "irrationally" (according to the individual calculus specified above) as to actually act *in accordance* with their collective interest? The answer that Olson – who is quite careful to avoid the use of any category such as "norms" or "values" – has to provide comes in either of two versions. Either the people do not, in fact, act "irrationally," because they are rationally attracted to contributing to the collective good due to the existence of some "selective incentives" that are made available to those who do contribute (in which case the collective good becomes a mere *by-product* of individual benefit-seeking). Or seemingly irrational behavior occurs because someone *forces* individuals to cooperate, in which case they do not *win* an individual *benefit* from contributing but *avoid* the punishment that would result from non-cooperation. With these two specifications, the main argument appears to remain valid: whenever someone contributes to the production of the collective good, she or he does not act irrationally if it can be shown that she or he does so on the basis of a rational motivation through either the gain from selective incentives or the avoidance of punishment; in all other cases, rational cooperation is not be expected.

This type of argument, however, works only as long as the punishment for noncontributors (to concentrate on this case alone) is imposed in a strictly *authoritarian* way, that is, without the option being open to the individual in question to *avoid* the alternative of either joining or being punished for not joining. The *democratic* citizen, in contrast, would in fact *have* the option to impose *his or her* will upon the government in order to prevent it from imposing *its* will upon the citizen (that is, compulsory contribution under the threat of punishment). Seen from this perspective, the problem of democracy is that it moves – in theory as well as in practice – beyond an account in terms of simple coercion. It does so "by introducing a framework wherein *legitimacy* may be tested."[30] Democracy puts citizens in a position in which they are able to coerce the coercer, and it becomes quite likely that they will use their democratic rights in this way if they have reason to believe that a sufficiently large number of other citizens will join this strategy to force state authorities to *refrain* from forcing citizens to contribute – unless they consider the state's authority legitimate. Among such reasons can be the following: (1) many people believe that many *other* people believe that the incidence of costs and benefits of a given program or legislation is redistributive in nature; therefore, it appears to be in their self-interest to adopt this belief themselves even in spite of individually available factual counterevidence, and to join those acting on the false belief that their action will be profitable. Such democratic evasion from collective goods contribution may also be attractive (2) for the reason that it is channeled through voting, that is, an institutional mechanism that renders individual behavior invisible (secret ballot) and noninteractive (simultaneous voting, which renders infeasible the emergence of an assurance game).

The paradox thus appears to be this: Unless citizens consider the state's authority legitimate, they can obstruct mandatory cooperation through the democratic ballot. As far as state provision for welfare is concerned, its legitimacy is not only dependent on the citizen's perception of the nature of the rulers or the government but also on the perception of fellow citizens and the anticipation of their action. If thus only a legitimate authority within a solidary society (that is, one consenting on the legitimacy of the authority) can enable the state to enforce cooperation, why is such authority necessary in the first place? Why can't it be fully replaced by voluntary collective goods production?

In other words: explaining collective goods production by reference to state authority and mandatory contributions is not really an explanation but the first step in an infinite regress that can only be halted by some axiom concerning the pregiven and unquestionable existence of state authority as the ultimate coercive power. Short of such an axiom, state authority that enforces collective goods must be considered a collective good in itself, thus suffering from the same problem that it supposedly solves. As Talcott Parsons demonstrated in a famous argument against Hobbes, no deductive link exists between the ideal selfishness of the inhabitants of the state of nature and the origin of state authority; Hobbes's suggestion that there is such a link "is really to violate his [utilitarian] postulate [and] to posit a momentary identity of interest."[31]

Consequently, the problem of selfish noncooperation cannot be explained away by the existence of state authority, because the latter owes its origin – and continued existence – to dispositions on the part of citizens toward cooperative action. A state that is necessary to deal with the collective problems of universal and pure selfishness is at the same time impossible (and *vice versa*) because it cannot originate from a condition of such selfishness. And neither can a state maintain itself in the context of pure selfishness, least of all a democratic state.

To be sure, the individual in a democratic polity would not be able to escape the binding force of authority as long as she or he remains the *only* one who wishes to stop the government from imposing a punishment on noncontributors. But, given a democratic polity, there is no reason to expect that she or he would *remain* the only one, given the fact that (by virtue of the bare minimum definition of democracy as the system under which dissent is not punishable) there would be a zero-cost attached to noncooperation by voting. For instance, citizens would vote into office a party that promises to do away with virtually all forced cooperation in the production of collective goods. What we would expect to see is a dynamic of actual defection, anticipated defection, anticipated anticipation, and so on, leading to a self-propelling or "autocatalytic" chain of causal effects.

This exercise in Olsonian logic of collective action seems to demonstrate that there is at least one case in which the logic does not work: that in which the "collective good" of *abolishing* the compulsory cooperation in the production of collective goods (or, for that matter, the "indirect" production of collective goods through the selective incentive effect) is to be had at a zero-price, which is actually the case in a democracy. But because zero-cost dissent is a real possibility, it would affect all production of collective goods (for large collectivities), which, according to Olson, can only be explained as resulting from the selective incentives or compulsory contribution effects. Consequently, we would be back to square one in our attempt to understand why, among rational actors, collective goods production occurs at all *in a democracy*.

Unless we want to stick – against the Parsonian argument – to the now questionable assumption that pure self-interest *can* lead to the constitution of an absolute authority that henceforth is immune from citizens choosing their opting-out option, we will have to take another road. The only alternative seems to be to hypothesize that actors produce collective goods not because of the rational capacity to maximize utility and to avoid punishment, but because of their normative disposition to do so, or because of the relationship of trust, reciprocity, sympathy, and fairness that they have experienced between themselves and their fellow contributors. For what, other than such legitimizing notions, motivations, and identities could lead them, in a democracy, to continue to cooperate, even though they *could* withdraw at zero-cost, thereby debasing the authority that compels them to act as rational contributors?

These theoretical considerations are less remote from the problem at hand than it might appear. The problem is to test the hypothesis in cell 2 of figure 8.2. For the arguments above lead us to conclude that (1) if a polity is a democracy and (2) if the state is also (and continues to be for any length of time) a welfare state, then this coexistence of structural features of the polity in question cannot be accounted for in terms of class interests (as in cell 1), but must be explained in terms of legitimizing values, attitudes, and practices that inhibit and prevent actors from behaving in ways that would effectively subvert collective goods production, but that still would be attractive from the point of view of pure rational individual utility maximizers. In other words, if a democratic state is a welfare state, this is not the case *because* of democracy, but *in spite* of democracy. It must be due to solidarities and modes of normative integration that underpin the continued production of collective goods and guarantee this production, notwithstanding the fact that democracy provides a greater and less expensive opportunity and even temptation to "opt out" and to obstruct this production than any other form of government.

To be sure, even the most ideal-typically selfish citizen would not necessarily be disposed to obstruct *all* collective goods production by the use of the democratic ballot. Mandatory liability insurance, for instance, might be an exception to this rule because it generates a collective good for the insured. This type of insurance, however, will be supported by the rational, selfish actor only as long as the operation of the insurance is perceived to be distributionally neutral. That is to say, the condition of rational consent to *mandatory* insurance is that provisions are taken that guarantee that no one can profit by exploiting the rest of the community of the insured. But this can be taken for granted only if access to the insurance is restricted to persons who regard each other as "our kind of people" or "the likes of us," whereas "cheaters" (who would be defined either as those who get away with less than their proportional contribution, or as those who extract more than their "fair share" of benefits) must be restrained or excluded. This problem is illustrated by the constant pressure on private liability, health, and life insurance companies to organize, by the differentiation of their rates and benefits, "homogeneous risk communities," so that no segment of the membership of the insured feels threatened by the systematic opportunity of other segments to exploit the collectivity of the insured.

Slightly more complicated cases in which rational utility maximizers will still be prepared to cooperate in the production of collective goods are those in which a redistributional game *is* being played but where the actor does have reasons to believe that, in spite of such redistribution effects, she or he will derive either (1) indirect benefits or (2) special advantages from her or his continued cooperation. They will derive *indirect benefits* if the redistribution involved helps to satisfy certain moral imperatives that she or he considers as binding for herself or himself (such as charity), or if such redistribution helps to serve the actor's own interest. Concerning the latter point, it is known that within business and employers' associations, the smaller firms often derive a more than proportional share of benefits while paying a less than proportional share in membership dues, thus making them clear net winners from cooperation. However, the reason that large firms find such subsidization of the small in their indirect interest, too, is to be found in the fact that otherwise the small firms might exit from the association, which would deprive all members, including the large ones, of the collective good of being able to speak in the name of the *entire* industry. It is thus exactly because of the redistribution component that everyone – and not just the winner – is better off. In such cases, even redistributive arrangements may be seen as being in everyone's interest – if only up to the point at which the small business sector within the association starts to make "exploitative" and hence "unacceptable" demands upon the collectivity. Again, the continued production of collective goods appears to be premised on some shared notion of sameness or nonrival commonality of interest.

The other case is that of *special advantages* provided for cooperation from the outside: while the weak gain more than the strong, even the strong receive more than they would be able to under any alternative arrangement that would become available to them through noncooperation. This is – or perhaps one should say this used to be – the case with many old age pension social insurance arrangements, where expected benefits for middle- and high-income participants are higher than can be anticipated from private insurance or individual savings alternatives, due to income graduation, wage indexation, and favorable entry conditions for higher income brackets. Such special advantages, which we could think of as a compensatory *external* subsidization of the *internal* subsidizers, were often used, in the 1950s and 1960s, as a political "bribe" designed to keep the better-off within the pro-welfare-state alliance, and to dissuade them from considering exit options.[32] But for this mechanism to work, it already presupposes on the part of the better-off in the cooperative game a considerable measure of trust that the promise of comparative advantage will be actually honored by any future government – a trust that in the field of old age pensions insurance is rendered notoriously shaky by current and foreseeable demographic and labor market trends. Again, there is a limiting case in which either trust in the willingness or ability of future governments to honor the deal is weakened and/or the price that the better-off demand for their staying within the alliance begins to be perceived as "excessive."

An interesting further case in which collective goods production (or abstention from the democratic option of opting out) is to be expected is weakness of will. I'll consent to being forced to contribute to some collective good (such as social security) if I think of myself as a person who is (for instance, for reasons of near-poverty) incapable of doing what his or her long-term interest would require him or her to do, namely, to save for consumption in old age. Similarly, I'll consent to mandatory insurance if the redistributive effect (for instance, in favor of those who live longer and at the expense of those who experience a below-average life span after retirement) is something that I approve of as a norm of solidarity, without, however, being sufficiently certain of my actual willingness and ability to live up to that principle in concrete cases. In both cases, the collective arrangement is accepted as a "self-paternalist" precommitment that is meant to protect me from the consequences of my own irrational inclinations to disregard either my own future well-being or that of my fellow citizens to whom I feel committed. A further rational motivation to join the collective arrangement may result from the consideration that its common-pool nature makes it more cost efficient: the more people participate, the less expensive (or qualitatively more specialized and adequate, as in public health services) the unit of output becomes.

But note that all these conditions are highly sensitive to empirical counterevidence and strategic fabrication of evidence under conditions of uncertainty. Under some conditions and perceptions, my willingness to cooperate may no longer make sense, which in turn can cause domino effects in the perceptions and attitude changes of others. For instance, if I conceive of myself as someone who is conscientiously prepared to provide for his own future needs, or if I think that others are either not deserving of a share of my income, or deserve only what I shall be willing to give on an *ad hoc* and *ad personam* basis, or if I feel that the expected economies of scale in collective services do not materialize, or are weighed by monopolistic exploitation by the supplying organizations, or must be paid for in terms of poor quality and excessive standardization – all this will damage my rational motivation for cooperating and, therefore, the collectivist arrangement as a whole. It is only my trust that my precommitment will not work out to my disadvantage, that others are worthy of participating in the common pool of resources, and that the latter will not be exploited by provider agencies that lead me to accept this "self-paternalist" arrangement.

In all these cases of cooperative production of public goods, the critical sociological variable is some notion of commonality of interest and fate, of "sameness," or a sufficiently binding conception of a durable collective identity, which is the ultimate resource that keeps cooperation intact beyond its initial phase. Operationally speaking, the notion of sameness, or of collective identity, is the threshold at which actors not only rationally calculate individual and instantaneous costs and utilities, and where they act on the basis of trust. Such trust also has a social dimension, trust in other people, and a temporal dimension, trust in the continued validity and bindingness of norms and institutions. At this threshold, individual actors shift, as it were, from an economic paradigm of choice and contingency into a sociological paradigm of normative bindingness and order. It is not only the durable production of public goods that is, as I shall argue, impossible without some underlying conception of sameness and collective identity; it is even impossible to define precisely the notion of a public good without making at least implicit reference to the idea of a collective identity.

The economists' definition of a public good is based on the criterion of nonexclusiveness: if the good exists at all, it serves all, not just those who have paid for it. This is exactly why no one would be rationally and voluntarily prepared to pay. This is also why payment must be enforced (or tied to selective incentives) in order to produce the public good. But the "publicness" of the good is not a quality of the good itself, but a reflection of the interpretive perspective under which people *view* the good. Take defense as a textbook example of a public good. Even here "inclusiveness' is not something that is inherent in a defense apparatus, but in the perspective under which it is regarded by agents in society. Its "publicness' is entirely dependent on that society's trust in the nonexploitative or nonredistributive nature of the good and its functions. In order for a "good" to be a "public good," there must be a collectivity, the members of which refer to themselves as "we." In the absence of such a collectivity (which in the case of defense is normally conceptualized as a nation or a bloc of nations), there would not be a referent to whom the good is a public good. The defense arrangement would not be seen as a benefit for "all of us" but as the outcome of a redistributional or exploitative game that takes place between taxpayers and defense contractors, military personnel and civilians, defense and civilian sectors of the budget, international-ist and national political orientations, pacifists and militarists, and so on. It is only the self-conception of a collectivity as a nation that puts an end to this type of reasoning in terms of individual and group pay-offs and replaces it by a discourse of collective benefits. This example should alert us to the fact that the "nationhood" of a collectivity can-not be taken for granted, as little as the existence of other collective self-conceptions can, and that without such notions of "sameness" and collective identity, public goods cannot be produced (or, if pro-duced, commonly perceived as "public" and as "goods") – least of all in a democracy, where there is, by definition, no ultimate authority that would be able to order such production by the fiat of its sovereign power.

If, in the course of social change, existing notions of sameness come under strain and stress, the seemingly self-evident public good under-goes a *Gestalt*-switch and turns into the object and outcome of a dis-tributive game. Before this switch occurs, a social policy, say the introduction of unemployment insurance, will be generally discussed and perceived in terms such as the creation of a just society, the guarantee of peaceful industrial relations, or the maintenance of aggregate demand. But *after* the switch, the very same policy will be viewed in categories of equivalence, exploitation, and redistribution, for example in terms of inappropriate burdens being imposed on the industrious and active parts of the workforce, and of undeserved benefits being granted to the unemployed. Note that, in this model example, the interpretive framework within which events are perceived has changed, *not* the policy measure itself. In education, the shift is typically from an emphasis on every person's right to the fullest development of her or his potential, or from human capital considerations, to an emphasis on violations of fiscal fairness or the autonomy of parents, on competitive distortions in the job market or on undue opportunities granted to teachers to promote their collective status interests. In each case, the underlying process is one in which dominant "parameters of sameness" are narrowed down: from the universalist notion of human rights of all human beings to the interest of the nation to the interest of certain categories of taxpayers, professional groups, and cultural communities, and finally to the interests of the individual. In all such cases, the decisive change is not on the level of objective events and facts, but on the level of interpretive frameworks and the strategic adoption of beliefs and expectations. The calculative attitude toward individual and short-term costs and benefits is therefore nothing that is inherent in human nature or an eternal standard of rational action; to the contrary, it is the product of disintegration and decomposition of cultural and structural conditions that constrain and inhibit such utilitarian orientations.

How can such a narrowing of parameters of sameness, or the fragmentation of collective identities, sympathies, and solidarities, be accounted for? Three approaches have been suggested. First, one can explain such shifts in terms of a moral or normative political theory, pointing out that broad humanitarian conceptions of human rights and human needs must be given priority over selfish or otherwise "narrow" interest orientations. To this group would also belong the philosophical idea of an evolutionary sequence of styles of moral orientation, be it linear along an axis of universalism (Habermas), or be it cyclical according to a model of "shifting involvements."[33] Second, the shift can be explained in terms of changing political elites, alliances, coalitions, conjunctures, and ideologies, as a consequence of which elites' strategies are seen to undermine and disorganize "large" collectivities and to entice and encourage citizens and voters to adopt a socially narrow and shortsighted perspective in defining their own political preferences. Thus analyses of the "right turn" in the United States[34] and the syndrome of "authoritarian populism" in Great Britain[35] have interpreted these phenomena as the outcome of a design of reactionary political elites to invoke selfish individualist attitudes, provide it with a moral pretext, and thus to divide solidaristic alliances, and even the nation as a whole, along the nonclass divide of respectable versus morally questionable and undeserving citizens and social categories. Socialist authors have at times shown an understandable, though in my view one-sided, tendency to rely on this "elitist" interpretation exclusively. Thus Krieger writes that

> the attack on the principles of the welfare state is only part of a broader project to reshape political community.... Particularistic and even explicitly divisive appeals replace the integrative universalist norms of the welfare state.... Policies ... are part of a strategy to reinforce particularism .... [and] to divide citizens in highly valuative categories of "us" and "them." ... "They" are blacks, the unemployed, the clients of the welfare state, the strikers.[36]

The problem with this approach is that it seems to assume that political elites are able to shape and change mass attitudes, opinions, and perceptions rather than merely providing excuses and justifications for reorientations that are conditioned by nonpolitical causes. As little can a pro-welfare-state climate of opinion be created by political elites, and an anti-welfare-state orientation be imposed through policies alone. This point is well expressed by Taylor-Gooby when he writes, referring to Habermas:

> The problem is that the social mechanisms that produce allegiance are not under the control of policy, because they originate in a different level of society.... The basic problem is that the political system cannot itself guarantee to produce the values required to assure loyalty to its policies. Values derive from culture which is independent of the state.[37]

Without denying the potential usefulness of either of these approaches, let me suggest a third, more sociological and at the same time more structural, approach. It starts from the assumption that collective identities and parameters of "sameness" are not chosen by individuals for morally good (or bad) reasons, and that the scope of sameness is not imposed upon social actors by either the laws of moral evolution or the manipulative efforts of political elites and ideologists. What we must look for, instead, are *structural* changes within modern societies that condition, suggest, and steer the prevailing interpretive patterns of "sameness." Within this perspective, it is assumed that the patterns of, for example, the division of labor, of cultural differentiation, of political organization and representation are underlying determinants of what kind and scope of collectivity people refer to when using the word "we."

Destructuration of Collectivities

It has often been observed that the most advanced and stable welfare states exist in those European societies that are highly homogeneous. Take Sweden as the prototypical case: an economy that is small and highly export dependent; a polity that is characterized by both long-term social democratic governance and hegemony and by a virtually unparalleled associational density of highly centralized interest associations; a society and culture that is, compared to other Western European countries, not only highly egalitarian (as a consequence of past redistributive welfare state policies) but also uniquely homogeneous as far as the striking absence of ethnic, regional, linguistic, religious, or other major cultural cleavages is concerned. A further characteristic has been Sweden's nonparticipation in supranational military (NATO) and economic (EEC) organizations – a trait shared by this country with Austria and (partly) with Norway, that is, with two of the other most advanced welfare states. All these features would suggest that in Swedish society the prevailing conception of "sameness" is very broad and inclusive, and that there exist powerful structural and cultural factors that effectively prevent the majority of Swedes from shifting to a view of their welfare state that would emphasize exploitation, unfair redistributional effects, free-riding, and similar utilitarian or "rational choice" perspectives. But even in this rather exceptional case of Sweden, new divisions, antisolidaristic strategies, symptoms of lack of trust in the welfare state's administration, and particularistic tendencies surfaced in the early 1980s that seemed to put into question major achievements of public policy and neocorporatist interest intermediation between large and centralized associational blocks.[38]

When T. H. Marshall[39] theorized the inherent tendency of parliamentary democracies to transform themselves into strong welfare states (see cell 1 of figure 8.2), he took for granted the existence of large, self-conscious, and well-organized collectivities and class organizations of labor that would use the ballot for strategies of social reform and expansive social policies. From the mid-1970s, however, we witness a fairly rapid decomposition or destructuration of such collectivities. There are many indicators suggesting that political preferences and orientations of increasing segments of the electorate are a reflection of this process of fragmentation, pluralization, and ultimately individualization of socioeconomic conditions and interest dispositions. Issue orientation versus party orientation in voting, the increasing significance of plant-level over sectoral regulation of industrial conflict, and of sectoral over centralized national regulation, social, economic, and cultural cleavages that crosscut the dividing lines between classes and class organizations are all frequently observed symptoms of societywide destructuration processes.

The disorganization of broad, relatively stable, and encompassing commonalities of economic interest, associational affiliation, or cultural values and lifestyles is in my view the key to an adequate understanding of the general weakening of solidaristic commitments. If it no longer "makes sense" to refer to a broad and sharply delineated category of fellow citizens as "our kind of people," the only remaining interpretive referent of action is the individual who refers to herself or himself in rational-calculative terms. This reorientation may be accelerated by political campaigns of the populist right that, as it were, "cross-code" people according to criteria of moral worthiness and unworthiness. Or it may be retarded by appeals to universalist moral standards that should not be sacrificed. But these appear to be variables of secondary importance, while primary significance rests with new forms of structural and cultural plurality leading to the virtual evaporation of classes and other self-conscious collectivities of political will, economic interest, and cultural values whose existence must be considered, as I have argued before, a necessary condition for solidary and collectivist attitudes and ideologies. The imagery of a fluid and mobile "patchwork" is often used to describe a newly emerging structure of society and pattern of conflict – conflicts no less severe than those represented in class-conflict modes, but that differ from them in that the new pattern is made up of a plurality of relatively small groups and categories rapidly shifting in size, influence, and internal coherence, with no dominant axis of conflict.

My thesis is that the welfare state as we know it as a major accomplishment of postwar West European societies is rapidly losing its political support for these reasons of structural change, and that this development cannot be fully explained either by economic and fiscal crisis arguments, or by political arguments emphasizing the rise of neoconservative elites and ideologies; nor can it be undone by moral appeals to the justice and legitimacy of existing welfare state arrangements. What this structural disintegration process leaves behind is an interpretive pattern that is deeply distrustful of social policies as "public goods," and that tends instead to unravel such policies in terms of gains and losses, exploitation, free-riding, redistribution, and so on – that is, in individualist "economic man" categories, the behavioral consequences of which are best captured and predicted by rational choice theory.[40]

To be sure, the destructuration process and its ideological and eventually political repercussions are not uniform across countries, social classes, income categories, gender groups, or groups defined by party affiliation, nor do they affect individual components of the welfare state, its programs and institutions, to the same extent. But some generalizations are in place in spite of these differences. One highly consequential destructuration occurs in the longitudinal dimension: the future is seen not to be a continuation of the past as far as economic growth, fiscal policy, and employment are concerned, and this anticipation undermines the plausibility of the traditional social democratic "solution of painless redistribution by funding welfare from expansion."[41] Another generalization concerns an increasing differentiation between the popularity that different components of the welfare state enjoy. Some programs and institutions – such as old age pensions and the health sector – find a greater acceptance than others (such as unemployment insurance, family allowance, youth programs, and social assistance), the intuitively plausible reason being that it is much easier to conceive of a broad and inclusive alliance of potential beneficiaries in the first case than in the second, where clients are much more easily marginalized and stigmatized. But given the fact that the most serious of the fiscal problems of the welfare state emerge in its old age pension and health programs, this relatively greater support for these programs is also qualified by the individually rational temptation to "opt out" and shift to private forms of provision. "There has developed during the last two decades a whole series of substitutes for publicly provided social safety nets, such as private life insurance, firm pensions ... which are even cheaper as they often pool 'good risks.' "[42] One might even suspect that, under these conditions, it becomes rational for some middle-class elements to express (insincere) support for the continued public provision of some minimal health and old age pension, because that would make the conditions for private provision all the more favorable – much in the way that it is rational to express strong and effective support for public transport while then expecting to be able to use private cars on the pleasantly uncongested streets.

Let me mention some of the underlying causes for the destruction of self-conscious interest communities in advanced industrial societies, and hence of the cultural and normative underpinnings of the welfare state.

(1) Within the labor force of these highly industrialized democratic societies, there are increasing disparities of life chances among the totality of wage workers. These disparities depend on variables such as industrial sector, ethnicity, region, gender, skill level, and so on. In view of such disparities, the organizational, political, and cultural

resources by which some measure of commonality of interest could be established and politically enforced become increasingly debased and powerless.

(2) The prevailing patterns of economic, industrial, and technical change generate the well-known disjunction between changes in economic output and changes in employment. As a consequence of this pattern of "jobless growth," the percentage of people who find themselves in the condition of open unemployment, hidden unemployment, or labor market marginalization, or who are rendered unemployable or discouraged from labor market participation, is rising. These categories of people, who are most desperately dependent on the welfare state's provision of transfers and services are, however, politically most vulnerable. This is so because there is little reason, either for the propertied middle classes and capital or for the core working class, to adopt the material interests of this "surplus class" as their own. Such a reason does not exist for the core working class because there is little empirical reason to fear that the "surplus class" could function as an effective "reserve army," that is, depress wages and undermine employment security in highly fragmented and stratified labor markets. Similarly, there is little reason for the middle class and employers to fear that the existence of a growing "surplus class" could lead to disruptive forms of social unrest and conflict, the prevention of which could be "worth" a major investment in welfare policies – or even the full maintenance of those that exist.

(3) Encompassing alliances of a pro-welfare-state orientation thrive in the "good times" of economic growth and full employment (that is, positive-sum games) and tend to decompose under zero-sum conditions. The potential for "public regarding" and solidaristic political commitments appears to be exhausted in many countries, both after the experience of real wage losses in the late 1970s and early 1980s and in anticipation of moderate growth rates and persistent high levels of unemployment and insecure employment. In that sense, the economic crisis of the welfare state generates individualistic political attitudes and orientations and thus translates, without much liberal-conservative mass mobilization and political organization needed, into a political crisis of the welfare state.

There seems to exist an asymmetry between the sociopolitical processes that result in the expansion of welfare states and those that lead to cuts and the eventual decay of social welfare policies. In the upward direction, what is needed are broad electoral and interest group alliances that converge on the institutionalization of collectivist arrangements. These arrangements will then persevere due to the inertia and entrenched interests of what has been set up. In order to survive, all that is needed is the absence of strong oppositional political forces. In contrast to the expansion, the decline is normally not initiated by reactionary mass movements and political forces. It normally originates from anonymous economic imperatives, such as budgetary pressures and fiscal as well as labor market imbalances, that suggest cuts in social expenditures. In the presence of such economic difficulties, the tendency toward cumulative cuts could only be halted if a strong and unified political alliance were in place to defend existing arrangements. But it is exactly the formation of such an alliance that is rendered unlikely by the fragmentation, pluralization, and individualization of interests. As a consequence, uncertainty in the social dimension (concerning which political forces and social categories could be relied on as trustworthy partners in a defensive alliance) is reinforced by uncertainty in the temporal dimension (concerning how much present sacrifice is likely to be compensated for by how much future gain in growth, employment, and security). In Western Europe at least, cuts in welfare expenditures do not typically occur as the political consequences of "tax revolts"; they simply "suggest themselves" as a consequence of changes in macro-economic indicators, and they can be implemented without much political cost in view of the weakness of resistance. While the rise of a welfare state requires mass mobilization and large political coalitions as a sufficient condition, its demise is mediated through economic imperatives as well as the silent and inconspicuous defection of voters, groups, and corporate actors whose heterogeneous structure, perceptions, and responses stand in the way of the formation of an effective defensive alliance. To put it somewhat simplistically, it takes politics to build a welfare state, but merely economic changes to destroy both major component parts of it and potential sources of resistance to such resistance.

(4) It is not only the *goals* and objectives of welfare state policies (which consist in the prevention of poverty, the guarantee of social security, and the provision of public health, education, housing, and other services) which meet with decreasing political support. It is also the *means* by which the goals have been traditionally implemented, namely bureaucratic and professional intervention, that seem to have lost much of their acceptance, and are increasingly seen in the corrosive light of a distributional and exploitative game. That is to say, these means are no longer universally considered as a rational instrument for the implementation of "public goods," but increasingly as a

highly effective strategy of a self-serving "new class" to cement their positions of power and privilege, and at the same time as an ineffective or even counterproductive ("dependency creating" and "decapacitating") way of responding to the needs of clients and recipients.

(5) A particularly important factor that helps in understanding anti-collectivist and anti-welfare-state reorientations of public opinion in Western democracies is the quantitative growth of the middle class, particularly the "new" or "salaried" middle class. As far as the *upper* strata of this broad social category are concerned, the welfare state has distributive effects that are clearly in their favor, a fact that can be partly explained through the logic of political "bribes" referred to above. Thus one author concludes that

> the members of the salaried middle class seem to be the main beneficiaries of the welfare state. In pensions, health, housing, and education it seemed that the better off you are the more you gained from the system. In terms of service, tax allowances and occupational welfare, the managers, administrators, professionals, scientists, technologicals working for large organizations benefited considerably more than manual and routine white collar workers.[43]

However, such special advantages and upward redistributive effects have failed to buy the political support of those who not only benefit from services and income-graduated transfers, but also from the secure and continuously expanding employment the welfare state had to offer them. The greater this income and privilege, the greater becomes their inclination to look for *private* alternatives to welfare state services, the most important of which are old age pension and health services. The higher the status and income that the welfare state provides you with, the *less* your rational motivation to have your privileges tied to (foreseeably precarious) collectivist arrangements, and the greater accordingly the inclination to look for – and to support parties that propose designs for – private market alternatives. The dilemma of the welfare state is clear enough: any emphasis on egalitarian "flat rate" policies would alienate those better off whose income would be used to subsidize the transfers to the less well-to-do. But the opposite policy – that of strong income differentiation and status maintenance – also would not help to keep the recipients of higher incomes within the alliance, for this policy reinforces and creates privileges that their beneficiaries are understandably unwilling to share with the rest of the welfare state's clientele.

As far as the *lower* middle class, including some segments of the skilled core working class, is concerned, its allegiance to the welfare state is notoriously questionable. Members of this "middle mass" have formed in various countries the political base of tax revolts and the "welfare backlash." Wilensky, who has conducted large-scale comparative studies of these phenomena, concludes that "as rich countries become richer, the middle mass as a political force becomes more fluid, torn loose from traditional political identities, and more strategic, larger and more potent as a swing vote." He sees a "developing political rage of the middle class."[44] This tendency described by Wilensky would reverse an old and strong positive statistical correlation between welfare collectivism and economic growth, and lead to a situation in which, as more people live in prosperity, they are *less* inclined to endorse such arrangements. It seems that dissolving "traditional political identities" are not openly replaced by pure individualism, but that such a shift to individualism is provided with a justification by the formation of identities of a moralizing and/or particularistic kind. What is least popular with the "middle mass" are programs that benefit those supposedly *morally* inferior categories (such as unemployed youth and single parents) and ascriptively defined minorities (such as ethnic or national ones).

A final observation concerning the widespread political defection of the middle class from collectivist welfare arrangements refers to the fact that since the mid-1970s much of the political energy of this social category has been invested, as it were, into issues and campaigns and conflicts of a nonclass, nonredistributive nature, ranging from civil rights to feminist to ecological to peace causes and movements. The reverse side of this shift in political style and emphasis of middle-class political activism is, of course, a deemphasis of conflicts having to do with social security, distributional justice, and solidarity.

(6) The disappearance of a plausible and mobilizing political program or project within the European left that would instill an idea of a mission or vision of sociopolitical transformation in the mass constituency of socialist, social democratic, and labor parties is a further important factor in the process of destruction of collective identities based on social class (or the nation in war or under the threat of war) and distributive interest. The failure of hegemonic projects – be it of etatist planning, be it of economic democracy – has left the traditional protagonists of the welfare state in a highly defensive position of "maintaining what we have" (*Besitzstandswahrung*), which in turn allows parts of their constituency to begin to think about evasive strategies in case this defensive position fails – a case that is predicted with considerable resonance by conservative and market liberal elites.

Three observations and perceptions tend to deprive the welfare state of the moral appeal of a just and "progressive" sociopolitical project. One concerns the evident incapacity of governments – including social democratic ones – to apply causal and preventive therapies to those socioeconomic problems that the welfare state must then solve in an ex post and compensatory manner by throwing ever-rising amounts of money at them. For example, generous unemployment compensation for those out of work is affordable only if an active and preventive full employment policy keeps the number of those who are entitled to such benefits relatively small – in much the same way in which, as Schumpeter observed long ago, the construction of faster automobiles does not so much depend on the invention of more powerful engines but on more effective brakes. Similarly, the idea of universal health insurance coverage of all employees and their families loses much of its moral plausibility if evidently no one is able to implement large-scale and effective preventive health programs and to control the "cost explosion" in health – that is, the price-setting behavior of pharmaceutical manufacturers, doctors, and hospitals. If, as a consequence, the proportion of income that is deducted for mandatory health insurance reaches record levels (13 percent in the mid-1980s in West Germany, without, incidentally, any objectively measurable improvement in the general health status of the population being shown), the *Gestalt*-switch referred to above sets in with particular force: what used to be thought of as a solidary arrangement guaranteeing the protection of the health of all irrespective of income is now seen as a giant redistributive game with widely dispersed and high costs for clients, and concentrated and even higher benefits for suppliers of services.

Second, the moral appeal of the welfare state resides in the perceived justice of its distributive effects. The more the interpretation finds a base in perceived reality that the distributive effects are much more intertemporal (that is, self-paternalist) in nature than intergroup (that is, redistributive), the appeal and legitimacy of the welfare state project as a secularized and modern version of Christian ideals of charity must necessarily suffer severe damage, particularly as the gap between the living conditions of those depending on social security systems and those depending on welfare, social assistance, and other means-tested and family-related programs becomes wider.

Third, pessimistic perceptions and interpretations both of the *effectiveness* of the welfare state, that is, its capacity to intervene causally into the need- and cost-inflating socioeconomic processes, and of the *legitimacy* of the welfare state, that is, its capacity to implement moral standards of redistributive justice, develop a self-reinforcing and self-propelling dynamic. This is so for the simple "sinking-boat" strategic reason that if one sees oneself as belonging to an alliance that is doomed to lose, one had better quit it earlier than others. Doing this, however, will convince others that defecting is the only remaining option for them, too. In view of giant fiscal problems that must be anticipated for the welfare state in connection with probable demographic, labor market, health, and family developments, such interactive chains of individual rational responses are something that is not only quite likely to occur, but also something that the traditional pro-welfare-state alliance of social democratic parties and unions is ideologically and hegemonically ill-equipped to prevent in most West European countries.

As a combined effect of these structural changes, we may anticipate the rise of behavioral orientations of voters and citizens that give support to anti-welfare-state policies – not primarily for reasons of bad intentions, irrational drives, or a sudden shift to neoconservative or market-liberal values and attitudes, but because of beliefs and preferences that are rationally formed in response to perceived social realities as well as to actual experiences with the practice of existing welfare states.

What all of this amounts to is the prediction that the neoconservative denunciations of the welfare state are likely to fall on fertile ground, thereby setting in motion a political mechanism of self-fulfilling predictions and interpretations. That does not mean, however, that the neoconservative analysis and the empirical arguments on which it claims to base its validity are "true" in any objectively testable sense, or that they are "right" according to substantive criteria of political legitimacy and social justice. They are, for all the reasons specified above, simply highly effective and self-confirming as a political formula with which electoral majorities can be formed, and with which existing large solidaristic communities of interest can be further disorganized. As a formula, it can be challenged only by a democratic left that moves beyond its traditional defensive positions and adopts new concepts, goals, and strategies whose outlines today remain largely uncertain.

Notes

1 Thomas H. Marshall, 'Citizenship and Social Class," in Marshall, *Class, Citizenship and Social Development* (New York, 1965; first published 1949).
2 Alan Wolfe, *The Limits of Legitimacy: Political Contradictions of Contemporary Capitalism* (London, 1977); Crawford Macpherson, *The Life and Times of*

Liberal Democracy (Oxford, 1977); Andrew Levine, *Liberal Democracy: A Critique of its Theory* (New York, 1981).

3 Anton C. Zijderfeld, "The Ethos of the Welfare State," *International Sociology* 1:4 (1986), pp. 452–3.

4 Ibid., p. 454.

5 Klaus Gretschmann, "Social Security in Transition: Some Reflections from a Fiscal Sociology Perspective," *International Sociology* 1:3 (1986) p. 232; Lawrence M. Mead, *Beyond Entitlement: The Social Obligations of Citizenship* (New York and London, 1986).

6 Ramesh Mishra, *The Welfare State in Crisis* (Brighton, 1984).

7 Jürgen Habermas, "Die Krise des Wohlfahrtsstaates und die Erschöpfung utopischer Energien," in Habermas, *Die neue Unübersichtlichkeit* (Frankfurt, 1985); Claus Offe, *Contradictions of the Welfare State*, ed. John Keane (London, 1984).

8 Habermas, *Die neue Unübersichtlichkeit*; Christoph Sachsse, "Verrechtlichung und Sozialisation: Über Grenzen des Wohlfahrtsstaates," *Leviathan* 14:4 (1986); Ivan Illich et al., *Disabling Professions* (London, 1977).

9 Mead, *Beyond Entitlement*.

10 Manfred Spieker, *Legitimitätsprobleme des Sozialstaates* (Berne and Stuttgart, 1986).

11 Mead, *Beyond Entitlement*.

12 Ibid., pp. 12–13.

13 Spieker, *Legitimitätsprobleme*, p. 328.

14 Ibid., p. 323.

15 See Sachsse, "Verrechtlichung."

16 Habermas, *Die neue Unübersichtlichkeit*, p. 151.

17 Richard Titmuss, *Essays on the Welfare State*, 2nd edn (London, 1963), p. 39.

18 Gilbert as quoted in Paul Whiteley, "Public Opinion and the Demand for Social Welfare in Britain," *Journal of Social Policy* 10:4 (1981) p. 455.

19 Göran Therborn, "Challenge to the Welfare State," unpublished paper, Institute for Political Science, Catholic University Nijmegen, Netherlands, 1986.

20 Else Øeyen, "The Muffling Effect of Social Policy: A Comparison of Social Security Systems and their Conflict Potential in Australia, the United States and Norway," *International Sociology* 1:3 (1986).

21 See Richard M. Coughlin, *Ideology, Public Opinion, and Welfare Policy* (Berkeley, 1980).

22 Seppo Pöntinen and Hannu Uusitalo, "The Legitimacy of the Welfare State: Social Security Opinions in Finland 1975–1985," Suormen Gallup Oy Report, no. 15, 1986, p. 26; Stein Ringen, *Does the Welfare State Work?* (Oxford, 1986).

23 Peter Taylor-Gooby, "Legitimation Deficit, Public Opinion and the Welfare State," *Sociology* 17:2 (1983), p. 175; Jens Alber, "Der Wohlfahrtsstaat in der Wirtschaftskrise: Eine Bilanz der Sozialpolitik in der Bundesrepublik seit den fruhen 70er Jahren," *Politische Vierteljahresschrift* 27:1 (1986).

24 Whiteley, "Public Opinion," p. 460.

25 While a full 81% belonged in that expansive category during 1950–74, and only 8% of the new legislation involved cuts, the federal legislative output of 1975–83 consisted of 56% of new laws implying cuts while only 27% of

the laws of this period led to increases (Alber, "Der Wohlfahrtsstaat in der Wirtschaftskrise," p. 31).

26 Claus Offe, "New Social Movements: Challenging the Boundaries of Institutional Politics," *Social Research* 52:4 (1985).

27 Adam Przeworski and Michael Wallerstein, "Why Is There No Left Economic Alternative?," unpublished MS, University of Chicago, 1986.

28 Habermas, *Die neue Unübersichtlichkeit*, pp. 149–52.

29 Harold L. Wilensky, *The Welfare State and Equality: Structural and Ideological Roots of Public Expenditures* (Berkeley, 1975); Jens Alber, *Vom Armenhaus zum Wohlfahrtsstaat: Analysen zur Entwicklung der Sozialversicherung in Westeuropa* (Frankfurt, 1982).

30 Taylor-Gooby, "Legitimation Deficit," p. 166, emphasis added.

31 Talcott Parsons, *The Structure of Social Action* (New York, 1968; first published 1937).

32 This problem would not be altered substantially if the possibility of democratic *rule*-making (of laws and constitutions) were taken into account as a further and rather obvious complication. Such rules can in fact perform the function of (self-)binding devices that make democratic decisions *temporarily* immune from revision and obstruction. But because such binding rules are never – be it *de lege* or *de facto* – absolutely and indefinitely binding, and as it appears highly questionable from the point of view of rational actors even to attempt to extend the bindingness of rules into the indefinite future, the "opting-out" argument itself is not affected by such rules, but only the rapidity with which the consequences can unfold.

33 Albert O. Hirschman, *Shifting Involvements, Private Interests and Public Action* (Princeton, 1982).

34 Thomas Ferguson and Joel Rogers, *Right Turn: The Decline of the Democrats and the Future of American Politics* (New York, 1986).

35 Stuart Hall and Martin Jacques (eds), *The Politics of Thatcherism* (London, 1983); Bob Jessop, Kevin Bonnett, Simon Bromley and Tom Ling, "Authoritarian Populism, Two Nations, and Thatcherism," *New Left Review* 147 (1984).

36 Joel Krieger, "Social Policy in the Age of Reagan and Thatcher," *Socialist Register* (London, 1987).

37 Taylor-Gooby, "Legitimation Deficit," p. 168.

38 Scott Lash, "The End of Neo-Corporatism? The Breakdown of Centralised Bargaining in Sweden," *British Journal of Industrial Relations* 23:2 (1985); Pöntinen and Uusitalo, "The Legitimacy of the Welfare State," pp. 20ff.

39 Marshall, "Citizenship and Social Class."

40 ... whose time seems to have come for exactly this "structural" reason. Its fundamental methodological assumptions are in their essence antistructural, antifunctionalist, antinormativist, and thus in a way antisociological (relying on psychological and economic paradigms instead). But it is exactly this new paradigm and the dramatic shift in the intellectual climate in much of the social sciences that lends itself to a sociology of knowledge interpretation: it corresponds to a centerless, atomized, and destructured condition of social life. Without having the space here to elaborate this interpretation further, let me just suggest that I find it fruitful not only for the understanding of the growth of rational choice theory, but also for its twin phenomena, namely the rise to prominence of 'postmodernist" approaches based on the work of Foucault and Lyotard.

41 Taylor-Gooby, "Legitimation Deficit," p. 171.
42 Gretschmann, "Social Security in Transition," p. 233.
43 Arthur Gould, "The Salaried Middle Class and the Welfare State in Sweden and Japan," *Policy and Politics* 10:4 (1982).
44 Wilensky, *The Welfare State*, p. 116.

9

The Acceptance and Legitimacy of Strategic Options in Social Policy

At a time when, in Eastern Germany and other postrevolutionary societies of Eastern and Central Europe, the project of a "social" market economy is gaining ground, in the West the very structural political-economic feature which was to moderate the market economy "socially," namely the welfare state, is beset by manifold doubts and uncertainties. To be sure, so far in Western Europe no mainstream academic voice or political group has declared *open* warfare on the welfare state. The institutions of and guarantees of entitlements to social insurance, health, state education and training, housing, assistance for families and social assistance are basic structural assets which are difficult simply to theorize or wish away. However, since the mid-1970s the signs have been of consolidation rather than expansion. If the welfare state becomes a public issue at all, it is treated as a costly ballast rather than as a set of indispensable guarantees of peace and social justice which ought to be developed further. The champions of the social or welfare state find themselves clearly on the defensive. Their position is undermined by a threefold doubt about whether the welfare state program can be financed, legitimated, or made effective.

I will restrict myself here to an outline analysis of the options, preferences, and strategies of actors participating in the social policy "game." Clearly, the issue here is not support for and justification of the welfare state system *as a whole*. For, for want of an extensive knowledge of an entirely different and superior alternative (and of how to achieve it!), the givenness of a state of affairs with a certain degree of complexity has to be accepted. The issue is far more the direction of *marginal changes* which can be described as rational and/or just. From this point of view, two questions arise. For what reasons and under what circumstances do these actors prefer, or accept, certain changes in the welfare state system? This is a question of (more or less rationally calculated or simply routine) support or *"acceptance."* And with what normative arguments, that is, arguments which are not tied to the situation of the players concerned, can these be justified? This is the question of how the welfare state can be grounded in principles, and in the case of their recognition, of its *legitimacy.*

I

The historical context in which the welfare state emerged is marked by the following problem (or the problem of how to acknowledge and confront it politically). In modern societies, characterized among other things by the development of a free market for labor and capital, individuals are typically exposed to a series of risks, which extend to their material life chances and opportunities for societal participation. These risks consist in the fact that, because of physical disadvantage or weakness (such as old age, inappropriate qualifications, homelessness, the burden of family duties or conversely the absence of a familial support network, and lack of employment opportunities), individuals are unable to gain, maintain, or regain access to the predominant form of societal participation, earning an income through dependent wage labor.

Furthermore, it may be said of this category of risks, typical in capitalist industrial societies, that, in the first place, the development and expansion of these risks are not a result of the shortcomings of groups affected by them. Therefore, it is, in the second place, implausible to expect from those affected an individual confrontation with, or uncomplaining acceptance of, their physical-material fate. In particular, the "Victorian" moralizing which links risk to poverty is rendered obsolete because, in the third place, these risks do not merely have objective social causes, but harmful *collective consequences* as well. These external costs include the danger of epidemics, which sprang from the overcrowded districts of nineteenth-century cities, and rebellious or revolutionary questioning of the social and political order. In this sense the privatization of some of these risks is no longer tolerable, for functional as well as moral reasons. For all these reasons the problem of how to deal with these types of risks forces itself on to the agenda of the state. They can no longer be dealt with through the old local charity organizations or forms of cooperative assistance and self-help which are independent of the state.

But the emergence and public *recognition* of a problem is one thing; coping with it institutionally is another. The solutions must not only be "adequate to the problem," but also "acceptable" to the relevant social actors. In general, and especially so in the German case, social security systems (such as arrangements surrounding accidents, illness, old age, and unemployment) are constructed in such a way as to ensure that the problem of acceptance does not become acute. The precondition of a system of social security being deemed acceptable for rational reasons and worthy of support by both sides of the labor market and their associations and political elites – despite the conflict between their interests – is their confidence, secured through robust institutional supports, that *two* reciprocally conditioned "undesired outcomes" will *not* occur. The two outcomes to be avoided, expressed roughly and schematically, are:

(a) those entitled to benefit from and those obliged to contribute to the social security system do *not* enjoy the benefits they should;
(b) the beneficiaries include those who have *not* become entitled through contributions or on other grounds.

In the first case, where those entitled do not receive what they "deserve," the security arrangement would founder on anticipations of its inefficiency, because it would demand from participants an unlikely degree of confidence in the future. In the second case, where "those who are not entitled" receive something they do not deserve, it would founder on "overdrawn" benefits. The distribution of these according to criteria of political and moral justice is controversial, so that in this case participants would be expected to display an equally unlikely degree of trust in the capacity of others for solidarity. Naturally, a really explosive mixture occurs when case (a) is seen as a *consequence* of case (b), that is, when feelings of "fear" are combined with those of "envy."

The purpose of these preliminary observations is simply to show the way in which the institutional structures of the German social security system are suited to channeling participants' motives toward conformity and acceptance. These structures can be reconstructed as a shrewdly worked out ensemble of measures which guarantee trust and ensure that neither of the cases which were to be avoided need be feared in fact.

1 That is true, first, of *"obligatory insurance."* This guards against case (a) by ensuring the expectation that the fund of collective capital

from current incomes will always be sufficient to cover new claims. At the same time it erects a barrier against case (b) in that, in contrast to voluntary insurance, it excludes the opportunity for employees to withhold their contributions to collective welfare provision and then, in case of need, to claim benefit.

2 Another means of guarding against case (a) is the principle of *state supervision*, and above all its *obligation to subsidize* in case of an insurance budget deficit.

3 The *equivalence principle* and the *conditional principle* ensure that the effects on redistribution and relief in case (b) are largely avoided. The equivalence principle, which concerns the size of the benefit, states that an intention to redistribute internally between worse and better placed cannot be carried out. Redistributions which do in fact occur among the "community of the insured" appear less drastic as a result of the fact that they take place unintentionally and are acknowledged only after the fact. A considerable internal redistribution does indeed occur between those in good and poor health, those in need of expensive and better-value treatment, families with many and with no children, and above all, those who live long and those who die young. But these forms of redistribution are not a strategic goal. Rather, they are ascribed to the noncontingent natural facts of human existence. Even where these occurrences cannot be treated as randomly distributed (and cannot thereby be rationally justified solely by the insurance principle of "risk pooling"), but are distributed among specifiable categories of people (for instance, accidents among blue-collar and white-collar workers, life expectancy among men and women), the conceivable internal redistribution remains morally unobjectionable. The corresponding sensitivities come into play only when a disproportionate withdrawal of benefits is no longer ascribed to fate, but is thought to result from contingent action (illness caused by addiction, the issuing of doctor's certificates for abortion according to social status, etc.). The conditional principle states that claims to benefit are in no way dependent on the assessment of need or want, but solely on satisfaction of the conditions for the claim. In this way, the better situated of those insured have no reason for the fear, corresponding to case (b), of losses resulting from an internal redistribution which benefits the less well situated.

4 Placing an upper threshold on obligatory income-proportionate contributions, by placing a *limit on the assessment of contributions*, does something more to ensure that the readiness of the better placed for solidarity is not overstretched. The introduction of supplementary insurance arrangements *within the enterprise* is designed to build up separate funds, with access to them being confined to those whose benefits and risks were relatively similar.

5 An essential method for avoiding case (b) is exemplified by the German social security system, and is related to capacity and readiness for *wage labor*. This excludes from benefits those who have either failed to prove their preparedness and capacity for dependent wage labor, or who do not at least have a dependent relationship to a family member in regular employment.

6 In contrast to financing through taxation, *financing through contributions* withdraws from executive and legislature the power to dispose over the social insurance budget, by excluding the use of these resources for purposes *other* than that of insurance. In this way, the collection and use of contributions is secured against redistributive temptations and ambitions which are "foreign to insurance," and firmly depoliticized. This structural principle gives those who are insured no cause to suspect the occurrence of either (a) or (b) and confers on the budget the status of collective private property.

7 This attitude of reserve vis-à-vis public policy, which resembles a disposition over private property, is reinforced by a quasi-public self-administration by the *bearers of social insurance*, and by the principle of *contributory parity*. This encourages representatives of employers and employees to work out their differences through negotiation, and in addition (similar to the case of free collective bargaining) it suggests that they have a common interest in social policy transactions which are largely free from state or politics.

This brief outline of the basic institutional features of the German system of social insurance is of interest here only from the following point of view. How can these features encourage individual and collective actors to support an "objective" collective interest in confronting the risks which typically face employees, and to do so out of calculations of subjective interest? The net effect of these features is to reduce the demands of *risk acceptance* (or of trust in the future) and moral demands for solidarity (or for trust in "others") to such an extent that rationally grounded reservations toward the social security system as a whole cannot easily be made. Ideally, the system makes no cognitive or moral claims: it makes it easy for each person to retain the subjective certainty that he or she receives what is owing to him or her, just as it nourishes the conviction that no one receives what is not their entitlement. It is to precisely this that it owes its remarkable historical robustness, seen in the fact the German system of social insurance (unchanged in most of the institutional features mentioned!) has survived an entire century and no less than four radically different state constitutions, and developed in unbroken continuity on the basis of these features.

II

The twofold question is: Will this cycle of a "motivating self-reproduction" continue to function under present social conditions and those of the foreseeable future? And will the system of social insurance, even in positive cases, be adequate to cope with all the significant collective risks to which these conditions give rise?

Every system of social security of the welfare state sort, that is, one which operates through the allocation of legal entitlements to (monetary) benefits, is janus-faced. It *guarantees* transfer and service benefits on the basis of certain conditions which serve to ground claims to them. But it *restricts* this guarantee to those who fulfill these conditions. Thus, every welfare state-style "inclusion" (Niklas Luhmann) goes hand-in-hand with an exclusion, simply because every sociolegal conditional program is constructed according to the formula "if–then," and implies the negation "if not–then not." It follows from this that the welfare state operates according to a logic which divides the population into *three* main categories.

1 The category of people (or needs) who have *no* entitlement because they count as already provided for, be it through markets for labor, private insurance, or commodities, or through the family. Their nonentitlement to assistance and benefits depends on a country's prevailing ideas concerning a normal living standard.
2 The category of those of whom it is acknowledged that they cannot be expected adequately to provide for themselves from their own resources, or to endure being unprovided for. Here, a recognition of demands for benefit always rests on personal or objective criteria – on an individual's income-earning history, on membership of a state, on expert medical judgment concerning the "necessity" of a particular treatment. The core group of welfare state clients enjoys an entitlement to a part of social "transfer capital,"[1] social security, which resembles a title to property.
3 The remaining category of those who, without belonging to the first category of those equipped with sufficient resources for independent self-provision or self-help, do *not* fulfill the conditions of entitlement which would include them in the second category, and are therefore excluded from state benefits (or included only to an extent which does not correspond to their needs, or only on the basis of a special assessment of those needs, and material conditions and restrictions).[2]

Clearly, as figure 9.1 shows, this tripartite division of the universe of people and needs is constituted by two lines of demarcation.

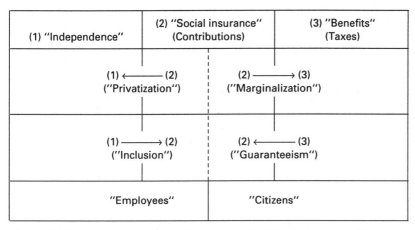

Figure 9.1 Strategies for transferring responsibilities between welfare state sectors

Accordingly, the welfare state's historical development can be reconstructed as a succession of "border conflicts" along these lines. Here, four political-ideological tendencies can be distinguished, which push the dynamics of these conflicts in one direction or another at one border or another. Each involves certain categories of people being shunted between three spheres and "transferred to another account."[3]

Historically, the dominant tendency has been toward *inclusion* ((1) → (2)). Persons and needs which "hitherto" were regarded as lying beyond the state's responsibility for welfare provision are "now" included in it. In Germany, beginning with Bismarck's social reforms, there was a cumulative recognition of additional circumstances in which social security was needed (such as unemployment in 1927), the inclusion of broader categories of people (such as white-collar workers in 1911), and an increase in the size of claims made on the basis of income (culminating in the pensions reform of 1957).[4]

Unless appearances deceive, the expansive dynamic of this tendency has now reached a state of permanent exhaustion. All proposals to include new types of need and new groups of people in the social security system, and at ever higher levels of benefit, have clearly lost their power to convince, and above all, their chances of electoral success. The reasons for this are clear. To begin with, technical and economic change, and lasting alterations in the population's attitude to work, have generated a permanent and serious imbalance in the labor market. But with unemployment, part of the income to which contributory obligations were tied disappears. (And the income of those employed is unlikely to rise as quickly as it would have under full employment). Furthermore, unemployment means an increase in the demands made on the social security system. Taken together these factors place that system in a financially parlous state. Secondly, this problem is exacerbated by demographic developments. If the servicing of existing claims (which, politically, can be reduced only with difficulty and in the long term) places increasing burdens on the fundraising side, that is, demands increased rates of pension contributions, then there is simply no room for further expansion.

Thirdly, in view of the federal budget deficit, brought about by social but also by economic policy, the determination of finance ministers to relieve the burden on the financial pillar known as the "state subsidy" will presumably be strengthened. In addition, political support for this form of budget relief is easily mobilized, as there is a majority of voters who give precedence to *universal* budget relief (in the hope of tax and interest rate reductions) over the fiscal subsidy for social security systems which always benefit *particular* groups and meet particular needs.

Fourthly, a well-established interpretation of the problems of social security and distribution (and one which has been proved correct in numerous respects) concludes that the economic function and effect of social security is thoroughly ambiguous. To be sure, on the plus side of the account stands a guarantee of social peace. Yet at the beginning of the 1980s in the Federal Republic of Germany expectations of a different sort meant that the breaking of the barrier of 2 million registered unemployed (and the much more uncertain material circumstances associated with it) in no way led to a discernible *threat* to social peace, but rather to its opposite. Awareness of (and strategic interest in) a message of this type, which is ambiguous to say the least, was heightened not only by the continuing poor state of the labor market, but above all by the impending introduction of a single European market (the catchwords here were "social dumping" and "Germany as an industrial center."

It is symptomatic, therefore, that the best-known social democratic proposals for structural innovation in social policy are directed not toward a further *expansion* of the social security budget, but toward an internal *redistribution* on both the income and expenditure sides. The first is true of "the levy on added value," the second of a "minimum wage." Yet both of these proposals are relatively ambitious given that there has traditionally been a systematic "underdemand" in the German social security system for "solidary sacrifices" from those insured. For the rest, the traditional champions of social policy expansion restrict themselves to an opposition to benefit *reductions* – with remarkably little effect, as the case of health reform demonstrates.

These observations and features all serve to justify the assumption that, at least for the foreseeable future, the honorable tradition of inclusion based on the principle of insurance has been superseded.

Just as old as this tradition is an opposing *tendency toward* (re)*privatization* ((2) → (1)), represented primarily by employers and their interest in relief from growing wage bills. Despite the emergence of new types of need, the restriction of the types and size of social benefit, and of the circle of recipients, or at least, opposition to further expansion, has received additional encouragement. This has come from a social policy of "deregulation" and "flexibility" based on conservative-liberal premises. This promises an improvement in the employment situation and, beyond that, a requirement from employees of that virtue known as "the art of finding one's way" (L. Späth). The political interest in relating categories of need and levels of benefit licensed by a social state to the sphere of "self-responsibility" is grounded in current and, given demographic developments, foreseeable budget deficits in the spheres of health insurance and pensions. But that means that it is grounded in a political decision to deal with these deficits from within the insurance system and by achieving a balance between its individual branches, not by means of a "state subsidy" from the central budget.[5]

A rationally motivated and electorally safe measure of support for such measures of consolidation is likely both from those insured as a whole, and from those among them who are better placed in terms of income and property. With a claim to "transfer capital" which can be realized in the future, that is, to the current incomes of the next generation, and faced at the same time with a choice between a "secure" income and a "high" one, those with insurance will give precedence to the value of security, and will not oppose a policy of consolidation they acknowledge to be "necessary." *A fortiori*, support from the better placed among them can be relied on, since their obligatory social insurance contributions will either seem to them like risk premiums for eventualities with which, in all likelihood, *they themselves* will not be confronted (as in the case of unemployment insurance), or produce a yield which is insignificant compared with possibilities for private insurance on the capital market. Moreover, they are not reliably protected against the feared "redistributive-political misuse" of transfer capital.[6]

But mention should be made here of quite different motives for a political critique of (a further expansion of) social security, motives directed at an "overprovision" of entitlements – which in the case of certain types of employee and benefit is undeniable – and at the fact that certain welfare state programs lead to the indirect subsidy of certain providers of services (for instance, in the housing and health sectors).

Historically, the policy field of social security and of benefits in health, housing, and education has been the preserve of social democracy. However, since the mid-1970s the formation and development of social democratic programs has clearly come to a standstill. Leaving aside contingencies of political development, the conjuncture of ecological and disarmament issues overlying social policy, intraparty elite formation and electoral performance, the relative political fruitlessness of the expansionist paradigm can be explained by the following model. At a time when the development of social security has reached an advanced stage, and under conditions in which social insurance and federal budgets are financially squeezed, further improvements in benefits or increases in the range and number of recipients are possible only if the social security system admits relatively *narrowly defined categories of supplementary need*. Therefore, the circle of prospective beneficiaries, and thereby of those directly concerned, be they classified according to age, position in the labor market, gender, state of health, or region, is always a minority whose security must be financed by contributors or the (far greater) majority of taxpayers. In particular, when the members of this majority have no reason to fear that *they themselves* might be in need of security (for example, through being one of the long-term unemployed, the inhabitant of a structurally weak coastal region, or an "old person in need of care"), expansionist initiatives in social security suffer a considerable loss of plausibility and electoral attractiveness.

Obviously, we are dealing here with a political logic of self-limitation. The further the expansion of social security has already progressed, the more will the *further* progress which is still possible suggest a distributional pattern of highly selective entitlements and very diffuse cost burdens. Such an unfavorable constellation of interests will make further expansion politically unattractive. In contrast, it is not expansion, but budgetary consolidation which is able to command majority support.

Turning now to the other front, that is, to the demarcation line between regular, licensed entitlements to benefit and the "special life situations" and assistance requirements which deflect attention downward and which must be assessed individually (the traditional distinction between the "deserving poor" and "undeserving poor"), an important factor is what one could call "marginalization" according to the "principle of the depth of the fall," or the "principle of distance" $((2) \rightarrow (3))$. This refers to the paternalism, embodied in most social policy arrangements, according to which, rather than have a (privileged) guarantee of social security, recipients are expected to attend to the rules of a "normal," "orderly," and "worthwhile" lifestyle. In both public institutions and in enterprises, this "hidden agenda" of social policy is clearly easier to carry out successfully the greater the depth of the fall for those who drop out of the status of "owners of entitlements" through their own actions, or who fail to acquire it. The welfare state's latent socialization and normative function can only be fulfilled when inclusion does not go "too far" and when the "second best" solution (in concrete terms, the road to the dole office) is decidedly worse, and thus a deterrent. Far beyond the rights which officials or bureaucrats have to services and welfare provision, the right to social security in general is bound up with more or less implicit injunctions and typifying ideas concerning "normal" biographies and gender roles within a "work-centered society." The "reward effect" of social security becomes clear only when there is a sufficiently large number of sufficiently visible people who, on a sufficiently low level, remain excluded from the benefits concerned and serve as a negative example.

In addition, those clients of the welfare state who have reason to view themselves as belonging among the "good risks" will have an immediate material interest in forcing the remaining "bad risks" into the third category. For otherwise the latter would enjoy net payments from the better placed, who would have to subsidize their security through higher contributions and/or lower benefit claims of their own. In this sense, under conditions of growing unemployment and an increasing average length of unemployment, those of the insured who are in stable employment will have a plausible material motive to resist enhancing the living conditions of their unemployed colleagues through higher contributions, or supporting their reincorporation through "active" labor market programs. Rather, they will wish to shunt and direct them on to another level of provision, where responsibility for financing it will fall not to those with insurance, but to the central state or local authority taxpayers. The solidarity of the "ins" would ultimately suffer if no demarcation line of nonsolidarity with the "outs" were laid down.

There are also motives of an opposing type along this front between the second and third categories. One could describe the movement (3) → (2) as "*guaranteeism*," and with this term refer to an old trade union social policy motif. This is based on a simple strategic consideration: only if a *universalistic* system of rules ensures that the living standards of those in ill-health, women, young people, the long-term unemployed, and the unqualified do not fall markedly below that of "normal" employees can the latter feel protected against dubious forms of low-wage competition from these disadvantaged groups. State guarantees of a minimum wage, of the universally binding character of wage agreements, and of low access thresholds to the universal system of social security, together with the exclusion from work of children and pensioners, are the types of prescription which can partially blunt ruinous competition between labor market suppliers by making extreme "special offers" more difficult.

However, in the 1980s in the Federal Republic of Germany, there came to the fore completely different variants of the strategy of "drawing up" members of the third category and introducing a regime of legally secured entitlements in areas in which assessment-dependent and individual case assistance had predominated hitherto. To be sure, that is more the case for the level of social policy *demands* made by, than for the *success* of, that antipaternalistic, nondiscriminatory "social policy from below" which emerged from the context of new social movements.[7] An example is the demand from self-help groups for fields of activity which are legally and financially secured. Those parts of the women's movement, too, concerned with social policy establish institutional bridgeheads with women's centers, women's quotas, and the employment of people responsible for women's issues. Immigrant support groups strive for a sociolegal category of membership valid for all those residing in a country. Better positions[8] and guarantees for women with "incomplete" income-earning biographies, for mothers and widows, encouraged notably by conservative-liberal governments, are designed to withdraw their material situation from the grey area of family supplement and social assistance, at least in a sociolegal sense. And the principle of "guaranteeism" is obviously the core of the much-discussed proposals from social reformist outsiders that, through a guaranteed basic income for all citizens financed by taxes, the legal claim to limited but adequate monetary payments be decoupled from engagement in wage labor.

Up to this point we have sketched the directions of social policy change with which strategic actors – individuals, members of particular categories of need and income, trade unions, associations, professions, parties or governments – respond in a rational way, that is, according to their particular preferences and perceptions. A rough estimate of the strengths of the four strategic orientations I have described would probably lead to the conclusion that for the Federal Republic of Germany (and elsewhere) in the period after 1974, the strategies represented in a clockwise fashion in figure 9.1 can be given a rank order. If one considers not existing social policy institutions but the marginal changes in and *shifts between* them, then on the level of both actually implemented strategies and scientific and political proposals, "privatization" has grown stronger than "marginalization," "marginalization" is stronger than "guaranteeism," and this in turn is stronger than "inclusion."

III

If we turn now to the question of *legitimacy*, that is, of how social policy arrangements can be grounded from the point of view of justice, it is necessary to adopt a position defined by John Rawls through the well-known "veil of ignorance." Here one has to imagine the position of an observer who, faced with the task of finding a just rule of distribution, would in an ideal case have to know everything about his own society but nothing about his own position in it. I refer to the first of these (naturally contradictory) requirements because the norms of justice to be arrived at in this way are supposed to be valid not for an imaginary society, but for an existing one, and must therefore "fit" the facts of this society, facts which cannot be treated as alterable at will.

One of these is the fact that the principle of social insurance, the lowest common denominator of the ranking system, has exhausted its potential for expansion and therefore will play no further significant role as an organizational model for dealing collectively with emerging needs or satisfying in a better way those which are already acknowledged. The efficiency of this organizational model no longer consists in guaranteeing social security and participation in the social state for the whole population. Rather, it consists solely (and even to a decreasing extent) in bringing together the great majority of the working population, the foot soldiers of the "work-centered society," so to speak, in an interest bloc which is relatively well protected against migration tendencies and internal rivalries.[9]

Assuming that this conclusion is valid, the next question posed by our Rawlsian theorist of justice is: from what point of view might the penultimate position on our scale, "guaranteeism," be defended? According to this position no longer would a society's usual risks be dealt with in such a way that assistance lying clearly below the society's average level was guaranteed through subsidy, discretionary payment, or in a way which sacrificed essential features of citizens' rights to freedom and privacy. Rather, a simple legal entitlement to services, transfer payments, and materially guaranteed autonomy of action would be granted. This would be independent of individual lifestyle, income-earning or family histories, etc. To our imagined observer, perhaps one advantage of such an arrangement would be that he would be secured against the dangers and losses which liberals and conservatives would hold in store for him in the case of his being in the (unfamiliar) position of one of those affected by their strategies of privatization and marginalization. But he would certainly be struck by the disadvantage that with the institution of such a system of unconditionally guaranteed entitlements, he would not only have to provide a large amount of money, but also exhibit a large amount of tolerance toward those who prefer lifestyles very different from his own – always assuming that he would find himself in the position of a net contributor to this generous arrangement.

Since the question cannot be decided in the field of tension between such extreme advantages and disadvantages, the observer seeks help from a further consideration. Since it is clear to him that a decision one way or the other could be supported only by a solid consensus, or at least a large majority, he begins to imagine which points of view (for and against) would emerge from a representative selection of members of the society in question, *if* they had to confront this question as people who, while bound to empirical positions and tied up in strategic games, were also capable of a certain abstraction from these empirical premises, that is, were subjects capable of exercising moral judgment. This necessary supplementary operation forces the observer to conduct a thought experiment (or practical argument experiment) to assess the potential acceptability of a series of arguments in favor. Only after the demonstrable failure of these arguments would it appear to him necessary to proceed to the next highest stage on our scale.

What might these trial arguments for the "guaranteeist" solution look like? A decision has to be made for or against a structural innovation such as the guarantee of legal entitlements to materially secured freedom of action. These are to be unconditional and dependent only on one's status as a citizen. If such a proposal for an allocation *without preconditions* to all citizens of a legal entitlement to material security is thought through to its end, the second and third groups in our tripartite division would in practical terms merge.[10] The concept of a "special situation" (in contrast, presumably, to a "normal situation"), so central to the right to social benefit, would lose its meaning. The welfare state would extend to *all* citizens without distinction or condition the right to a material share, and thereby remove the means by which "deserving" and "normal" members of the community might be symbolically and materially distinguished from the less deserving and less normal.

In conclusion I would like to discuss five arguments (and partial counterarguments) for the "guaranteeist" social policy solution, which I would expect to be pertinent to a discourse on justice of the type referred to above.

1 The distinction between "special" and "normal" life situations and modes of conduct would be abolished. One could give positive grounds for this, seeking to justify it in the name of the overarching priority of the principle of equality between the citizens of a state. More hopeful seem to me to be negative grounds which at the same time shift the burden of proof. A negative grounding rests on the fact that nobody has at their disposal (or in a "modern" society *can* have at their disposal) the authority or the evidence with which to privilege certain lifestyles as "normal" and discriminate against others. Out of this difficulty, and according to the measure in which the bindingness of a certain lifestyle has become questionable, there arises the opposite conclusion, namely that under these conditions *all* lifestyles must be treated equally. The problem also has a noteworthy empirical side: should one wish to demand that the "normal" mode of life of an adult male be one of full-time, lifelong, professional employment, then this demand is only plausible if it is simultaneously made clear that everyone *can* conform to this model if only that person makes the requisite effort, or exhibits the requisite discipline or self-limitation. But the degree of "requisite effort" obviously varies considerably according to the economic cycle, and is dependent on numerous features of social structure and personality. So paradoxically, if, as would be fairer, one wanted to hold the pressure to conform corresponding to the norm of "requisite effort" *constant over time* and *for all*, it would be necessary to *vary constantly* the material criteria according to which this effort was measured. But this would bring with it such a degree of "measurement error," observational contingencies, stigmatization, arbitrariness, and legal uncertainty that it would more likely be the *renunciation* of the use of such criteria – even were there thought to be sound objective reasons for them – which would reduce the probability of error.[11]

2 The negative motivational effect of a guarantee of material entitlements to all citizens, as in proposals for a basic income, is often overexaggerated. According to the counterargument, many people would simply not work if they were entitled to a limited but adequate transfer payment. The fear that a further fall in the birth rate is likely unless families are placed in a significantly better position than childless marriages, or that a more generous provision of medical services by health insurance companies would lead to an immeasurable increase in the use made of them, appeals to analogous motivational effects. As a result, all these cases indicate a more or less soft regime of material stimuli and penalties. While these stimuli clearly prove able

to steer conduct in individual areas, this "economistic" calculation ignores the role of what sociologists call "intrinsic" motives, which are nourished and reproduced by the enactment of particular forms of life themselves, and not by the allocation or withholding of external rewards. The hypothesis that persons able to achieve an adequate income without working would therefore stop work in dramatic numbers is just as foolish as the fear that entitlement to free health treatment would result in people constantly visiting their doctors. In these cases there is a failure to take into account the intrinsic value of income-earning activity and its social environment, or the intrinsic indignity of being a patient.

3 If particular modes of life, biographical patterns, sexual divisions of labor, etc., can no longer be privileged or discriminated against, social policy loses its traditional mandate, via rewards and punishments, to contribute to the cultural anchoring of a hegemonic mode of life. This means that it maximizes only the value of "optimality," not that of "conformity." In the course of such a paradigm shift the positive goal of adaptation to certain images and normal biographical patterns would be subordinated to the negative goal of avoiding dead-ends or the marginalization of people and their irreversible attachment to particular types and spheres of activity. Relevant proposals have been developed in such varied policy spheres as working hours, health and rehabilitation, professional and further education, and feminism. Their net result is the maintenance and extension of the horizon of available options and the relaxation of typifying restrictions and categorizations through the guarantee without preconditions of physical, material, and legal conditions.

4 It could be argued, in favor of a "guaranteeist" social policy, that in a "rich" society such structural innovations are a "requisite" and therefore much-needed social sacrifice. To be sure, in the context of (almost) universal prosperity, such an argument is ambiguous. It makes the innovation dependent on economic as well as political circumstance. So that if it turned out that, as a consequence of the innovation, or as a result of negative stimuli brought about by the innovation, a society did not *remain* as rich as it had been, or was prevented from increasing its wealth further, then according to the same logic a withdrawal of the innovation would be justified. Politically, too, a majority could easily be found which believed that in such cases other people ought to tighten their belts, and that social policy "luxuries" should be adjusted downwards. Therefore, the presuppositionless legal entitlement to income and benefit cannot be solidly grounded with an argument about wealth. There is a possible further argument which would base such entitlements not on material sur-

plus but, on the contrary, on a society's institutional deficits. It would state that guarantees of a certain material status even to such citizens as have not (according to the insurance principle) earned this through their own efforts is justified on the grounds that society clearly does not contain the institutions and mechanisms required to develop and employ the talents of these people, or to acknowledge them. In this sense, guaranteed material benefits would be the punishment society imposes on itself for manifest failures. It would thereby act as a self-created stimulus to lighten the burden of this punishment through appropriate institutional innovations.[12]

5 A further potentially fruitful argument for "guaranteeist" social policy innovations could be derived from a negative consideration presented as an answer to the question: "What happens if nothing happens?" The strategy would then be justified by the foreseeable costs of its neglect. The extent of these costs would become clear and convincing should a careful assessment of foreseeable social and political developments lead to the conclusion (as worked out in more detail above) that the effectiveness of inclusion strategies is exhausted, and that at the same time the scene is dominated by tendencies toward reprivatization and strategies of marginalization. In the face of such a scenario, which can be deduced not only through calculation from models but partly from the reality of political developments and social conditions in Britain and the USA in the 1980s, a consensus would then be possible for a social policy without conditions, which as an emergency brake, and despite the unacknowledged normative problems it might contain, could at least avoid a possibly greater evil.

Notes

1 A. de Swaan, *In Care of the State* (Cambridge, 1988).
2 On the distinction between the second and third groups and their institutional and material delimitation, see the contributions in S. Leibfried and F. Tennstedt, *Politik der Armut und die Spaltung des Sozialstaates* (Frankfurt, 1985).
3 The schema is based on the following assumptions and principles of construction. In one direction there is a political "right–left" dividing line, and the other is related to the question of whether it is the status of the *employee* (as in inclusion or reprivatization) or the *citizen* (employed or otherwise) which is at stake. Clockwise, beginning with "privatization," the four cells can be labeled approximately according to the political positions of liberals, rightwing conservatives, greens, and traditional socialists. In accordance with this, alliances and strategic combinations in a vertical direction are logically excluded, but in the horizontal direction are normal and diagonally are easily imaginable and partly familiar with actual practice.

4 See the rich collection of comparative data on these three expansionist tendencies in J. Astner, *Vom Armenhaus zum Wohlfahrtstaat* (Frankfurt, 1982).

5 W. Heine, "Wie sicher ist die gesetzliche Alterssicherung?" in B. Riedmüller and M. Rodenstein (eds), *Wie sicher ist die soziale Sicherung?* (Frankfurt, 1989).

6 See C. Offe, "Smooth Consolidation in the West German Welfare State: Structural Change, Fiscal Policies, and Populist Politics," Zentrum für Sozialpolitik, Bremen, 1990.

7 B. Roth, "Soziale Arbeit und gesellschaftliche Entwicklung. Soziale Probleme, soziale Bewegungen, und die Veränderungen institutioneller Praxis in der Bundesrepublik Deutschland," unpublished MS, Free University of Berlin, 1989.

8 See G. Schmidt, *Sozialpolitik. Historische Entwicklung und internationaler Vergleich* (Opladen, 1988), p. 89.

9 This case would be another application of the story of the drunken sailor who searches for his lost key in the light of a street lamp, but at the same time knows for sure that he did not lose it *here*. On being made aware of the contradictory nature of his action, he justifies himself by saying that of course he won't find the key here, but he does at least have the light in which to look.

10 See M. Opielka, "Das garantierte Mindesteinkommen – ein sozialpolitisches Paradox?" in T. Schmid, *Befreiung von falscher Arbeit* (Berlin, 1984).

11 R. E. Goodin, "Toward a Minimally Presumptuous Social Welfare Policy," unpublished MS, Canberra, 1989.

12 On the question of appropriate complementary institutions for a guaranteed basic income, see chapter 10 below.

10

A Basic Income Guaranteed by the State: A Need of the Moment in Social Policy

WITH

ULRICH MÜCKENBERGER AND

ILONA OSTNER

In this chapter we wish to defend the thesis that a basic income guaranteed by the state is a social policy necessity; that, given the present and foreseeable employment crisis, its introduction fulfills the obligations of a social state; and that, even under these circumstances, such a basic guarantee for all citizens can be realized and also financed.

The plea for a universal basic guarantee entails a fundamental change of perspective. It should be possible to make the right to an income independent of the fact and extent of an individual's income-earning activity. As a first step toward a universal basic guarantee we recommend that a guaranteed minimum, which already exists in security and transfer systems,[1] be systematized, and then gradually transferred to those security systems which do not yet include one. In the course of this harmonization a sociocultural standard of need can be defined which can serve as the basic form of a guaranteed income for all.

Below we show, first, why a basic income guaranteed by the state seems to us a social policy necessity. The aim of these observations is *not* to work out or give a foundation for particular concrete arrangements for a basic income (BI), nor to analyze how they might be financed. But we do sketch here the general type of BI we favor. It is regrettable yet unavoidable that important parameters – above all, the exact size of the BI – remain undefined: without integration into a thoroughly worked out and realizable conception of BI, they will remain arbitrary.

Our basic points of orientation are these:

1 A sum total will be arrived at as a BI related to a material and cultural standard of need and distribution. The actual size of this sum total must on the one hand maintain a financial incentive to paid work, and on the other avoid tendencies toward poverty and division which characterize existing benefit arrangements.

2 Priority will be given to a version of "negative income tax,"[2] that is, BI will not be paid out in advance as a subsidy, but, within the framework of taxation procedure, income will be increased by the amount by which it falls short of the level referred to in (1) (for calculations see below). The expected total cost of financing this mode will be considerably less than that of subsidy in advance, since in cases of expected income-earning activity the repayment of negative income tax becomes wholly or partly irrelevant.

3 Incomes below the level of BI will be only partially credited (for example, up to 50 percent). In this way, a financial incentive to work for an income will be maintained even below the BI threshold.

4 BI will be financed essentially through a social redistribution of tax burdens. Therefore, the determination of tax rates for income above BI has enormous significance. It should (a) generate the volume of finances required by BI, and (b) burden first the highest, and then the upper-middle income groups. The rate which would best achieve this would have to be worked out on the basis of calculations which we can neither present nor summarize here.

5 A BI financed through taxes will have no direct impact on the existing system of social insurance, but it will have an indirect one. In contrast to conservative-liberal proposals, it will not lead to a "privatization" of social security beyond BI, but it does emphasize functional flaws in the system of social insurance. On the one hand, in the sphere of lower incomes it leads to greater equality and less social division than that associated with the principle of insurance. On the other, the system whereby the legal burdens of insurance are transferred to the social benefit budgets of local authorities will be dismantled.

6 Transfer incomes from social insurance will be fully accounted to BI. Accordingly, BI will be maintained by welfare payments.

7 There is no agreement about whether the BI model should be based

on the household or the individual principle. In both a horizontal (partners) and a vertical (parents–children) direction, the individual principle favors tendencies toward dissolution within the (family) household, and households with high incomes. On the other hand, it encourages independence from the constraints of traditional gender roles and family authority, and in no way excludes the free development of familial relationships (that is, relationships free of financial constraints). Therefore, our preference is for the individual principle, though we are unable to make a definitive statement about possible restrictions which might be placed on it in future.

A Challenge and Call for Action

The need for a reorientation of social policy arises because, for more and more members of society, paid work is decreasing in significance as a mode of securing a livelihood.[3] In the Federal Republic of Germany after the beginning of the 1980s, more people were out of work than ever before. The unemployment rate hovered at around 9 percent. In addition to more than 2 million registered unemployed in May 1986, there were at least a million who were not registered. The outlook is bleak: in the 1990s there will conceivably be a shortage of at least 3 million workplaces. The capacity of the labor market to absorb wage labor under "normal working conditions,"[4] that is, professional, continuous, full-time productive activity within enterprises, *is falling*. The areas at the margins of the employment system, where the connection between wage labor and subsistence is uncertain, is beginning to grow. The saving on labor power through technical innovation is proceeding at a faster pace than the satisfaction of a need for employment and income-earning opportunities among the growing number of people who seek them. An increasing proportion of the population has an ever-decreasing expectation of the possibility of securing a livelihood through permanent employment and is being forced into part-time and/or discontinuous and/or undervalued and/or unprotected employment. The division of the workforce into full-time or "normal" workers, on the one hand, and those in multiple forms of marginal employment, on the other, a process developing during the phase of full employment, is now more clearly established. There is much to suggest that the social division between the shrinking group of those in permanent well-qualified, professional work, and that of those pursuing all manner of strategies for earning an income, or "escaping with an income," will sharpen in future.

The growth of unstable employment conditions is codetermined by the strategies of economy and flexibility adopted by firms, and is paralleled by a neoconservative policy of a *"deregulation of labor relations."* This has a direct effect on the household. The crisis of the labor market, that is, of the predominant form of labor and income distribution, cuts many households off from the natural and "normal" source of their provision. For in a capitalist "work-centered society," the system whereby existence is secured, and the system of primary income distribution and social security, is *centered on dependent wage labor.*[5]

This social organization of labor and income proceeds from the assumption that, in principle, income from waged work suffices for individual and collective self-provision (of the employee and the members of the household dependent on the employee), and that forms of security provided by the state are required only for narrowly defined categories of person or types of need, and only for a limited period. The substitutive mechanisms for the securing of existence are also coupled to income from work: this is true for social security, where there is a link between contribution and benefit, and for the security of the family by means of its maintenance entitlements. A lasting imbalance in the labor market thereby affects the entire system through which a livelihood can be secured, in particular the system through which social security is financed. With an expansion of what was hitherto the periphery of the employment system, with the growth of short-time and short-term employment, with "old" (over 45) employees being forced out of the labor market, the confrontation of risk by means of insurance tied to employment – and ultimately, the maintenance of the family – are a precarious business for a growing proportion of the population.

Already in 1985, 60%, or DM 23.2 billion, of the federal employment office budget had to be paid out in unemployment benefit (in 1970, it was DM 0.7 billion).[6] Increasing expenses (unemployment benefit or assistance; health and pensions insurance contributions for the unemployed; social assistance and housing benefit) are accompanied by decreasing incomes in the spheres noted, as well as by losses in income tax and indirect tax. In the year 1984–5, the average cost of an unemployed person rose from DM 24,000 to DM 24,700. With an annual unemployment figure of around 2 million, the total cost was around DM 57 billion. This amounted to fully 3% of the gross domestic product and one-tenth of total public expenditure. By no means all of those unemployed were entitled to unemployment benefit or social assistance. By the end of 1985 approximately 32% of the unemployed received no support from the employment office, compared with 24% in 1980 and 14% in 1975. This means that an increasing number of unemployed people had been out of work for so long that their entitlement to benefit lapsed. And an increasing number of those in first jobs did not even meet the criteria of entitlement. At the same time, after 1975, the range of those entitled to benefit, and the length of benefits, were limited through a series of changes in the law. The unemployment benefit (*Arbeitslosengeld*) paid out by the employment office in 1987 was 68% (for someone with children) or 63% of the last net income, the unemployment assistance (*Arbeitslosenhilfe*) only 58%. As a result of unemployment, the number of those receiving social assistance continuously increased. In 1986 almost one-third of recipients said that the reason was that one or more members of the family had lost their jobs (in 1980 it was 10%).

Today, this development is discussed under the heading of "*new poverty*," which overlays contemporary changes in the sphere of the old poverty. One aspect is the large proportion of widowed women who, for lack of previous employment, have either no entitlement to a pension or one which is too small – a situation which will grow more acute with the crisis surrounding the achieving of security through employment, and with demographic changes. In 1986 the number of those receiving social assistance broke through the 3 million barrier for the first time (an increase of 7.35% on the previous year).[7] It thus doubled in only 15 years (1970–85). Payments increased from DM 3.3 billion to DM 20.8 billion, or sixfold. Approximately 5.5% of the population, or 1.7 million women and 1.3 million men, were drawing social assistance. A distinction is made between assistance for maintenance (income supplement) and for particular circumstances. In March 1984, according to the Federal Statistical Bureau, 2.2 million people were receiving ongoing support for the meeting of such basic everyday needs as accommodation, food, and clothing. The increases in payments of this sort represent a great burden for local authorities, on whom the prime responsibility for financing social benefit falls.

However, for *women*, wage labor has never been the "normal case" in the sense of an independent means of existence.[8] When the labor market's capacity to absorb full-time workers declines, it is still more difficult for women to gain access to it through anything other than work which is discontinuous, undervalued, and without employment protection. It even appears that, despite the labor market crisis, women have additional employment opportunities. For years the participation in work of married women and especially mothers has been increasing (25% in 1950; 42.5% in 1985), an increase traceable to an expansion in part-time work. Even if there has been an increase in the types of work with no social insurance obligation attached (14 hours per week or less), there has clearly been a growth in part-time work for women in the protected sphere. This has proved to be not very vulnerable to economic circumstances, which explains why in the recession of 1981–3 the number of men and women in *full*-time work fell sharply, while that of women in part-time work increased. The proportion of women among those in employment as a whole has increased continuously since 1980, in terms both of the number employed and, in almost the same measure, the volume of work done.[9] This means that in the Federal Republic of Germany more and more women followed a pattern typical for the Western industrialized countries, remaining in part-time work, at least, even during the so-called "family phase," when one or more small children have to be cared for. The fact that the Federal Republic of Germany (and the Benelux countries) lagged behind the Western rate of part-time female labor can be traced to regulations making it difficult to combine child(ren) and work. The dismantling of barriers of this sort and the increased availability of part-time work would lead to a further increase in such figures.[10]

All this justifies the conclusion that wage labor on a part-time basis is beginning to be a universal phenomenon among women.[11] Yet for the majority of women who seek it, there is no prospect that it will provide an independent means of support on a level which compares with that of men. At the same time, many women are not so able to secure their existence on a continuous basis within marriage. This is because, on the one hand, the labor market crisis makes maintenance through wage labor precarious and discontinuous; and, on the other hand, it coincides with already existing societal trends toward individualization and the individual grounding of choices. This provides the background not only for the growing involvement of women in waged work, but also the growing number of marriages ending in divorce: the ties of maintenance or provision are loosened. This may mean that *neither* on the *labor market* – with its falling capacity to absorb continuous wage labor and the claim to a living wage – *nor* through *marriage* are women able to earn enough to secure a livelihood. The other side of this "abnormality" of female wage labor and of the uncertainty of provision through marriage is the poverty of older women, and the paucity of their labor market participation. In 1982, of 25 million women (the female population over 25), 74.5% had no independent income, or had one below DM 1,200 (the figure for men was 25.5%).

The principle of derived material security continues to operate in the sphere of *job creation*. In 1984 38.4% of unemployed women received no benefit. The example of women's life circumstances demonstrates that a policy which continues to be centered on wage labor will in future run up sharply against principles of equality and equal participation. Without decisive changes in the mode of distribution of labor and income, there is no realistic prospect that sexual inequality and the conflict which revolves around it might be overcome by a policy of growth, employment, and professional training.

The *development of the social state* has also been largely dependent on wage labor, growth, and full employment, and has presupposed the "normalization" of ever more people as "working citizens," that is, the *universalization of normal working conditions.* Today, this universalization runs up against barriers which call into question the inherited model of the social state, a model which ties the participation of citizens in state and society essentially to their status as employees. Only through this relationship is (the chance of) freedom, social justice, and welfare for individuals thought possible.

By contrast, the *crisis of the labor market*, that is, of the predominant principle according to which work and incomes are distributed, creates a situation in which unemployment and bottlenecks in the social budget can no longer be regulated simply by balancing different elements (contribution rates, conditions and size of entitlement, range of those with insurance obligations, etc.) *within the framework* of existing institutional structures and premises of economic growth. The Keynesian model has long since been called into question: it is hardly plausible to trace the current labor market crisis to the simple connection between consumer and labor demand, or to regulate it through an expansive economic and fiscal policy. Since the mid-1970s none of the political parties has been prepared to commit the sums required to stimulate demand. The reduction of the working week to 38.5 hours had no significant effect on employment. Nor did trade union policies on working hours halt trends toward a deregulation of working conditions. Full employment and growth in the traditional sense can be created neither by means of state intervention nor through a system of wage agreements.

As long as the project of the social state flourished against a background of full employment, the fact could remain hidden that in neither the intentions of its advocates nor the results of its functioning was it capable of overcoming social inequality. While the development of the social state and its institutions has failed to fundamentally reduce social inequality,[12] at the same time, new forms of inequality and dependence have been added to the old divisions. It is often the case that social inequality is merely legitimated in a different way. Thus one can speak not only of the social state's economic failure, but of its *moral failure* as well. The social state has remained divided. The old separation between policies on work, social insurance, and poverty remain. Redistributive processes, social service and social insurance benefits, fiscal measures, and workplace regulations have developed unevenly and in no way benefited those most in need. It is primarily the better informed and educated who profit most from the development of social services. In many cases, a claim to assistance means direct dependence on experts and a devaluation of the context-bound knowledge of the client. It is questionable, therefore, whether the development of the social state as a whole has improved the conditions for citizens' participation and equality. Its development encouraged not a generalized *culture of giving*[13] (to those who are unknown or unfamiliar), but, in view of persisting inequality, utilitarian conduct on the part of status groups with different amounts of power, and the competition between them for *particular benefit gains.*[14] The encouragement of a potential for traditional self-help and of attention to the ecological consequences of social and political development were neglected.

Contemporary *demographic developments* make it clear that wage labor, which is still the most important basis for the social opportunities of the citizen, embraces an ever shorter time-span, and makes a claim on an ever smaller proportion of our lives. The average proportion of total working time to total lifetime has fallen to 8–14 percent, due to longer periods of training, earlier retirement, etc. Taking both factors together – reduced opportunities for wages work and current demographic trends – it is already clear that in the near future a smaller number of those engaged in (predominantly discontinuous) wage labor will have to raise the transfer incomes for a growing number of older people. At the same time, traditional forms of familial and communal care are already stretched to their limits, so that a further substitution of money or rights by "solidary" forms of need satisfaction organized beyond the state cannot automatically be assumed.[15]

These trends can be summed up as follows.

1 There is overwhelming evidence of a crisis of the labor market and of the social state, a crisis which cannot be resolved with the means available hitherto.
2 The failure of a model of sociopolitical progress resting on full employment, economic growth, and social state security reveals its negative side all the more clearly: namely, wage labor as the focal means of leading a "normal" life within industrial society; a gender-specific inequality of access to the labor market; the destruction of those traditional forms of life not regulated through the labor market or state administration; and the overburdening of infrastructure and environment.
3 A traditional strategy for full employment, be it through "more

growth through more market" or "growth through state intervention," appears illusory. A return to the apparently "normal" model of a society of work and wage labor insulated by a welfare state is (a) economically undesirable, (b) ecologically indefensible, and (c) socially unacceptable.[16]

It may be useful to expand briefly on (a), (b) and (c), and the way they block our return to the old model.

(a) If the growth rates which can be secured by the continuous, expansive reproduction of capital are uncertain, then those which would produce full employment are wholly unthinkable. The decoupling of employment from growth and investment, conditioned by both technology and the organization of labor, makes a successful renewal of the developmental model of "full employment through growth and modernization of capital stock" extremely doubtful, even with "favorable" demographic developments.

(b) However, even if the strategy of employment through growth were realistic, it would quickly run up against ecological barriers, due to an increase in the consumption of raw material, land, and energy which would inevitably accompany it. In addition, the idea that a consistently carried through environmental protection would draw us nearer to full employment rests on mistaken assumptions. Environmental protection involves the restriction or halting of certain forms of production and types of product, not an allegedly labor-intensive "cleaning-up operation." Moreover, the advocates of this idea often make the casual, optimistic, and mistaken assumption that the distributional battle which would break out between the "winners" in an industrial system which destroys the environment and the potential beneficiaries of a "reconciliation of economy and ecology" has already been won.

(c) Finally, a resurrection of the traditional goal of full employment is socially unacceptable. Even if empirical research shows that in many cases assumptions about "postmaterialistic" values are unconvincing, and even if a traditional understanding of work should remain a standard for the life-plans of most people, this idea still implies a discrimination against nonmarket activities, forms of work, and individual orientations, and consequently discrimination against all those who (wish to or must) live "differently," that is, outside the labor market. Moreover, the priority given to full employment has until now strengthened rather than destroyed hierarchical divisions, such as those between policy on social insurance and policy on poverty, between masculine and feminine spheres of work, and between living standards and quality of life.

The call for full employment is not an appropriate response to the current problems of unemployment, mass poverty, social underprovision, and the exhaustion of individual and collective resources. Even assuming the need for a state-run employment program, this would have to fit a framework which is not identical with the image of full employment. In a basic income guaranteed by the state we see a necessary element of a social policy perspective for the phase of modern society which now lies before us, one in which full employment through continuing industrial growth has lost its plausibility and attraction. A basic income is one component of a bundle of ideas and measures in which there is a place for income *through* employment and also a secure income *without* employment. This bundle is not a package of emergency social policy measures, but is conceived with a view to and as an anticipation of a still-to-be-created organization of work and life, individual and society, and individual and collective integrity.

Normative Foundations for a Strategy of Social Policy Reform

The reform strategy of which a basic income[17] is part assumes that a return to traditional "full employment" is unrealistic. It also assumes that its reestablishment would be accompanied by circumstances and developments which would be undesirable in themselves. *Within* the framework of existing labor market and social security institutions, "full employment" would be conceivable only under circumstances in which the wage levels, social security, and working conditions of those in employment markedly deteriorated. Furthermore, there would exist the danger that "full employment" would be reestablished not so much through an increase in the demand for labor as through restrictions of access to the labor market, the consequences of which would be borne by female employees in particular. For all these reasons, and in a situation of structural unemployment which is now setting in and will continue for the foreseeable future, there is a need to develop and put into practice ideas about political order and social security which at least make it possible to preserve the levels of social security and distributive justice attained during the phase of full employment.

A central building block of a social policy which might do justice to these realities and political-moral demands is the idea that *individual income entitlement* can be *decoupled from actual income-earning activity,* and that it can become an acknowledged right of citizens as members of a society, even when they do *not* "make themselves available for work." This change of perspective, from one centered on wage labor to one which decouples wage labor and the securing of an individual income, leads to the idea of a *basic guarantee*. In Western Europe in recent years much interest has been shown in, and much attention given to, ideas about *social justice and security outside growth and full employment*, ideas which go hand in hand with the demand for a basic income. In several countries they have become an established compo-nent of social policy debate and actual social policy development, primarily in those (such as Great Britain, Belgium, The Netherlands and Denmark) suffering from particularly high and persistent unemployment.

The core idea of a decoupling of income entitlement from wage labor embraces several features of social-economic distribution.

- The funds for financing social security should no longer be drawn solely from the income-proportionate *contributions* of those in work or from the contributions of employers. Instead, a growing propor-tion of social security is likely to be *financed by taxes*. This method of financing will result in *a clear redistribution* of capital and peak incomes toward those on low incomes or without means, and relieve supplementary wage costs.
- Claims to transfer benefits which guarantee adequate social security will no longer be dependent on the *wage-earning biography* of the claimants (which usually means on the length of employment in work to which a social insurance obligation is attached) and no longer either on their *family circumstances* or on their *means*, or, finally, on their *willingness* to "make themselves available" on the labor market.
- The size of the income entitlement will be measured according to the *principle of need*, not according to individual or professional criteria of entitlement or living standards. The decoupling of a mini-mum guarantee from the system of wage labor thus has the egali-tarian consequence that it loosens and ultimately dissolves the connection between size of income and size of transfer benefit.
- Finally, on the basis of the *principle of the individual* (which would be restricted in some cases) social security can be decoupled not only from wage labor but also partially from legal relationships between (marriage) partners and members of different generations. In this way, materially based relationships of control and dependence among family members and relatives, which are codetermined and reinforced by the crisis of the labor market, can be gradually neutralized.

The social policy response to the crisis of the labor market consists, thus, in a new form of social security (*basic income*), through which incomes are detached from wage-earning situation and wage-earning biography. This decoupling is given concrete form by the principle of financing social security through taxation, through doing away with means testing and assessment of willingness to work, by the gradual replacement of the principle of equivalence by that of need, and finally through the principle of the individual as the basis for entitlement. By transforming the social security system according to these principles, it is possible to carry over welfare state values of freedom, equality, and social justice into the phase of development which capitalist welfare states have now entered, a phase in which the goal of full employment has receded beyond the horizon of what is realistic and desirable.

However, the fact cannot be ignored that in scientific and political debate the demand for a guaranteed basic income and the detachment of social security from the system of wage labor according to the principles outlined above meets with serious as well as trivial objections and fears. We can dismiss as trivial the claim that the champions of this fundamental innovation merely wish to promote a "right to laziness," or have succumbed to the insane idea that industrial society has reached a stage of abundance which might (according to taste) be confused with paradise, the land of milk and honey, or with the communist end state described by Marx, which would recognize the basic distributional principle of "to each according to his needs." Those who advocate a guaranteed basic income are concerned precisely to *prevent* the labor market crisis and the disappearance of the goal of full employment from undermining those bases and levels of social security and social justice which have already been achieved. Turning to the principle of the individual and its effect on the relationship between marriage partners, it might be objected that a basic income "liberates the husband first,"[18] that is, liberates him from his traditional maintenance responsibility, before the wife's earnings have reached a comparable level.

Three further objections deserve evaluation and analysis. (1) The objection raised by social democrats, traditional socialists, and partly also feminists, that the decoupling of social security entitlement from wage labor, and the introduction of a basic income, would lead to a deeper and more firmly *cemented division of society* into the camp of those to whom wage labor is "permitted" and that of those who are excluded, and "maintained" by a basic income. Traditional social policy makers object (2) that a basic income would ultimately give succour to new market-liberal ideas. The aim of these would be to "insure" the unemployed at the *lowest level*, which would *therefore act as a deterrent*.

In this way, mediated by a deregulated labor market, the compulsion to earn a wage and subordinate oneself to labor market relations would grow. Finally (3) the libertarian and antiauthoritarian critique of the welfare state argues that a basic income would lead to the *"state's increasing responsibility for reproduction,"* and ultimately exchange individuals' dependence on the labor market for their dependence on state decision-making processes, which would be even harder to regulate.

With respect to (1): We grant that the social policy intentions bound up with a basic income would be seriously mistaken were they to result in a division of society into the privileged with work and the underprivileged unemployed. But according to our conception such a division can safely be avoided by means of *allied strategies*, whose goal would be to open up real possibilities of choice between income earning and other forms of activity, and which would be bound up with a basic income as part of a package of measures (see the next section below). Conversely, one can ask whether the representatives of this view are not caught up in nostalgic, nebulous, or utopian ideas about the possibility of full employment, and because of this make light of the real divisions between those in work and a growing "marginal population" of the unemployed, unqualified, and irregularly employed.

With respect to (2): This fear is directed not at the principle of a basic income, but at its level. Here, a suspicion may lurk in the background that the *trade unions*, as bargaining organizations on whom the level of wages (and indirectly of social incomes) depends, would be partly *driven out* of their role as control center by the introduction of a basic income. Against this it can be argued that, under the assumed conditions of structural and long-term unemployment, trade unions will lose this function in any case, and thereby their function of guaranteeing both wage levels and the numbers to benefit from them. Under these premises trade unions will come to adopt a long-term rational strategy of seeking alternatives and supplementary forms of *politically* mediated income security. This would have the desirable additional effect of reducing at least part of the "supply-side surplus" in the labor market. It could be brought about especially by the decisive adoption of a policy to *reduce working hours* (see the next section below).

With respect to (3): The fear that a transferral to the state of responsibilities for distribution and reproduction could lead to an institutionalization of poverty also appears to be a serious objection. But on closer inspection it turns out to be based on an unjustified and pessimistic judgment of the executive, which is always bound to processes of democratic will formation. Only if a basic income were to remain restricted to a *minority* of legitimate claimants would a majority of "net payers" and a minority of "net beneficiaries"[19] stand opposed to one another in these processes. But as soon as we adopt a model which assumes that a majority or even the whole population actually or potentially benefits from a basic income, then it will no longer be in the rational self-interest of voters and parties to object either to the release of social security from its ties to the labor market, or to an increased significance for state organs and processes of will formation. For the rest, any solution to this problem would require a legislative-technical prescription, and thereby make a "downward modification" of basic income entitlements already in existence dependent on a two-thirds majority, or even stricter provisos.

A "Package Solution" Avoids the Undesirable Consequences of a Basic Income

These objections to a decoupling of income from income-earning activity and to the resulting demand for a basic income are justified up to a point. But they do not compel us to drop this demand and to acquiesce in the foreseeable financial crises of the social insurance system or in the "new poverty" which is institutionalized through social assistance. Behind the facade of everyday political rhetoric there is widespread agreement that the crisis of the welfare state and of traditional institutions of social policy cannot be resolved along conservative lines. A basic guarantee is a building block of a progressive and socially just solution – but only if it is *one* building block placed together with two others. Only such a "package solution" can counter objections raised against the allegedly "universal solution" of a basic income.

The two supplementary elements of a comprehensive solution are, first, a comprehensive *reduction in working hours*, promoted in all its variants; and, second, the *political stimulation* and development of the "informal sector," of organized independent labor, *and all other forms of socially useful work which are not mediated by the labor market*.

With respect to the first, further drastic reductions in daily, weekly, annual, and lifetime[20] working hours would mean that shrinking opportunities for wage labor and therewith for earned income could be distributed equally among all those seeking work. This solution is based on the principle of equality and avoids current trends toward a social division between those in work and a marginal labor force. But it cannot be put into practice by means of quotas alone. This is because individual employees and trade unions have long been caught in an unresolvable dilemma between individual and collective interests. This is exemplified by reductions in working hours, whose intention is primarily to improve the income-earning opportunities of the *un-employed*, but which must be paid for by *those in employment* with considerable losses of real earnings (or of the increases in income which would otherwise be possible). As a result, an acceptable framework for these sacrifices of income has to be maintained through partial compensation in the form of subsidiary state benefits. These could be organized in such a way that the total income of those in work is no longer paid as wages. Rather, the income entitlement resulting from the labor contract increasingly takes on the character of income which is "additional" to basic income. For example, were employees to draw only a third of their income as net income based on a contract, but the other two-thirds as guaranteed basic income, it is likely that even with a linear reduction in earned income proportional to a reduction in working hours, this "sacrifice" would be more acceptable, and the reduction in working hours easier to carry through, than under present circumstances. In this sense a basic income (or a partial, preliminary version of it) is a necessary condition for the realization of interventionary reductions in working hours.

But, conversely, an interventionary reduction in working hours is a necessary condition for a basic income's proving to be a solution which does not bring with it unintended and undesirable side-effects. As has been said, social democratic critics fear that with basic income the mere appearance of a solution is being promoted, and that in practice it will only produce a division of society into relatively well-placed full-time employees and necessarily marginalized unemployed or part-time workers. But this fear is ungrounded if access to paid work is more evenly distributed as a result of reductions in working hours, if the difference between full and part-time work is leveled off, and if a new type of "full employment" is created for all those who seek paid employment – even if this means that – as Gorz first proposed[21] – the proportion of a lifetime spent by each individual in formal wage labor is decisively reduced. In this way, not only would social division be prevented, but partial account would be taken of the feminist critique of the gender codification of the labor market. In addition to reductions in working hours, a particularly effective way of avoiding social division and disintegration would be to encourage processes of socialization, qualification,[22] and in some cases rights of access to waged work (quotas, entitlement to be taken on or to be reemployed after a break, etc.), which would make *all* workers aware of the labor market and of the income-earning opportunities open to them. Just as reductions in working hours would create a universal *demand* for labor power, so the educational measures developed alongside them would ensure that the *suppliers* of labor power were actually able to fill the places offered. As long as we recall this functional connection between basic income, a reduction in working hours, and education policy, there can be no talk of "opting out" from work or of the marginalization of certain categories of worker.

As well as the compensations for loss of income which a basic income provides, a further stimulus to reductions in working hours would be the possibility that individual employees, in accordance with their own needs and obligations outside work, could themselves choose the *particular* hours, days, weeks, or years in which their working hours would be reduced. This right to choose to do "less work," and to determine how this would be organized, could be legislated for, and would markedly increase the attraction of reduced working hours for individual employees. For in this way entire blocks of time would be at their disposal, blocks whose individual utility would be much greater than a uniform reduction in working hours of, say, 30 minutes per day. Such "labor time flexibility" *on the part of the employee* would merely be a justified and easily legitimated counterweight to those forms of labor time reduction already in existence which are aimed solely at the needs of the *enterprise* (for productivity, orders, etc.).

The second key component of the "package" proposed here is the encouragement, development, and formal recognition of "informal" independent labor and activity in associations, cooperatives, neighborhoods, and self-help organizations, and under voluntary arrangements. Given falling labor market demand, the explicit purpose of a basic income is to rid employees of the need to tie themselves to the labor market and to seek employment through it. For this carries with it a high risk of pauperization. But the option of voluntarily forgoing waged work over a shorter or longer period would be a realistic one for most employees only if, instead of being ignored, their demand for useful activity and for the social worth and recognition associated with it were directed into channels which lay outside the labor market but which were freed of the stigma of work which was devalued or held to be a deviation from a "normal" way of leading one's life. There is no doubt that in the course of capitalist industrialization and modernization the spheres of such activity, external to the labor market and to the field of economic "autonomy," have shrunk, and that today they have congealed into a small residue. For these structural reasons, and also for cultural ones, the prospect of a return to "original" forms of cooperation in extended family, neighborhood, local community, and voluntary association is hardly a good one.

But since interventionary reductions in working hours have created a demand for such forms of activity, and for the concrete services and forms of production associated with them, the only realistic course is to establish and maintain such forms of activity through encouragement from the state, legal guarantees, and political recognition. A basic income is a vital presupposition of this. It guarantees an "income without work," in the short or long term, as the sole basis of the existence of those who "work without income." Conversely, the development of independent work and production, and of local and cooperative self-provision, is necessary if a basic income, which can be precisely calculated in the short run, is to be an acceptable form of social security. For basic income can only be that form of social security – that is, one which does not discriminate through poverty – if, within the framework of these forms of activity and the networks of mutual assistance and exchange associated with them, those services can be maintained which would otherwise have to be created through the market and through the use of monetary income.

There is a relationship of mutual presupposition not only between basic income and reductions in working hours and between basic income and new forms of independent labor, but also between new forms of independent labor and reductions in working hours. Clearly, the prospects for such new forms of independent labor are good only if these activities are not restricted to the "free time" of full-time employees. Rather, supplementary periods of time will have to be deducted from that devoted to wage labor. Conversely, it will be possible to stimulate the interest of individual employees in reductions in working hours only if they are made aware that such activities are possible.

Basic Income in the Field of Political Conflict

Those who advocate a strategy of social reform in which a basic income plays a central role are not pursuing new, let alone revolutionary, goals. Its main purpose is to secure those ethical standards which are already recognized as binding – prevention of poverty, equality of opportunity, solidarity – against losses and regressions which, *without* the introduction of a basic income, would inevitably accompany certain current and future socioeconomic developments (such as falling growth rates, absence of full employment, demographic "overdemand," the existing social security system's "dependence on employment," the increasing ineffectiveness of laws on maintenance).

Because basic income has this "conservative" purpose, the burden of proof falls to its opponents. Either they wish to put an end to the postwar social ethical consensus, or they must show that their demands can be met in the long term by means *other* than that of a basic income – something which, for reasons already given, seems to us highly doubtful.

Aside from this social policy front, where the opponents of a basic income are challenged either to provide a better alternative or become the champions of regression, there is the question of the *group interests* from which support for a basic income can be expected. The following is a review of such socioeconomic categories and their associations and representatives.

The recipients of social assistance and unemployment benefit, but also all those with legitimate claims on the social security system, are disposed toward support for the basic income model. They have an interest in an adequate income which is secured against fluctuations in the state of the economy and of unemployment. This holds for those with social insurance, especially those in pension schemes, because this model would allow them to rely on a basic "pillar" of monetary income, without preventing them from achieving a standard of living which goes beyond it. They might do so through the accumulation of private means and/or through additional paid work. Those receiving social assistance are likely to give their support for the additional reason that they would be spared having to prove their "availability" for work or to accept a means test for family supplement.

Under circumstances in which the long-term future of employment is difficult to estimate, the *trade unions,* as bargaining organizations for employees, have a rational interest in a BI model. This is because the chronic "oversupply" of those seeking work inevitably leads to price competition among employees, and threatens a disintegration of trade unions and a restriction of their room for maneuver. For trade unions, a basic income would solve this problem by restricting the labor supply. All employees would be given the chance of opting out of their role as employees, either in the short or the long term, and contenting themselves with the subsistence which a basic income secures. This would be particularly tempting for those in badly paid or unattractive jobs. Its result, which trade unions would welcome, would be that employers would have to provide their employees with better paid positions, to phase out routine or unskilled tasks, or at least to take steps which significantly increased their attraction.

A social security system financed by taxes gives *employers* in labor-intensive and medium-sized firms the advantage of a relief from supplementary labor costs. It also equalizes competition with large industrial and/or capital-intensive branches of the economy. For these reasons one can expect a weakening of the ideological and political resistance of these groups, and under certain circumstances their unequivocal support.

A basic income is also of considerable interest from the point of view of *policy toward women*. A guarantee of such an entitlement would make it easier for women to avoid having to choose between a form of life secured only by the law on maintenance, and participation in work which may be marginal, undervalued, or discontinuous. Instead, they would be able either to reject both, or to make *fully valued* employment the condition of their engagement in paid work.

Finally, where local authorities are responsible for social benefits, they will have a clear interest in the introduction of a basic income. Not only would they no longer have to shoulder the responsibility for social benefit, but the resources released could be used, directly or indirectly, to stimulate employment. Following the introduction of the entitlement to a basic income, they could thus help to reduce the number of occasions on which the insufficient absorptive capacity of the labor market meant that it was actually claimed.

This apparent paradox, that fewer people *will* claim a basic income the greater is the circle of those who, as citizens, *can* do so, is also produced by some of its other socioeconomic effects. Far from being an excuse for "laziness," inactivity, and the egotistical exploitation of public resources, it is precisely suited to putting a stop to the widespread squandering of the productive potential of human labor power. It may do so through the stimulation of "informal" modes of work organized outside the rigid forms of a labor contract, or through the generation of employment arising out of fiscal relief granted to businesses and local authorities. It does not seem too far-fetched to assume that in wealthy industrial societies, employees who are accorded the right to withdraw from paid work without penalty and at the cost only of loss of income (but not poverty!) will as a result be better motivated, better qualified, and in a better physical and psychic condition to engage in it (for then they would be choosing it "voluntarily") than those from whom this choice is withheld, and who must consequently work knowing that nonengagement in paid work (or the failure of an attempted engagement in it) carries the threat of material need and social stigma.

Notes

1 See Stephan Leibfried, "Soziale Grundsicherung. Das Bedarfsprinzip in der Sozial- und Gesellschaftspolitik in der Bundesrepublik Deutschland," in Georg Voruba (ed.), *Lohnarbeitszentierte Sozialpolitik und sozial Grundsicherung* (Frankfurt, 1988); on pensions see Winfried Schmähl (ed.), *Verkürzung oder Verlängerung der Erwerbsphase?* (Tübingen, 1988); Dieter Schäfer, "Alterssicherung in der sozialen Marktwirtschaft," *Zeitschrift für Sozialreform* 34:5 (1988).

2 We arrive at this option fully aware of the political objections of which Philippe van Parijs has reminded us in a detailed commentary. The most important difference between a "negative income tax" and a basic income of the "social dividend" type is that in the first case the transfer payments basically take place at the end of a period (a month or the tax year), but in the second case are a prepayment. So with a negative income tax we accept the principle of first waiting to see whether income was earned in the previous year (or how high it was) before a transfer payment is made. That does not rule out the possibility that in individual cases of insufficient market income, generous prepayments would be combined with conditional backpayments. This would already undermine the neoliberal version of "negative income tax," which due to need and hunger would drive potential recipients into (low-paid) jobs before they could make good their (anyway extremely low-level) entitlements. Our proposal resembles that of Milton Friedman in name only. On the other hand, the ex post rule, with conditional entitlements to prepayments, might improve the chances of putting the proposal into practice without having to reduce the level of benefit.

3 Claus Offe, "The Future of the Labour Market," in Offe, *Disorganized Capitalism*, ed. John Keane (Cambridge, 1985); Michael Opielka and Ilona Ostner (eds), *Die Zukunft des Sozialstaats* (Essen, 1987), Introduction, pp. 7–22.

4 Ulrich Mückenberger, "Die Krise des Normalarbeiterverhältnisses. Hat das Arbeit noch eine Zukunft?" *Zeitschrift für Sozialreform* 31:7 and 31:8 (1985); and "Deregulierendes Arbeitsrecht," *Kritische Justiz* 18:3 (1985).

5 Stephan Leibfried and Florian Tennstedt (eds), *Politik der Armut und die Spaltung des Sozialstaats* (Frankfurt, 1985).

6 Data here and below from *Datenreport 1987*, ed. Statistisches Bundesamt, Schriftenreihe der Bundeszentrale für politische Bildung (Bonn, 1987).

7 Data from Statistische Bundesamt, March 1988, and *Datenreport 1987*.

8 Ilona Ostner, "Prekäre Subsidiarität und partielle Modernisierung – Die Zukunfte von Haushalt und Familie," in Johannes Berger (ed.), *Die Moderne – Kontinuität und Zäsuren*, special issue 4 of *Sozialen Welt* (1986).

9 *Mitteilungen aus der Arbeitsmarkt- und Berufsforschung* 19:3 (1986), p. 363.

10 Ibid., p. 431.

11 *The Integration of Women into the Economy* (OECD, Paris, 1985).

12 T. H. Marshall, *Class, Citizenship and Social Development* (New York, 1964), pp. 65–122; Richard Titmuss, "The Social Division of Welfare: Some Reflections on the Search for Equity," in Titmuss, *The Philosophy of Welfare* (London and Sydney, 1987), pp. 39–59.

13 Richard Titmuss, "Social Welfare and the Art of Giving," in Titmuss, *The Philosophy of Welfare*.

14 See chapter 8 above.
15 Wolfgang Glatzer and Regina Berger-Schmitt (eds), *Haushaltsproduktion und Netzwerkhilfe* (Frankfurt and New York, 1986).
16 Compare Göran Therborn, *Why Some People are More Unemployed than Others* (London, 1986); John Keane and John Owens, *After Full Employment* (London, 1986); Claus Offe, *Contradictions of the Welfare State*, ed. John Keane (London, 1984), and "The Future of the Labour Market." See also the discussion between Keane/Owens and Mike Rustin in *Critical Social Policy*, no. 18 (1986–7); no. 22 (Summer 1988); no. 21 (Spring 1988).
17 For an introduction see Michael Opielka and Georg Voruba, *Das garantierte Grundeinkommen. Entwicklung und Perspektiven einer Forderung* (Frankfurt, 1986).
18 For this position, albeit with a view to the politics of sexuality, see Deirdre English, "The Fear that Feminism will Liberate Men First," in Ann Snitow, Christine Stansell and Sharon Thompson (eds), *Powers of Desire: The Politics of Sexuality* (New York, 1983).
19 Schäfer, "Alterssicherung in der sozialen Marktwirtschaft"; see also chapter 8 above.
20 Claus Offe, Karl Hinrichs and Helmut Wiesenthal (eds), *Arbeitszeit Politik* (Frankfurt and New York, 1982).
21 A. Gorz, *Paths to Paradise* (London, 1984); see also *Kritik der ökonomischen Vernunft* (Berlin, 1989), part 3.
22 Ulrich Mückenberger, *Die Ausbildungspflicht der Unternehmen nach dem Grundgesetz* (Baden-Baden, 1986).

PART IV

The New East

11

The Politics of Social Policy in East European Transitions: Antecedents, Agents, and Agendas of Reform

The Scope of the Problem of Social Policy in Postcommunist Societies

Postcommunist political economies face three problems of transformation: property must be privatized, prices must be liberalized, or "marketized," and the state budget has to be stabilized in order to relieve strong inflationary pressures. Corresponding to these three transformations, and in fact motivating them, are three cost considerations: privatization is mandated by the consideration that it will reduce production costs; marketization will reduce transaction costs (including the transaction costs resulting from perverse incentives generated by soft budget constraints); but stabilization, if strictly pursued, does not economize on costs, but leads to *increases* of costs of a special kind, namely "transition costs" (comprising the vast devaluation of both physical and human capital, the fiscal crises ensuing therefrom, and the concomitant pressures on transfer, service, and infrastructure budgets), thus generating political resistance to marketization and privatization.[1]

The social policy implications of economic transition are fairly straightforward. The economic transition, which evolved slowly and gradually in Hungary throughout the 1980s and much more suddenly and hence chaotically in the rest of the Comecon world, triggers four interrelated social policy problems.

1 Employment is being gradually marketized and becomes contingent on labor contracts rather than state-guaranteed rights and duties to work. The contractual nature of employment means that security of *obtaining* employment, security of *durability* of employment once it is obtained, and security of the level of *real income* attached to employment are simultaneously reduced.

2 Business firms are forced to turn into "functionally specific" organizations; once they can no longer rely on soft budget constraints, this means giving priority to issues of productivity and profitability and abandoning all or most of the social policy functions that were traditionally implemented by them under state socialism. Abandoning social policy functions is an imperative that is also enforced by banks and (foreign) investors, and it is also supported, as a rule, by employees, who must give highest priority to promoting the competitiveness and economic viability of the enterprises, in the interest of maintaining their jobs.

3 The need to unburden the state budget and the politically adopted principle of price liberalization result in the discontinuation of price subsidies for items of mass consumption, and thus in sharply declining real incomes.

4 Marketization of labor and privatization of production have jointly created the need for specialized complementary social policy agencies and institutions capable of absorbing the increased risk associated with the new conditions and of substituting for the former integrated way of performing social security and service functions. Such new institutions have to operate in an environment that is simultaneously characterized by sharply rising demand for transfers and services, an equally sharply decreasing supply of fiscal resources, and a lack of established specific legal and institutional routines and acknowledged practices by which the two are to be mediated. There is a rather sharp division between countries that developed a fairly elaborate social policy system in their precommunist past and which therefore can reactivate institutional patterns established in the interwar period (such as the largely Bismarckian social insurance systems of Hungary[2] and Czechoslovakia[3]), and those countries which must design and introduce an entirely novel system.

What I intend to do on the following pages is to give a preliminary and exploratory, at times also speculative, outline of the modes of social policy making, its historical and political context, its antecedents, its agents, and of the further agenda of social policies in the East Central European transition.

Modes of Social Policy Making

The scope of social policy responses to these unprecedented challenges which present themselves in postcommunist societies is much broader than what is to be found on the social policy agenda of Western societies. I wish to distinguish three broadly consecutive steps: emergency measures; institution building; reform and adjustment within established social policy institutions.

First, "transitions costs"[4] will have to be alleviated by very special types of social policies. The labor market and real income situation call for a variety of ad hoc emergency measures, which are being taken through various parabudgetary funds (such as the Hungarian Employment Fund) or temporary rules, benefits, and exceptions (such as the strange East German arrangement of "zero hours short-time work" whereby people stay nominally employed and receive pay which is higher than unemployment benefit, without, however, having any work to do). Before conventional social policies can become operative, these special policies of coping with the emergencies of the transition must be adopted and implemented. In apparent contrast to the principles now adopted of privatization and marketization, these transitory emergency measures tend to be highly etatist and discretionary in form, since they cannot yet rely on institutionalized routines and established divisions of powers and domains. The typical mode of decision-making appears to be negotiations between top executives in the ministries of finance, privatization, and labor. In addition, these negotiations (about such issues as the adjustment of transfers and benefits to inflation) have to be conducted under great time pressure[5] and within a short time horizon. It does not come as a surprise that these measures were often "realized in a hurry and thus had the flavor of improvisation,"[6] and that the legal-technical quality of these ad hoc rules is described as deplorable.[7]

"Transition costs" are a mixed bag of items. Two of them should be highlighted, and their paradoxical relationship emphasized. On the one hand, the rather dramatic changes resulting from unemployment, abolition of services, and budgetary cuts must now be compensated for through a "separate corrective system";[8] however, this is not yet in place and must be substituted for in discretionary ways. But simultaneously, old enterprises that would have to be considered obsolete by market and efficiency standards must be granted, as it were, an "artificial" spell of life, because the level of social and economic disruption would be even greater if the market were allowed to take over without delay. In order to avoid some of the social burdens and political risks that might follow from the rapid adoption of marketization and privatization, these reform moves, or so many policy-makers believe, must be stretched over time, thus generating economic opportunity costs of *foregone* efficiency increases. Thus two types of income support expenditures (even if they are not labeled as such) will be needed, one corresponding to the state of marketization to the extent that it has been accomplished, and one corresponding to the premarketization condition to the extent that it is still preserved. Some amount of employment, even though inefficient, must be subsidized, *and* efficiency-induced *un*employment must be compensated. Taken together, these two kinds of transfers may constitute a fiscal burden of intolerable proportions, which in turn may work as a momentous impediment to the privatization process itself and interfere with the policy goals of stabilization.

Economic burdens and uncertainties are relatively easy to justify in normative terms if economic policies of transition and marketization are conducted in such a way that the poorest are ascertained to be the first to benefit from the growth dividend and to make progress in absolute terms. This is the combination of growth and progressive distribution. Inversely, the scenario that must be avoided under all circumstances, according to this normative principle, is one in which no growth occurs

	progressive redistribution	regressive redistribution
+ growth	1	2
− growth	3	4

Figure 11.1

and redistribution takes place in favor of the already privileged (that is, stagnation plus regressive redistribution). These extremes, as well as intermediary combinations, are represented in figure 11.1.

Two contrasting preference orderings – partly based on implicit economic theories about sequences – concerning economic and social policies can be highlighted. One is the social democratic reliance on the market economy's tolerance for – or even dependency on – redistribution, that is, $1 > 3 > 2 > 4$. Its major political opponent is the conservative-liberal ordering $2 > 1 > 4 > 3$, which sees social inequality not only as the direct result of economic growth, but a lasting functional precondition for it, serving to maintain the appropriate incentive structure. There may also be agents who consider 1 and 2 to lie outside the feasible set, and who thus prefer 4 to 3. The relative political strength enjoyed by the proponents of these implicit economic and normative theories and their preferred equity/equality mixes will determine much of the nature of the initial emergency measures adopted.

At the same time, there is the task of initiating a process of social policy institution building, which mainly means creating corporate actors, domains, and specific functions, as well as organizing a process of devolution from the overburdened or "underpowered" center to specialized agencies.

It is only after these two steps of emergency measures and institution building have been taken that, third, "normal" social policies, including the ongoing process of institutional reform and adaptation, can be pursued. Social policies, as conventionally understood, consist of statutory mechanisms that are designed to do two things. First, they absorb and provide for those standard risks which occur as a side effect of the normal operation of a capitalist market economy and which are assumed to be of such a nature and volume that the persons affected by them cannot cope with them through their own resources alone. Obvious examples of such risks are unemployment, health problems, lack of market income due to old age and disability, family burdens, poverty, and inadequate housing. The other aspect of social policies is interpersonal redistribution based on the normative notion that the more fortunate members of the community owe the less fortunate the fulfillment of a solidaristic obligation. Both of these functions, risk absorption and redistribution, are carried out, coordinated, and continuously fine-tuned through an established network of agencies (such as legislatures, national, state, and municipal governments, self-governing bodies, corporate actors, interest associations, and professional associations) acting according to largely uncontested routines, traditions, and domain demarcations.

In contrast to this somewhat simplified model of the "normal" social policies of a steady-state political economy of democratic capitalism, what is called for in postcommunist societies undergoing transition is much more. In short, the risks that must be absorbed are much greater, both in terms of the volume of need and the social incidence of need, because of the disruptive impact of the breakdown of the old regime and the incipient economic transformation, and because the institutional, financial, as well as the political and cultural resources available to accomplish the task are much more limited. While the politics of social policy in established capitalist democracies consists mainly in rather undramatic marginal adjustments to ongoing demographic, economic, budgetary, medical, and institutional changes, the politics of social policy takes on a much more dramatic form, since the transition itself both increases the level and urgency of security and redistribution problems that need to be addressed *and* renders obsolete the institutional and other resources through which these problems can be dealt with. In addition to the standard problem of normal policy making, namely, "doing the right thing" within an established setting of agencies, domains, and routines, the extraordinary problem must be tackled of setting up these agencies, domains, and routines.

The tasks of institution building and policy making must be resolved simultaneously. Under the unprecedented conditions of the postcommunist transition, it is clearly not enough just to carry out the functions of social policy. For before they can be carried out, an institutional policy system must be put in place that is fit for the task. As in many other policy areas, the old-fashioned question of "What is to be done?" loses much of its significance relative to the logically prior question of constitutional design: "Is there anyone capable of doing it?" – or "Who should be in charge?"

Political and Historical Contexts: The West and the Past

The urgency of finding an answer to both these questions in their proper logical sequence stems from the fact that, in sharp contrast to the historical evolution of Western welfare states, East Central European transformations take place in the dual context, or cognitive frame of reference and comparison, of "the West" and "the past."

As far as the "West" is concerned (meaning mostly continental Western Europe, to which the Poles, Hungarians, Czechs, as well as the populations of the Baltic states wish to "return"), it provides them with a model of a political economy within which all four consecutive steps of political modernization have already been accomplished, namely:

1 the formation of consolidated nation-states;
2 civil liberties and negative freedoms protecting life and property;
3 democratic political rights;
4 positive welfare state rights.

The presence and high visibility of this model is likely to encourage popular aspirations in the light of which the accomplishment of anything less than the full set of these modernizing steps, for instance the presence of (2) and (3) combined with the absence of (1) and (4), will be widely regarded as a positive failure of the entire transformative effort.[9] Given the extraordinary deprivations and disruptions caused by (2), that is, the privatization of the economy, the absence of compensatory mechanisms (4) will be felt all the more strongly, particularly as the people are now endowed with the political resources (3) that allow for "voice" and hence possibly resistance. Needless to say, the level and social scope of positive rights (4) that can be afforded also depends on the favorable economic effects triggered by privatization and marketization (2). But, in contrast to authoritarian capitalism of the Chilean type, under democratic capitalism in East Central Europe this affordability and feasibility assessment will always be mediated through democratic participation (3).

In societies that have become used to comparing themselves to the West and are now involved in the project of imitating Western political and economic institutions, the threshold of patience with poverty and insecurity is likely to be much lower than it can be assumed to be even in the contemporary newly industrializing societies of South Asia or South America. All of which is not meant to suggest that majorities in the East European transition countries do actually press for social security and protection and support political forces advocating the respective legislative reform. It only suggests that unless such reform is initiated autonomously by political elites, the aggregate medium-term effect is likely to be any combination of disruptive social conflict, symptoms of social disorganization, and emergent longings for the more attractive aspects of the old regimes.

The transition to a market society uproots individuals by rendering sizable quantities of labor power economically superfluous, partly due to the shrinking demand for labor per unit of output and partly due to the obsolescence or nonconvertibility of skills acquired under state socialism. During the industrial revolution in Western Europe, it was only through the possibility of relocating large masses of surplus labor power to other parts of the world through emigration, largely to the virtually "empty" continent of North America, that the hardship of the transition to a market society could be gradually diminished. As the emerging proletariat had no voice, they resorted to departure in massive numbers. No equivalent to this "no voice–empty space" scenario is available today, and Western European political elites and publics will take an active interest in seeing to it that their countries are not mistaken for "empty space."[10]

It follows that the long delay that occurred in the West between the accomplishment of civic rights, political rights, and eventually social, or positive, rights (T. H. Marshall) cannot be allowed, even from the point of view of Western European states, to repeat itself in the East, and that the scope and level of social protection and social security that is requisite in the early stage of the latter case is much greater than it was in the former.

On the other hand, and as far as the (communist) "past" is concerned, it is clearly and highly unfavorably remembered for its failure to accomplish (2), (3), and in many cases also (1). But at the same time, its accomplishments concerning (4), that is, security and equality, do sometimes appear remarkable in absolute terms, and perhaps to some even comparatively attractive in relative terms if compared to the present condition of turbulent and often painful transformation. Even if the past is not "sincerely" appreciated as providing greater security and equity, a pretended and misrevealed preference for the past may well be resorted to as a lever of political mobilization.

Given these two cognitive references as they are widely adopted within East Central European societies, the combined net result is likely to amount to a massive discontent with the current situation. Both looking back and looking to the West will generate a social demand for protection and security that is not easily met by the newly emerging economic and institutional structures and resources.[11] This discontent threatens to delegitimate the new regime and to confer a measure of retrospective legitimacy on the old. Given the fact that both production and employment are sharply declining, while at the same time income inequalities surpass by far not only what people in these societies, but also what people in Western societies are used to, sizable portions of the population of postcommunist societies will be inclined to reason that "we have given up many of the beneficial aspects of the old regime without having been able to redeem the promises of the new." Needless to say, this kind of evaluative perception is quite likely to help to mobilize political forces of a reactionary, populist, authoritarian, and chauvinist kind, which in turn is equally likely to jeopardize the accomplishments of (2) and/or (3), thus reversing even the partial modernization that has actually occurred.[12] A keen awareness of these contingencies transpires in many official pronouncements of political leaders, such as in that of President Havel of June 1990, when he stated that "economic reforms must be accompanied by a social system that safeguards human rights and prevents social upheaval ... [by protecting] those most likely to suffer in the transition."[13]

Thus political elites of the new regime appear to be largely aware of the need to respond to demands for social justice that arise in the process of transition. The requirement for such responsiveness is all the more pressing since the societies of the newly democratizing countries of Central and Eastern Europe have acquired the political resources to vote those elites out of office if they are regarded as frustrating demands for social justice. People in these societies are not used to coping with insecurity. What they expect and demand is an improvement over what they have experienced in the past, not a regression to conditions that the old regime prided itself on having overcome. The new political elites have to take seriously sensitivities of this sort concerning matters of social justice. However, there are three kinds of responses, clearly inadequate, which consist of measures which are not social policies in the technical sense. Due to the limited range of options available to them, elites will nevertheless be tempted to resort to these inadequate responses.

In the first, social justice is meted out not by providing for security and transfers to the masses affected by the burdens of economic transition, but by punishing the old elite, whose members are held personally responsible for the economic decay of socialist societies.[14] Another kind of social policy surrogate (*Ersatzhandlung*) is to adopt confiscatory measures or criminal punishment, both of which remain largely symbolic in nature and are aimed against the most conspicuous *winners* of the new economic game, not its less conspicuous but clearly more numerous losers.

In the second, it is being suggested (adopting Milton Friedman's rule that the only social responsibility of the business firm is to make a profit) that societies undergoing economic transformation cannot afford the extra burden of expanding social security, as such a move would be bound to delay the economic process and hence make everyone worse off, compared to the rapid achievement of a fully privatized growth economy.

In the third, the diametrically opposite position is taken by some of the remnants of the political left who argue that, as the supposedly therapeutic "short sharp shock" of privatization will probably neither be short nor therapeutic, all political efforts must now be concentrated on delaying it. What is advocated instead is the continued protection of state enterprises for the sake of a continuation of the relatively egalitarian, security-maximizing social policies implemented in them.

Such policy prescriptions are often issued by ex-communists, such as Meciar in Slovakia or the leadership of the BSP in Bulgaria, who also tend to emphasize nationalist motives and the need for interethnic redistributive measures, to be adopted at the expense of minorities. Slowing down the pace of the three economic reforms (privatization of property, liberalization of prices, stabilization of the value of the currency) is a recommendation that is also, together with an emphasis on institutional reform, advocated by (mostly Western) social democrats.[15]

Short of a full-blown political reversal, there will also be, in the absence of adequate policies addressing the problems of insecurity and inequality, "spontaneous" substitutes for social policies by which people try to escape some of the burdens of the economic transition. Such "spontaneous" substitute practices are so widespread and common in today's postcommunist societies that one hesitates to term them "illegal" – which most of them[16] technically in fact are, in spite of the fact that the respective laws often cannot be enforced. Such practices include smuggling, stealing of state and private property, bribes and "tips" paid for public services, robberies, illegal employment, tax evasion, large-scale illegal exports, black market activities, civilian violence, extortion, and corruption of state officials and civil servants. These mass phenomena, for which Richard Rose has coined the term "uncivil economy,"[17] have the combined effect of depriving political authorities of their political credit, governing capacity, and fiscal resources.[18]

So far, I have argued four propositions:

1 Postcommunist transitions pose demand-side problems of social policy that are unparalleled in Western welfare states.
2 They also pose supply-side problems which amount to the need to set up a full and mostly new institutional system of social policy, including its actors, rules, and financial resources, and effective as well as efficient administrative capacities.
3 The failure to accomplish this dual task will lead, because of the cognitive reference to the "West" and the "past," to political turbulences that are likely, at least in some of the postcommunist countries, to challenge their post-1989 political and economic accomplishments.
4 This failure will also give rise to illegal substitute practices of a scope and volume that is bound to paralyze much of the state's governance and future reform capacity.

Inherited Patterns and the Reversal of the Logic of Social Policy

In order to understand the scale of the transformative effort required, or the distance that must be traveled, to rebuild the social policy system, we must look back at the "logic" governing the old system. Socialist societies are quintessentially production-centered, or "productivist" (if certainly not particularly "productive") societies. Organizing production, increasing production, and participating according to one's capabilities in the productive process are uniformly declared the moral essence of socialist society, as well as the condition of collective survival and individual status. The proportions of the population engaged in paid work exceeded Western labor market participation rates, most markedly in the case of women. Enterprises were the location where all the central life interests – in the officially declared sense – of workers converged: education, consumption, social services, health, political propaganda, even defense. The "work collective" paralleled and perhaps even replaced the family as the functionally most diffuse form of social organization, that is, the one that performs all those functions which are not taken care of by other, functionally more specific organizations. The legitimacy of every institutional sector, with the possible exception of the military, but certainly including the party, the state bureaucracy, the school system, academia, the production and allocation of housing, was to be derived from its successful performance of a role subservient to production.

The ideological and institutional centrality of the sphere of production is epitomized by the principles that governed the life of workers-citizens of socialism, or "*Werktätige.*" First, preparation for, orientation toward and continuous participation in production (or in functions that supposedly were subservient to production) was the prime demand that society made on its members.[19] Second, and in return, society offered its workers-citizens three rewards. These, in a steeply decreasing order of the degree of actual implementation, were security of employment; a relatively high degree of equality of remuneration; and the prospect of ever-increasing production and, consequently, consumption. Given the low and only slowly increasing level of productivity, the absorption capacity of the employment system was virtually insatiable, and shortages of (skilled) labor power ubiquitous and permanent. Given the relative equality of income and working conditions, job mobility was limited, due to the nonavailability of dismissals and of substantial wage differentials, both within and between enterprises. Thus, entry into the production system and movement within this system were at best only marginally determined through mechanisms of market and contract, but were determined rather through status rights and obligations.

Attached to the status rights of the workers were a variety of benefits, allocated in largely paternalistic ways, that is, without an enforceable claim attached to them in accordance with the principle of formal legality. These benefits ranged from day care to housing to health services to vacation homes to routine opportunities to use the facilities and tools of the enterprise, as well as the social networks mediated through the place of work, for private purposes.

Given the system of authoritatively enforced duties and status rights in which socialist labor relations were embedded, enterprises (as well as the equally state-controlled trade unions) were by no means constituted exclusively as organizations of production (or organs of workers' interest representation), but at the same time served as comprehensive social policy agencies performing many of those functions which in capitalist societies are performed outside, and in relative independence from, the business firm. As a consequence of this integrated approach, "social policy" was not considered a separate policy area with its specific institutions and actors. It clearly lacked the feature of a "policy area," with its corresponding institutional "policy arena." Even the term had disappeared in some countries, while in others, such as the German Democratic Republic, it only began to be invoked in the early 1970s, after having been rejected for a long time as inadequate, in order to emphasize the stereotypical (institutional as well as fiscal) "unity of economic and social policies."[20] What is largely absent under state socialism is the institutional distinction between the domains of welfare state and business firm, as well as that between the interests of employees, as represented through unions, works councils, etc., and the interests of employers and investors. Such lack of differentiation (of politics and production in general, and of social policy and production in particular) was deemed by the protagonists of the system as a definite advantage of state socialism.

The underlying philosophical assumption leading to the "unity" postulate is this. To start with, there are the needs of the worker.[21] These needs must be satisfied, and the most economical way to do so is to satisfy them at the point of production (and with a close look at both the need itself and the worthiness of the worker as a loyal and productive person). The *outcome* to be achieved through this investment is a *more productive worker*. "One of the goals of social policy was to direct labor resources where the Government felt the need was greatest."[22]

Thus the socialist enterprise is the locus not just of the utilization, but at the same time of the social construction of labor power through the satisfaction of the needs of the worker.[23] Socialist social policy follows a "downstream" logic, as it is seen as an essential instrument to generate a productive and loyal workforce. The state socialist welfare state has been described as "a mechanism whereby a state-directed economy geared to production for production's sake organizes its population to ensure the maximum availability of its labour power at minimal costs."[24] This is also the case with the heavily natalist family policy, which was – and has remained so far – particularly generous in Hungary, and which was here as everywhere else designed to offset the negative demographic impact of extremely high (by Western standards) female labor participation rates. Potucek captures this downstream logic nicely when he says that "the reproduction of working power – and not the working performance – was decisive for the policy of salaries and social allowances."[25]

The social policy performance accomplished in the pursuit of this logic in Central East European communist countries deserves a mixed, but generally not unfavorable, evaluation. In retrospect from the present point in time and amid the current turmoil of unemployment, institutional breakdown, and fiscal crisis, it may even be seen by some as a paradise lost, with the potential political consequences mentioned above. More realistically, I think the following is a fair though summary assessment:

- State socialism has provided a free and universal system of health, education, and vocational training to its citizens;
- it also provided heavily subsidized housing, which, however, remained scarce and qualitatively deficient in most places;
- formal unemployment was virtually unknown,[26] an accomplishment[27] that was paid for in terms of vast inefficiencies of production, partly resulting in involuntary (as well as voluntary[28]) "unemployment on the job";
- childcare services were generously provided in order to free female labor for employment,[29] and also in order to maximize state control over the political socialization of children;
- many mass consumption items were heavily subsidized, again causing vast inefficiencies;
- income inequality was significantly smaller than in market societies,[30] but disposable income was also lower;
- but many quality consumption items were unavailable in the market or excessively highly priced or allocated through mechanisms other than income and prices, such as connections and patronage;

- retirement incomes were extremely low by most Western standards;
- health and other services were of poor quality in many places;
- enforcement of positive rights and claims was difficult, as many of
  the transfers, services, and benefits were allocated through mechanisms of paternalist managerial, bureaucratic, or professional dis-
  cretion, while rule-of-law principles remained at best rudimentary.

This list indicates that the overall picture is at best ambiguous if
measured against the institutional practices and accomplishments of
Western welfare states. One Hungarian critic complains that "social
policy [under state socialism] has come to be associated with widely
unsatisfied needs, unacceptable bureaucratic regulations, haphazard
provision of services at more and more unacceptable levels."[31] These
deficiencies do not, however, preclude the rise of nostalgic sentiments,
given the current social policy and income situation in many East
European countries and regions. As is also obvious from this list,
social policies were highly integrated into the production process and
consistently designed to promote production and to create and maintain its human capital base.

In contrast, in a market economy need satisfaction and productivity
are tied to each other through the reverse logical link: as workers have
unfulfilled needs, these needs will operate on them as incentives and
induce them to be productive; as the anticipated and hence motivating
(as well as proportionate) *outcome* of demonstrated productivity, *needs
will be satisfied* through individual income in the marketplace, which
takes precedence over collectivist provision.[32] Collective social security
arrangements play a supplementary role and take effect in an ex post
way. They are restricted to those risks and contingencies which are
considered beyond the control and/or beyond the means of the worker,
and they are tied, as is the case with unemployment insurance and old
age pensions, to the duration of previous employment and the level of
income derived from it. Thus social policies in capitalist market
economies mostly follow an "upstream" logic, that is, they are contingent on rights acquired through employed work; "if ... then" *rules*
(instead of "in order to" *decisions*) specify a legal precedent on which
claims and eligibilities depend. In the first ("downstream") case,
social policy is primarily seen as producing the labor force in accordance with its (other-attributed and licensed) *needs*, in the second case
it is primarily seen as distributing income in accordance with workers'
rights and *deserts*.

Given these vast differences in the underlying philosophies of social
policy in state socialism and democratic capitalism, the design problems that must be solved in the transition from one to the other are

clearly momentous. In the first place, a highly *integrated* social policy must be replaced with a *separate* institutional system, which under state socialism consisted only in the rudimentary form of a state-operated universal pension fund, as well as state-financed health and other service organizations. Secondly, the operational logic must be reversed from the "downstream" to the "upstream" type, which implies the need to generate an elaborate set of rules, hitherto nonexistent, to specify legally enforceable rights, duties, and claims in relation to individual workers, plus rules regulating the budget, administration, and enforcement of the system with the claims and duties it allocates. Thirdly, the narrow perspective of channeling virtually all social benefits and services through the enterprise must be broadened so as to include in the social policy agenda other focuses that are no longer (or have never been) taken care of at the point of production, such as services for families, children, youth, the elderly, or tenants.

These three interrelated and tremendous tasks are further compounded by two complications. For one, the nature of the process of postcommunist transition causes enormous time pressure. With the disintegration of the institutions and routines of the old regime, and with the serious problems of economic decline, unemployment, social insecurity, and inflation caused by their breakdown and the incipient privatization process, a veritable emergency operation of institutional design is called for if the institutional interregnum is to be limited to a tolerable duration. This time pressure does not allow for those time-consuming processes of mutual partisan adjustment, experimentation, and incremental change that have been so characteristic of the history of Western welfare state developments. There is no time for political learning, that is, for consideration, deliberation, and the formation of viable compromise.

Agency and Social Policy

The other complication is the absence of strong, competent, mutually recognized, representative, and cooperatively minded collective actors within civil society (such as political parties, trade unions, business and employers' associations, professional associations, as well as a corruption-proof administrative apparatus) which could, as they have done in the West, play a guiding role as designers and proponents of social policies and social policy institutions.[33] What we would therefore expect, in the light of these two complications, is a pattern of the politics of social policy that remains – beyond the initial period of emergency measures – erratic, shifting, fragmented, clientelistic, and based on the bits and pieces of state power that derive from transient parliamentary majorities or presidential rights to issue decrees.

The classical protagonists of social policy and labor market regulation, namely social democratic parties, are conspicuously absent or weak in the East European transition. Nor is it hard to find an answer to the question of "Why is there no socialism in Eastern Europe?" Virtually everything that starts with "social" – not just "-ism," but also "social democracy" or "social policy" – tends to be discredited with postcommunist political elites. In comparison to continental Western Europe, East Central European countries have developed a spectrum of political forces that is clearly shifted toward market liberal, nationalist, and conservative ideologies and policies of the political right.

Given the disruption of production and trade, the priority of these political elites seems to be on economic reconstruction through privatization and marketization. This priority is clearly enforced by international pressures, coming from the International Monetary Fund as well as Western European governments and banks, to adopt measures designed to control inflation, reduce budget deficits, and adopt currency convertibility.[34]

Furthermore, not only are political forces "biased" to the right, but the newly formed political parties are also organizationally weak, often relying more on networks of trust and personal charisma than on formal rules. The same applies to unions, employers' and professional associations, self-governing collective actors, and local governments. Organizational domains of these collective actors tend to be fuzzy, demarcation lines between policy arenas contested, membership support shaky and fluctuating, bargaining routines missing, interassociational alliances fragile, representativeness questionable, the bindingness of decisions hence very limited, ideological orientations unsophisticated, and cleavages more often local, regional, occupational, and sectoral rather than national and comprehensive. Most observers suggest that Hungary, again, is the most consolidated and crystallized case in all these respects. But even in this country "the political profile of the newly-emerged parties has not yet settled down; it is both unusually mixed and shifting."[35]

At present, it is not clear how Eastern European societies will be able to extricate themselves from this associational wasteland which, with the possible exception of agricultural interest intermediation, must today be described as a pluralist-syndicalist-populist hybrid that is a far cry from Western European patterns of corporatism, tripartism, federalism, municipal self-government, self-government through chambers, *Sozialpartnerschaft*, *folkhemmet*, *économie concertée*, *transicion pactada*, or *verzuiling*.

Now, much of the available comparative historical evidence suggests that the coincidence of liberal-conservative political predominance with the symptoms of general associational weakness is the worst possible structural background for the emergence of social policies and social policy institutions.[36] Associational weakness may well be a stronger impediment to the evolution of social policy institutions than it is for any other policy area. For social policies, be they concerned with old age pensions, unemployment insurance, health, assistance to families, housing policy, or welfare policy, always involve interpersonal, intertemporal, interclass, intergenerational, or interregional redistribution on which *both* of the respective sides, the givers and the takers, must somehow be brought to agree and on which they must make a commitment to cooperate. It is mainly through strong collective actors operating as virtual "private governments," being linked to each other by networks of professional expertise and personal trust relations and enjoying a substantial measure of representativeness and control over their constituency, that such redistributive agreements can be reached and reliably honored.

Conversely, in the absence of associational strength that might help to accomplish just this, we would expect social policies to be given low priority by parties and governments. We would also expect that problems of social insecurity and poverty are left to, or explicitly delegated to, either the "marketplace" or institutional settings outside the network of territorial or functional representation, namely, parties and associations. We would therefore expect a largely "parapolitical" set of social policy practices to be advocated and implemented in the name of "subsidiarity," in which the family, clans, the neighborhood, the company, the church, ethnic communities, and charitable or philanthropic associations play key roles, and where, on the other hand, the notion of social citizenship, and state-guaranteed positive rights granted to citizens, remain at best of marginal significance. Proposals for "self-help" and "welfare pluralism" are actively promoted, and self-employment advocated as a way out from unemployment (rather than policies designed to restore "full employment"). It is exactly this pattern that recent legislative developments in Hungary and other East Central European states seem to confirm.

If associability, or the strength of collective actors, is hypothesized to play such an important role in a society's capacity to develop a social policy system, what in turn accounts for associability itself? I wish to suggest two answers to this question. First, associability is correlated to people's perception and expectation, to a reasonable extent validated by experience, that the game they are involved in is actually a positive-sum game in which cooperation pays and defection is therefore not self-evidently preferable. Well-grounded optimism concerning the economic development of the country will generate such cooperative and associative dispositions, while pessimism in this regard, or a habitual "limited good"[37] perspective on the world, will lead people to adopt "lifeboat strategies" much more readily.

Second, for strong associability to emerge, cleavages must be clear, expected to remain stable over time, and still be amenable to compromise. The best example of this pattern is, of course, a social democratic version of class conflict based on the notion that the parties to societal conflict are stable, but the outcome of conflict variable, namely, open to negotiation, compromise, and comprehensive progress. If, in contrast, people do not have reliable ideas as to where they belong, whom they must fight, how to reach compromise, and what the next day is likely to bring, large-scale and comprehensive associative action is meaningless. Postcommunist social structures are often described as "amorphous" or "atomized," which I take to mean that people find it difficult to detect reliable clues as to their own position in society, their relation to relevant others, and their likely future. On the one hand, virtually all individuals are exposed to the turbulences caused by the transition; on the other hand, social positions and the life chances attached to them are not easily typified, since all kinds of individual attributes can make a decisive difference as to whether a person ends up as a clear winner or an unequivocal loser in the transition. Instead of a clear-cut class structure, what determines the allocation of future privilege and power, or of marginality and poverty, are complex and opaque patterns of "asset convertibility"; having the right past, knowing the right people, speaking the right languages, living in the right place, belonging to the right age and gender category, and working in the right sector are rightly expected to make substantially more of a difference in the determination of future life chances than individual engagement in collective associational efforts on the basis of the assumption of broadly shared interests. Those who "make it" under the conditions of postcommunism are much more likely to succeed through clever moves in and between labor, capital, real estate, and information markets, as well as the use they can make out of past political affiliations,[38] than through formal association and collective action.

As so much depends — and is known to depend — on accidental assets, liabilities, and opportunities, there is no clear-cut pattern that would serve as a guide as to where people should locate themselves, who is going to win, and who to lose. Conversely, actual losers and actual winners tend to have little in common in terms of a shared "independent variable," such as location within the system of the division of labor; hence they will tend to relate to each other as might passengers traveling on the same bus, rather than as members of the same class. As the cognitive basis for comprehensive interest aggregation is missing, regional or ethnic codes may be taken to be the most likely ones resorted to in organizing collective action.[39]

The problem of "agency and social policy" with which we have been concerned in this section on a political macro level can also be transferred to a psychological micro level. In making that transfer, we would be presented with the inverted question: how do given social policies and positive rights affect the behavior and decisions of clients and citizens, which in turn will affect economic and political outcomes? It is easy to see how the preference for certain changes in social policies is often motivated by – as well as justified in terms of – implicit psychological theories about the behavioral impact of social rights and the positive and negative incentives and normative standards built into them. For instance, some Western social policy experts have claimed that welfare rights will generate a syndrome of "welfare dependency" in clients, and must therefore be viewed skeptically, while others argue that positive rights will activate the clients' sense of recognition, pride, community, obligation, and effort. It is on the battlefield of these more or less implicit behavioral theories that social policy controversies are usually pursued.

If, as many observers claim, men and women in postcommunist societies must to some extent be "reeducated" in order to perform properly in a pluralist polity and a competitive market economy, the question concerning the "formative" impact of social policies on the citizenry is even more central. Let me just briefly enter this debate, as it pertains to postcommunist transitions, by offering a classification of implicit theories that I have encountered in this field, both inside and (mostly) outside academia.

First, there are a number of ideas and assumptions that can be stereotyped under the heading of "*homo sovieticus* theories." Under the old regime, people have become used to unconditional, though not rights-based, security at a low level of prosperity. As a consequence, they have developed bad work habits, a contempt for effort and initiative, fear of innovation, and an inclination to trade the expression of their loyalty and submissiveness for patronage and protection. Once the past and its mental as well as moral residues are framed in these terms, and socialist social policy is charged with "spoiling the population by overprotection,"[40] the social policy prescription for a rapid and successful transition is unambiguous. People must learn that only effort pays, and that prosperity and security are contingent on productive accomplishments in the labor and other markets. Thus a social policy is called for that rewards effort and thereby serves, through its simultaneous "demonstration effect," to undo inherited cultural patterns and psychological states of mind.

Second, "*homo oeconomicus* theories." They start with the assumption that the aversion to hard work and effort is a general rather than culture-specific feature of human nature. In addition, the basic defect and cause of the eventual failure of the state socialist economic system is said to consist in its lack of an effective mechanism of obsolescence which would eliminate both unproductive workers as well as inefficient assets from the system. If such a mechanism is introduced through an (at best) minimalist version of social protection, human nature will respond in the desired way, albeit this time not to the carrot of prosperity, but to the stick of imminent misery.

Third, there is a group of assumptions and intuitions for which the label "*homo hungaricus*" may apply. Economic virtues such as effort and inventiveness have, according to this view, in fact been nurtured and cultivated under the old regime, if in hidden, distorted, and repressed ways. After all, if people live in a society where nothing works, where spare parts and other supplies are constantly missing, where command lines are opaque and decisions dictated by political opportunism, at least many of them will be quasi-automatically trained in practicing the moral antidotes of self-reliance, flexibility, inventiveness, and entrepreneurship in order to cope with these inefficiencies. These "unofficial" virtues, as they were cultivated under the old regime, must now, or so it is concluded, be recognized, generalized, and rewarded with "official" recognition. But it is exactly this desirable set of behavioral patterns that is likely to vanish unless it is complemented by social policies that help to make the risk bearable – while the market, if left to itself, will operate as Polanyi's "satanic mill" that cannot but discourage the preparedness to take risks, which now carries, in the case of a negative outcome of the risk-taking, the sanction of economic ruin. The social policy lesson to be learned if this set of assumptions is held valid is also obvious: workers (as well as investors and entrepreneurs) must be provided with an extensive variety of rights, guarantees, and services which will limit risks to acceptable proportions.

The Agenda of Social Policy

The political elites of postcommunist societies are forced to actively promote – and to take full responsibility for – a process of institutional "creative destruction," with the visible implication that the demolition of the old order comes first and the creation of the new order only after a more or less lengthy interval. This interval is filled with problems of social policy. As I have argued before, failure to address these problems will jeopardize the hoped-for outcome of democratic capitalism. But, at the same time, "excessive" attention to these problems will also endanger the desired outcome, as it will be likely to amount to imposing "protectionist brakes" on all three of the economic transformations, namely privatization, marketization, and fiscal and monetary stabilization.

It is clearly too early to assess or predict the mix of action and inaction, attention and neglect through which this social policy dilemma[41] will be tackled. Political forces are not crystallized enough for that, and institutional domains and jurisdictions are not sufficiently established. What alone is fairly certain is the nature and scope of those social policy problems that fill the interval between "destruction" and "creation." The following is an attempt to compile a rather comprehensive list of these problems.

Concerning each of them, possible approaches range from selective neglect, to executive emergency measures, to the installation of institutional routines. The eventual aim in this exercise is to arrive at a descriptive account as to which problems are to be addressed by which approach by what kinds of political forces in which of the postcommunist countries. For the time being, I limit myself to listing the problems.

1 The subsidization of mass consumption items (basic food, housing, transportation) is no longer affordable[42] and in some cases explicitly prohibited or discouraged by IMF-imposed rules; the result is loss of real income per average earner of income. This affects most seriously those groups in the population with least command over institutional resources necessary to protect their relative and absolute income status in the market or through collective bargaining, most obviously pensioners[43] and the unemployed.

2 Not only must the government accept the discontinuation of subsidies to achieve liberalization of prices and stabilization of the currency, which is a necessary condition for becoming eligible for foreign loans; it must also play an active role in an incomes policy that freezes public sector wages below the rate of inflation, thus imposing considerable sacrifices on what for some time (that is, until privatization is accomplished on a large scale) will remain the majority of the population. Also, cuts in unemployment benefits have been urged by IMF representatives, for instance, in discussions with the newly elected Bulgarian government in October 1991.[44]

3 Effective and universal wage bargaining and industrial relations

systems are not yet installed which could protect employees' real wages from inflationary pressures and help to increase them in line with productivity gains. As most social security benefits are tied to wages, and as wages are still a matter of statutory regulation (minimum wages plus legislated, irregular, often targeted, nonautomatic adjustment to inflation) plus individual- or company-level contracts, not of sector-wide collective agreements, a sizable portion of the population suffers from poverty due to inadequate wage or transfer income.

4 As all institutions switch to the logic of "functional specificity," enterprises, in particular, find it necessary to abandon social services, such as nursery schools, and schools will abandon the provision of meals. All this takes place before substitute mechanisms of provision are established, with the likely consequence of heavy burdens of self-provision falling on families and households, at least transitorily. This shift of burdens depresses both the previously very high rates of female labor market participation as well as the average number of earners per household, and hence income per household. These consequences for household income are all the more serious since wages in state-socialist societies were not typically "family wages," and "most families needed two incomes to survive."[45] At the same time, the relatively generous family allowances and maternity benefits that have prevailed for a long time in Hungary are presently up for targeting, means testing, and general cuts.

5 Income inequality is bound to rise in many dimensions: interpersonal, intersectoral, between the state sector and the private sector, between the employed, unemployed, and self-employed. This is a sensitive social policy issue in a society that is "used to" a great deal of "equality of outcomes."

6 Lack of capital, budgetary austerity measures, lagging productivity, and the breakdown of much of international trade have generated a decline of production which now translates, contrary to past experience, into rising unemployment originating from the sector of the economy that has been privatized already. But the hoped-for efficiency increases of industrial production, once accomplished, will also lead to layoffs, if perhaps only temporarily. As the fiscal as well as institutional means of anything like an "active labor market policy" are largely not available, applying in many places to simple labor exchanges, and as protection of the unemployed is very limited by levels of benefits and by duration, pressures for migration will continue to mount. What is also clearly increasing is an exclusionary mass response to structural unemployment that tries to reserve jobs (as well as other sources of income) to primordial (family, ethnic, and

racial) categories and thus adds to the potential for violent ethnic conflict,[46] conflict, moreover, that the police apparatus of the former regime is no longer in a position to repress.

7 As housing can no longer be subsidized and maintained through the state budget, it must be privatized. Privatization (including restitution) of residential housing will have the consequence in part of dramatic rent increases, only partly and reluctantly offset by targeted housing subsidy payments, and eventually rising homelessness.

8 All these problems amount to a rising general precariousness of income and to poverty, which is expected to increase steeply in the near future. High levels of inflation – together with the absence of price subsidies, of robust collective bargaining arrangements, of automatic wage indexation, and, of course, of economic growth – has led a society such as the Bulgarian society, for instance, into a situation where 45.2 percent of the population find themselves below subsistence level, 64.6 percent below the poverty line, and where (according to the news service *The Bulgarian Watcher* in 1992[47]) "the average wage may soon reach the poverty line." Social assistance is entirely left to local governments, with no fiscal subsidies being made available to them by the central state (and with mostly no tax base of their own so far) to enable them to perform this function.[48] One consequence of this is interlocal unevenness of provision.[49] To say the least, there is certainly no mechanism in place that would implement the Rawlsian principle of justice, also advocated by Kornai,[50] that the poorest should be first to make absolute progress in their income situation.[51]

9 Everywhere the transition from state socialism to democratic capitalism involves giant fiscal crises. As John Campbell has argued, these crises are generated in an opposite way from fiscal crises in the West. "Whereas fiscal crises in capitalist . . . states occur due to expenditures rising faster than revenues, fiscal crises in post-Communist states occur due to revenues declining faster than expenditures."[52] Revenue decline is due to a combination of factors: the shrinking tax base resulting from the privatization of state-controlled economic activity, privatization at undervalued prices, the initial recession following privatization, the lack of development of the tax laws, deficiencies in the extractive capacity of the internal revenue administration which permit large-scale tax avoidance, and the fiscal favors that must be extended to both foreign and domestic investors for both political and economic considerations. Budgetary alternatives to taxation are also excluded, except for the inflationary recourse to printing money, as the IMF makes loans contingent on the state deficit not exceeding 5 percent of GNP. As a consequence of the combined effect of all these circumstances, social policy expenditures financed from the state

budget are likely to be pushed very far down the list of financial and economic priorities by liberal-conservative governments.

10 The move from universal and free services to devolution, privatization, subsidiarity, and welfare mixes, including the transformation of badly underfunded public health systems into two-tier health systems, is bound to deprive sizable portions of the population of their coverage. The uneven and largely very poor quality of social services is due not only to fiscal constraints, but also to the lack of properly trained social service professionals and administrators and the absence of a tradition of professional control and autonomy in service delivery.[53]

This tremendous agenda of social policy transformations is made even more difficult by the fact that the intermediate actors, administrative agencies, and political forces that would all have to play a role in the design and implementation of social policies are in a rudimentary or nascent state and need to be constituted and strengthened. At least in those countries where there is no tradition of a social policy system to be rediscovered from the precommunist past and now adopted as a guiding model (as is most clearly the case in the former Czechoslovakia), the building of collective actors and administrative agencies is likely to be a process beset by polarizing conflicts rather than converging ideological and political forces. These conflicts can be described as those between protectionist stagnation and free market orthodoxy, reliance on ad hoc emergency measures and institution building, and tightening state control versus devolution of social policy tasks to local and otherwise decentralized actors.

Most importantly, perhaps, a problem must be solved that at the same time is clearly outside the range of problems that public policies are normally thought to be capable of solving, namely, a change of the political and economic culture, including the strengthening of the relationship of "social trust," in both of its relevant dimensions: trust in others and trust in the future. Unless this kind of social trust develops, the habits, attitudes, and expectations inherited from and nurtured under the old regime are unlikely to be overcome. These consist in a syndrome of political and economic cultures which emphasize paternalistic state-sponsored security and protection, on the one side, and the informal provision of resources through families, relations, social networks, barter, and the second economy, on the other. Everything that we would associate with a well-functioning, firmly institutionalized welfare state and social policy system must be created in the largely empty space between these twin ills of the old regime.

Notes

1 Peter Stania (ed.), *Agenda '92* (Vienna, 1992).

2 Zsuzsa Ferge, "Social Policy Regimes and Social Structure: Hypotheses about the Prospects of Social Policy in Central and Eastern Europe," in Zsuzsa Ferge and Jon Eivind Kolberg (eds), *Social Policy in a Changing Europe* (Frankfurt, 1992).

3 Martin Potucek, "Quo Vadis, Social Policy in Czechoslovakia?" Department of Sociology and Social Policy, Charles University, Prague, 1992.

4 The social costs of the transition from state socialism to democratic capitalism have never before occurred in history. But it is noteworthy that many social policies, labor market policies, and industrial relations policies in the West, too, have their historical origins in a context of a transition crisis, namely the transition from a wartime economy to a peacetime economy. Examples range from the *Betriebsrätegesetz* to the GI Bill to the British National Health Service.

5 It is interesting to see that where time pressure has been relatively mild, as in Hungary, institutionalization (as opposed to policies of emergency measures) has made the greatest progress. Hungary's long prehistory of creeping privatization, marketization, and economic reform pre-1989 left that country sufficient time to develop a range of social policy institutions (such as unemployment insurance, adopted as early as 1989); where this is absent it must be compensated for through discretionary ad hoc measures.

6 Potucek, "Quo Vadis," p. 3.

7 Herbert Szurgacz, "Die neuere Entwicklung auf dem Gebiet des Sozialrechts in Polen," *ZIAS* 5:3 (1991), p. 283.

8 Julia Szalai, "Outline for the Radical Reform of Social Policy in Hungary," in Bob Deacon and Julia Szalai (eds), *Social Policy in the New Eastern Europe* (Aldershot, 1990), p. 91.

9 Steps (2), (3), and (4) are of course the same stages of political modernization as those conceptualized by T. H. Marshall. The notion of a cognitive model or frame of reference invites the thought experiment that, had social reformers of the late nineteenth and early twentieth century had a realistic foresight about what would come to be possible in terms of welfare state development in the then distant future of the 1960s and 1970s, they might well have dismissed their own demands and accomplishment as overly modest, opting instead for maximalist radicalism that would have remained sterile in the earlier period. Should some mechanism exist of such a "veil of ignorance productivity" or "the cunning of modesty," it is certainly inoperative in East and Central European countries.

10 Volker Ronge, "Social Change in Eastern Europe: Implications for the Western Poverty Agenda," *Journal of European Social Policy* 1:1 (1992).

11 There is little consistent evidence concerning the social policy preferences of the electorate in general in postcommunist electorates. While political parties advocating or promising strong social protection are clearly not on the rise, the possibility must be considered that voter preferences, within ideologically poorly consolidated Eastern European societies, are largely inconsistent (or "rent-seeking"), following the logic of "strong protection for me, and the free market for everyone else."

12 In view of this danger, Vaclav Klaus's brave standard announcement,

made in many statements and interviews, that what he wants to install is a "market economy without an adjective" (the missing adjective being "social") can either not be taken seriously or, if actually pursued, must be seen as having contributed to the strengthening of the socialist-nationalist forces headed by Meciar and thus to the effective split of Slovakia from the CSFR caused by Meciar's movement.

13 Quoted by Igor Tomes, "Social Reform: A Cornerstone in Czechoslovakia's New Economic Structure," *International Labour Review*, 130:2 (1991), p. 191.

14 Cf. Akos Róna-Tas, "The Last Shall Be the First? The Social Consequences of the Transition from Socialism in Hungary," Working Papers 1992/34, Juan March Institute, Madrid, 1992, p. 2.

15 Cf. Stania, *Agenda '92.*

16 Other and perfectly legal substitute practices for the decaying social policy arrangements consist in a significant resort to and reliance on primordial networks of solidarity, such as families, localities, resources of the second economy, ethnic groups, and church-organized charity, or access to underground labor markets abroad. One effect of this turn to communities is to establish a new and additional axis of inequality between those who do have access to them and those who do not.

17 Richard Rose, "Towards a Civil Economy," *Journal of Democracy* 3:2 (1992).

18 These corrosive consequences would have to be taken seriously even by those economic liberal political elites who believe that a "market economy without an adjective" is not running the risk of a political backlash but would find broad majority acclaim.

19 More specifically, the production-centeredness of social policies pertains to the *subjective disposition* of workers and their activation for employment, that is, to their skills, efforts, loyalty, discipline, willingness to cooperate, and compliance with rules and authorities. Much less, or so it appears, does it apply to the objective protection and preservation of the labor power of workers. An indication of this biased emphasis would be the level of rules pertaining to health and safety at work, as well as the stringency of the enforcement of such rules, both of which seem to have been remarkably deficient by Western standards of labor law and labor protection. See Bob Deacon et al., *The New Eastern Europe: Social Policy, Past, Present, and Future* (London, 1992), p. 3; Adam Szalkowski and Jacek Olbrycht, "Social Function of the Post-Socialist State," Seminar Papers 10, Academy of Economics, Cracow, 1992, p. 13.

20 Paul Adams, "The Unity of Economic and Social Policy in the German Democratic Republic," in Deacon and Szalai, *Social Policy in the New Eastern Europe.*

21 The monopoly of interpretation of what the "needs of the workers" are resides with the party, which determines them in the light of its own need, or the so-called collective needs of socialist society. This paternalist and authoritarian political structure allows and invites the discretionary use of social policy benefits and their allocation for political purposes, such as selective discrimination and punishment, or as a premium for loyalty and "worthiness." The extreme and sometimes obscene privileges in access to health, recreation, and other services that the higher ranks of the nomenklatura enjoyed are well known.

22 Tomes, "Social Reform," p. 192.

23 Cf. Szalkowski and Olbrycht, "Social Function of the Post-Socialist State," pp. 9–10.

24 Adams, "The Unity of Economic and Social Policy," p. 140.

25 Potucek, "Quo Vadis," p. 2; working performance would be "upstream."

26 The fact that unemployment could be excluded as a contingency to be reckoned with, together with the fact that the job meant not only a source of income but the locus of comprehensive need satisfaction, is bound to make the actual experience of joblessness a much more painful one of deprivation to those affected by it than it would be in a market society where people have been brought up with a very different perspective on the job, unemployment, and positive rights.

27 An ambiguous accomplishment, to be sure. The reverse side of the right to work was the obligation to work. Furthermore, dismissal from jobs was often used as a kind of social ostracism to brand "hostile elements," who were therefore not entitled to any kind of unemployment benefit.

28 Following the famous rule of "as long as they pretend to pay us decent wages, we just pretend to be working."

29 This pattern is linked to another shock effect of subjective deprivation. As enterprise-based day care facilities are being discontinued, and as available jobs sharply decline, an extreme disparity between female and male unemployment rates emerges. Compared to any continental West European country, female joblessness is experienced as more scandalous in a society which was "used" to and considered as "normal" a female labor force participation of up to 90 percent, and where family budgets typically consisted of two incomes.

30 This statement must, however, be qualified by the "redistributive privileges" built into the administrative system of the allocation of income, services, and housing. Cf. Ivan Szelenyi and Robert Manchin, "Social Policy under State Socialism: Market Redistribution and Social Inequalities in East European Socialist Societies," in Gösta Esping-Andersen and Lee Rainwater (eds), *Stagnation and Renewal in Social Policy* (Armonk, N.Y., 1987).

31 Szalai, "Outline for the Radical Reform of Social Policy in Hungary," p. 92.

32 An extreme example of how enterprise provision takes precedence over market provision under state socialism is the fact that a large producer of light bulbs in East Berlin had a full-time pastry baker on its payroll. A major part of his job was to produce cakes for family festivities of employees.

33 For a concise elaboration of the essential role of intermediary collective actors in the process of postsocialist transformation, cf. Helmut Wiesenthal, "Sturz in die Moderne. Der Sonderstatus der DDR in den Transformationsprozessen Osteuropas," in Michael Brie and Dieter Klein (eds), *Zwischen den Zeiten* (Hamburg, 1992), pp. 171f. Julia Szalai ("Outline for the Radical Reform of Social Policy in Hungary," pp. 93, 96) has argued convincingly that social policies must be based on a "social self-defence system controlled by the population," rather than on the ruins of a "state donation system," and that such a self-defense system of civil society presupposes for its emergence "institutions functioning in the interest of the independent and autonomous members, groups, and communities of the society," such as trade unions, self-governing institutions, and local autonomies, plus the appropriate bargaining procedures between them.

The crucial problem, however, is that state actors of the old regime have in many countries and institutional sectors retained sufficient "negative" power to prevent such collective actors from constituting themselves, while at the same time their "positive" power is largely discredited and hence insufficient to organize and lead the process of transformation.

34 Cf. Bob Deacon "The Impact of Supranational and Global Agencies on Central European National Social Policy," conference paper, Faculty of Health, Leeds Polytechnic, 1992.

35 Ferge, "Social Policy Regimes," p. 218.

36 I am inclined to believe, following some ideas of Esping-Andersen, that the second of these two independent variables has a yet stronger negative effect on the evolution of "welfare-stateness" than the first.

37 The term "limited good," as taken from the work of George Foster on peasant societies, is employed by Ken Jowitt to analyze the premodern patterns of political culture preserved by Leninist regimes, see Jowitt, *The New World Disorder* (Berkeley, 1991), p. 2.

38 Róna-Tas, "The Last Shall Be the First?" pp. 11–13.

39 Cf. Claus Offe, "Ethnic Politics in East European Transitions," unpublished paper, Center for Social Policy Research, University of Bremen, 1992. This situation is partly reminiscent, if for very different reasons, of what have been described as "postmodern" features of the social structures of Western societies; the outcome concerning associational weakness and its impact on social citizenship may well be comparable.

40 Zsuzsa Ferge, "Human Resource Mobilization and Social Integration: In Search of New Balances in the Great Transformation," unpublished MS, 1992.

41 The nature of this dilemma boils down to whether "static antagonism" or "dynamic complementarity" is seen to govern the relation of economic modernization and social policy. The reasoning behind "static antagonism" is this: the more spending there is on social security, services, and transfers, the fewer resources will be available for economic reconstruction. The opposite belief is that the more spending there is on social transfers, the more people will be willing to trust the beneficial outcomes of the economic and political transformation, and the more this transformation itself will be guided by incentives of long-term efficiency, such as the development and protection of human capital and the prevention of non-institutional social conflict. One question related to this dilemma is, of course, which of these two implicit theories is "right." Another, equally relevant question is the adoption of which of them is thought by political elites to generate the greater electoral support.

42 At the time of the first liberalization of prices in Czechoslovakia in July 1990, "the Government abolished subsidies on retail prices worth some 60 million crowns, which at the time represented about 20 per cent of the total annual wage bill" (Tomes, "Social Reform," p. 193).

43 According to the Polish Prime Minister Olzowski (interviewed in *Der Spiegel*, no. 7, 1992, p. 156), the problem with the level of subsistence of pensioners in Poland is no longer one of patience and endurance, but the fact that "they have come dangerously close to the biological threshold of survival."

44 Deacon, "The Impact of Supranational and Global Agencies," p. 27.

45 Tomes, "Social Reform," p. 193.

Social Policy in East European Transitions   253

46 Deacon, "The Impact of Supranational and Global Agencies," pp. 12–13.
47 *The Bulgarian Watcher*, May 21, 1992, p. 10.
48 Ferge, "Social Policy Regimes," p. 209.
49 Katalin Lévai, "Towards a Reform of Social Policy in Hungary," Discussion Paper 6–91, Hamburger Institut für Sozialforschung, Hamburg, 1991, p. 31.
50 Janos Kornai, *Vision and Reality: Market and the State* (London, 1990), pp. 124–9.
51 And neither is there any mechanism that would make sure that another rather plausible intuition of distributive justice be complied with, namely the intuition that the privileged groups of the old regime should not be allowed to emerge as the privileged groups of the new: cf. Elemér Hankiss, *East European Alternatives* (Oxford, 1990), pp. 234–65.
52 John Campbell, "Reflections on the Fiscal Crisis of Post-Communist States," conference paper, Department of Sociology, Harvard University, p. 1.
53 Potucek, "Quo Vadis," p. 6.

12

After the Democratic Revolution: New Burdens of Proof

There is no point in belaboring the obvious fact that democracy has now become the universal norm for the political and constitutional practices of modern societies. As this norm is virtually universally shared as a standard providing internal legitimacy and external recognition to regimes, it also becomes vague. There are so many hopes, meanings, and supposed implications attached to the notion of democracy that the concept is in constant need of elaboration and precision.

This is particularly the case as we look at the newly democratizing countries of Central and East Europe. After all, the now obsolete regimes of real socialism also described themselves by the term "democracy," or even, in a strange pleonasm, as "people's democracies." Thus the conceptual task is not to define democracy in contrast to openly nondemocratic regimes (of which there are few), but to explore, in order to avoid premature and shallow consensus, varieties and antagonisms within the concept of democracy itself. For this concept has been claimed as the basis of legitimation by the most diverse regimes that we find in the modern world. Let me do so by distinguishing two models of democracy.

Democracy as the vehicle of progress Subsumed under this model are all conceptions of democracy that can be traced back to the French and eventually Russian revolutions. Their common characteristic is that political forms – such as rights, modes of representation, the scope and extent of participation, and the division of power – were all seen to serve some substantive collective purpose or project, ultimately to be furthered, in the case of real socialism, through the political monopoly of the communist party. In this instrumental perspective, the test of the democratic nature of a polity is in its outputs and outcomes. Democracy is virtually defined as whatever provides the right kinds of political elites with the necessary power resources in order to make the right kinds of decisions – the correctness of which is established by the supposedly superior insight of ideological truth about the laws of motion of society and history. One implication of this "output" model of democracy is that, should democratic forms (such as freedom of the press, equality of political participation) fail to contribute to the promotion of some preconceived "progress" or the victory of "progressive forces," these forms must be abandoned (by way of repression and even the open "putschist" violation of the constitution) in order to continue to achieve progress or to maintain the ruling position of the monopolistic party. Another implication is that what bears the adjective "democratic" is not the procedure of politics, but the outcome of policies; whatever the mechanism that brought it about, economic growth, technological advancement, the provision of jobs, schools and housing, or the buildup and maintenance of defense systems are all described as "democratic" by virtue of the alleged contribution these policies make to some notion of universal "progress." Still another implication of this model of democracy is that political power is seen in rather an optimistic perspective, not so much as a potential threat to citizens and their rights and liberties, but primarily as a precious resource to promote the progressive transformation of society.

Democracy as procedure The roots of this liberal model lay in the American revolution and the constitutional system of checks, balances, participation, representation, and liberties. The supreme goal within this model is the prevention of dictatorship, including the tyranny of the majority. No one is entitled to sacrifice procedural correctness for some alleged notion of progress or substantive justice, on which there is bound to be irreconcilable controversy anyway. Only rules and procedures (which, if contested, are to be decided on by properly constituted independent courts) count as democratic, and whatever the policy outcome of democratic procedures is, it must be accepted as democratic and thus binding. The virtue of democracy is not the *use* of power for collectively beneficial and progressive ends, but, to the contrary, the *taming* of state power, the dangerous and destructive potential of which is seen to be much greater than its creative promise. Democracy means certain procedures with uncertain outcomes (Adam Przeworski).

To be sure, both of these models of democracy are extreme and ideal-typical abstractions. But they serve to build a scale by which the democratic revolutions in East Central Europe can be measured. For the generations of those who have been too young to be conscious witnesses of the military as well as moral defeat of Nazi barbarism, this peaceful democratic (and, on top of everything else, hardly expected and predicted) revolution of 1989 may well stand out as the happiest political event of our lifetime. If we try to locate this event on the analytical axis just defined, the result is obvious. This revolution has been a giant and consistent move from one democratic doctrine to the other: from progress to procedure, from content to form, from trust in the benign effects of an omnipotent party state to distrust of unaccountable power.

Political theory, just as with any other kind of theorizing, involves burdens of proof. Its propositions are likely to meet with hard questions and dissent concerning their validity, and the strength of a political theory (such as either of the two versions of democratic theory just sketched out) depends on how compellingly it can answer such questions and doubts. Let us see what these burdens of proof are in the case of each of the two democratic theories.

The (hardly any longer bearable) burden of proof of "progressive" theories (and practices!) of democracy is that it must somehow justify its pretense of (1) knowing what progress "is," and (2) how it can be brought about through the means of monopolistic party and state power. Such an arrogant pretense of having the right theory and practice has clearly fallen into abysmal disrepute, and the nakedness of the emperor is evident to all. Its Achilles' heel is its circularity: if the authors of supposedly true propositions are themselves party to or subject to the power that their truths are in turn to justify, power becomes tautological and normatively empty as it loses all independently established reasons.

There is, however, a reciprocal burden of proof to be carried by the now victorious liberal theory of democracy that relies on procedures rather than outcomes. As we all share the enthusiasm over the democratic revolution, the formidable weight of this burden of proof may be obscured for some time. While ignoring the size of some task may be temporarily useful advice in practical politics (because knowing all that is knowable would inhibit the motivation for action), this pragmatic rule cannot be followed by intellectuals. What I therefore want to do in my brief remarks is to explore the theoretical as well as the practical burdens of proof with which democratic theory in general, and the newly democratizing countries of East Central Europe in particular, are fraught.

If democracy is the combination of certain procedures and uncertain outcomes, democrats need to think about two questions that immediately emerge from this formula. First, what makes those "certain procedures" actually certain? Second, if outcomes are no longer determined by some authoritatively imposed notion of "progress," but instead become "uncertain" and contingent on emerging majorities and coalitions, resources and identities, how can we be reasonably confident that these outcomes will be at least *tolerable* and accepted as such even by those whose interests appear to be violated by them? These two thorny questions are transparently interrelated: if those uncertain outcomes are considered "good enough" by most of the people for most of the time, the people are likely to support the democratic procedures, and in this way *make* them certain. But the opposite case also needs consideration: if the outcomes, as left to the contingencies of competitive party politics, market forces, are seen as positively detrimental for at least some of the time by at least some relevant portion of the people, and also if the initial hope and enthusiasm invested in the newly established democratic institutions should evaporate, what mechanisms will then be able to effectively safeguard the certainty of procedures?

To the first question concerning the sources of the certainty of procedures, there are a number of reassuring answers, some of which I wish to briefly review. First, the durability of the democratic institutions and procedures can be assumed to rest on the *constitution*. The constitution declares procedures sacrosanct, guarantees the rights and the liberties of the people, and accordingly sets limits to the power resources that the state apparatus, in both its civilian and military capacities, can employ. But the mere presence of a constitution that does all this is not enough. As the attempted coup of August 19–21, 1991 in Russia demonstrates, the constitution can be violated, and it must be actively defended if it is to survive such violation.

This raises the question as to who is to guard the constitution if it comes under stress and pressure. As an answer, *nationhood* and a widely shared sentiment of national identity as it emerges from a common past and common destiny, common religion and common language is cited as the second source of democratic "certainty," as these sentiments and passions can activate the willingness of the people to support and defend the constitution. The energy flowing from this source, and its certainty-generating potential, were also in clear evidence during the Russian revolution of 1991. Reliance on this source provides a viable answer to our certainty question wherever the boundaries of the state and the boundaries of strong sentiments of national identity do in fact coincide. But none of the Central and East European states find themselves in that fortunate position of being homogeneous nation-states. All of them, not only the Soviet Union as it was, have either sizable internal or external ethnic and national minorities. Consequently, an appeal to national, religious, and linguistic identities may well turn out to be divisive and to undermine the certainty of the constitutional rules rather than invigorating the validity and acceptance of these rules.

Third, the role of charismatic and widely trusted political *leaders* has been cited as a major underpinning of democratic stability and certainty. In fact, such individuals with exceptional leadership qualities, although with very diverse political statures and outlooks, have emerged in most of the newly democratizing countries of Central and East Europe. There are figures such as President Vaclav Havel. But still, there is no certainty that leaders like this will always emerge, nor is there a certainty that charismatic leaders will always and uncompromisingly lead the defense of the constitutional order.

Fourth, one might think of sources of certainty and stability coming from the *international system*. The post–World War II transition to democracy in what then became West Germany was certainly safeguarded by the occupying forces of the Western Allies. But there is clearly no direct equivalent to that certainty-generating mechanism visible today – except, perhaps, a prudent use of moral, political, and economic support coming from the countries of the European Community that would have to be designed to assist the certainty and irreversibility of the transition to democracy and constitutionalism. But then, such assistance might serve other and less respectable purposes, either by intention or by perception, and it can easily be denounced as a new strategy of Western empire-building.

Fifth, we have good reasons to believe that what is known in Western political science as *"collective actors"* can play a decisive role in providing robustness and durability to the newly forming democracies of Central and East Europe. By instilling the appreciation and a favorable attitude toward the routines of democratic participation and representation into their respective social domains, and also by developing a strong interest in their own respective role in the making of public policies, independent trade unions, employers' associations, leagues of farmers, professional associations, political parties, etc., can reinforce the popular consensus that supports the constitution and the practice of democratic government. Apart from the fact that such collective actors might also try to bypass and even to subvert constitutional government, a further skeptical note must be added that it is exactly the absence of strong collective actors performing this certainty-generating function that is one of the most conspicuous characteristics of the postcommunist societies.

All of these solutions – a formal constitution, a strong sense of national identity, charismatic leaders, a favorable international environment, and strong collective actors representing and at the same time shaping the forces within a differentiated (rather than atomistic) civil society – are probably necessary, though ultimately insufficient, conditions for the certainty of democratic procedures. What is also required, in addition, is a "civic spirit" or a political culture which is widely shared within the population and which constitutes a democratic political community inspired by a sense of "constitutional patriotism" (Jürgen Habermas) that transcends the boundaries of ethnic, religious, or linguistic identities.

This rather intangible "moral infrastructure" of the democratic polity may initially be generated by the intrinsic enjoyment of democratic practices that now become available to the mass of the population, by the excitement of the transition itself, and by the fresh memories of the lies and arrogance of power, of repression, and of isolation which were the most prominent features of the old regime. But, again, the durability of these moods and sentiments cannot be taken for granted, particularly if they are exposed to frustrations of economic aspirations and intensifying divisions of material interest, which can now be expressed and pursued in a much less restrained manner than before the transition. In order to consolidate the moral infrastructure of a democratic polity, much will depend on formative processes in the course of which people "get used to," accept, and even derive some intrinsic pleasure from their role in the democratic polity. As it is not well understood how the essential ingredients of a democratic political culture come into being, let me speculate for a moment about their nature and origin.

Communist societies have been opaque societies, reminiscent of the old lady who has removed all mirrors from her house. The arts and techniques of reflection, self-monitoring, and self-observation were dramatically underdeveloped. Reliable knowledge about what was going on was a privilege of the planners and the secret police, and even they lacked the techniques of capital accounting or an adequate assessment of the subversiveness of ideas, or, for that matter, an assessment of the lawfulness of some action through an independent court system or an assessment of the real costs of production through a mechanism of market prices. In contrast, democratic political institutions, with a free press, free science, free practice of religion, free arts, free public debate, and free markets generate an abundance of information about what is going on. The absorption and consumption of this self-evaluative information is likely to become habit-forming, even addictive. To be sure, it may also give rise to stress, information overload, and the ensuing cycle of apathy and overdoses of simplistic images. Nevertheless, the availability of information and the chance to observe, to compare, to learn, and to discover will shape the cognitive practices of people in irreversible ways.

Another way in which civic virtues that are so essential for the growth and stability of a democratic polity are likely to be cultivated under the impact of democratic institutions is this. As people are given choices – both in the marketplace and in political life – they are likely to develop (and become reflexively aware of) tastes, preferences, and criteria by which they actually make such choices. As a consequence, they are likely to distinguish (and to learn that others will apply the same criteria to themselves) between honest work and careless practices, personal interest and public duty, private moral beliefs and general norm, and trustworthy as against deceptive and ideological messages and modes of communication. It would probably be asking too much to expect (as Rousseau did) that democracy by itself will make *better citizens*; but it certainly inculcates the *criteria* by which a citizen can tell a "good" from a not-so-respectable citizen.

But then again, these speculations about a favorable formative impact of democratic institutions on the moral and cognitive practices of citizens may be rejected as idle hopes. For a sober and realist assessment of the situation of the newly democratizing societies suggests that the citizens of these societies have plenty of reasons not only for pride in the newly won liberties of their republics, but also for intense feelings of uncertainty and fear. Vehement ethnic conflict with the potential to turn into civil violence, economic crises of transition of unforeseeable duration, and the anticipation of possible reactionary countermoves designed to topple the still fragile democratic order combine to generate such feelings of uncertainty and fear – feelings that are not exactly known for their conduciveness to the evolution of a robust civic culture. In the light of these dangers, it does not come as a surprise to see that the nascent democratic virtues are not immune from disappointment, frustration, alienation, resentment, panic, and the temptations of utterly selfish *sauve-qui-peut* strategies. In a situation where many have a great deal to win and even more numerous others have virtually everything to lose, cooperation toward some common good does not come naturally.

At this point, and by way of conclusion, I wish to at least touch on the second of the two sizable burdens of proof which the theorists and practitioners of liberal democracy must bear. If such a democracy means certain procedures with uncertain outcomes, how can we make sure that outcomes stay within the limits of what is accepted as just and tolerable by all? If democratic politics leads to results that – by intentional commission or by default – create a class of the impover-ished, excluded, hopeless, alienated, and marginalized, then there is not much to redeem democracy in the eyes of these citizens. The situa-tion has been much easier in most of the West European countries, where an interval of several decades elapsed between the introduction of political democracy and the rise of a fully developed welfare state and its underpinnings in an economic policy geared to full employ-ment. But given the tumultuous circumstances under which political democracy and the free market are being introduced into East Central Europe, and also given the emergent territorial reorganization of the region, it is quite unlikely that massive programs designed to favor the least privileged can be postponed for a comparable length of time without creating a "dualist," deeply divided society in which demo-cracy would find it exceedingly difficult to take root. As far as housing and schooling, old age pensions and unemployment insurance, a modern health system and benefits for families are concerned, social policies must be thought of not as a relatively late fruit of democracy, but as a precondition for its consolidation and survival. It is in this sense, at least, that the notion of social progress and concerns about distributive justice, discredited though they partly are by the arrogant proclamations of the old regime, have not been entirely rendered obsolete by the most recent turn of history.

Index

action 22–3, 43–4, 45, 72–3; *see also* collective action
actors: collective 115–16, 258; functional differentiation 8–9; rational 28–9, 154–5; self-location vii–viii; social 6, 8, 9, 70; validity 44, 160–1
Adorno, T. 12, 14, 39
agency vii–ix, 239–44
altruism 134, 155–6
Apter, D. E. 66
associative relations: collective action 65; free-riding 43; institutions 45–9, 53–4; postcommunist countries 241–2; public spirit 44–5; societal 32, 42–9, 65; steering capacity 117–18; transformative 53–4; weakened 76; *see also* social movements, new
Austria 68
authority 24, 137, 147–8, 164
autonomy 6, 32
autopaternalism 101

basic income: entitlement 210; ethics 217; funding 218–19; as guarantee 197–8, 201–3; levels 213; political conflict 217–19; solutions 214–17
Beck, U. 33, 34–5
Bell, Daniel 116, 123
Benjamin, W. 41
black economy 128–31
Bobbio, N. 13–14
borders, penetrable viii, 73
Britain 50–1, 67, 68, 131
Bulgaria 247
bureaucracy 7, 28, 86

Campbell, J. 247
Catholic doctrine, employment 152–3
citizens: coercion 162; and democracy 90–1, 260; empowered 99–100; equality 197; and politicians 95; self-limitation 85; state authority 147–8; welfare 148; will 43, 112; as workers 197, 199 (n3), 235–7

civic spirit 259, 260
civil liberties 231
civil society 87–8, 107, 112,
  115–16
class structure viii, 33–4, 50, 53,
  62
coalitions, distributive 78–9
coercion 43–4, 162
collective action: associations
  65; costs 32; limitations
  15–16; moral dimension 46;
  public good 161–4; rational
  154–5; social-structural
  114–17; unorganized 117–19
collective actors 115–16, 258
collective good 44, 77–8, 161–4,
  166–7; *see also* public good
collective identities 32, 80, 110,
  169, 170
collectivities, destructured
  171–9
command economies 98; *see
  also* postcommunist
  countries
committees 94
common good: *see* collective
  good; public good
communicative action 22–3
communitarianism 137, 142
community 11, 12, 136, 173–4
conflict 7, 76–8, 112–13, 154–5,
  158, 217–19
Conrad, G. 98
conservatism 37, 229
constant sum principle 13
constitution 38–9, 257
consumption 122, 123–4
cooperation ix, 140, 166
cooperation circle 141, 142–4
coordination 13, 15, 22, 64, 68
corporatism 69
cultural reproductions 7
culture industry theory 14

Dahrendorf, R. 108
decision-making, rational 63
dedifferentiation 87–8
democracy: *see* liberal
  democracy
democratic welfare states: *see*
  welfare state
demographic changes 158,
  208–9
dependency creation 176, 213,
  243
deregulation 72–4; alternatives
  85–8; labor relations 204; and
  political conflict 76–8;
  sacrifices 76–7; as state
  intervention 75–6
Dialectic of Enlightenment
  (Horkheimer and Adorno)
  12, 39
differentiation 15;
  dedifferentiation 87–8;
  functional 8–9, 246; internal
  42–3; political preferences 96
discourse ethics 35–6, 41–2,
  53–4
distributive justice 178, 195–6
do-it-yourself activities 122–3,
  126–8

Eastern Europe: *see*
  postcommunist countries
education 46, 169
elites: modern society 12;
  political 94, 99–100, 152, 156,
  169, 233; reactionary 169–70;
  social conflict 154; welfare
  state 152, 156
Elster, J. 38
employees: *see* workers
employment: black economy
  128–31; Catholic doctrine
  152–3; changes 174;
  citizenship 197, 199 (n3)

employment – *cont.*
   235–7; as duty 152;
   environmental problems 209;
   formal/informal 127, 131,
   140; full 140, 208–10;
   marketized 226; paid 121;
   and unemployment 203–4;
   see also labor; wage labor
End of Ideology, The (Bell) 116
equality 135, 139, 197, 214
essentialism 21
etatism 66, 105–9
ethics 31–2, 217
ethics of responsibility 17, 23,
   44
ethnic factors 234, 247, 258, 260
Europe, Central and Eastern: *see*
   postcommunist countries

family 79–80, 125, 203; *see also*
   household
family supplement 194
Ferge, Z. 226
Fraenkel, E. 69–70
free-riding 43, 161
freedom 135, 137–8, 139, 147–8
Frisch, M. 47
functional differentiation 8–9,
   246
fundamentalism 42–3, 53, 55
   (n27)

game theory 42, 43, 45, 49, 50;
   negative-sum game 33;
   prisoner's dilemma 25, 47–8
German Democratic Republic
   98; *see also* postcommunist
   countries
Germany, Federal Republic:
   coordination 68; do-it-
   yourself 126–7; new social
   movements 97–8; political
   party funding 115; social

policy 194; social security
   185, 187, 190; unemployment
   203–5; welfare 152, 157–8
Gershuny, J. 123
globalization viii, 73, 78
Goodin, R. E. 48
Gorz, A. 215
guaranteeism 193–4, 195–9

Habermas, J.: lifeworld 31–2,
   42; loyalties 170, 259;
   modernity 14; morality 36,
   169; procedural rules 43;
   welfare state 159
Havel, V. 98, 258
health expenditures 178, 248
Hegel, G. W. F. 31, 55 (n27)
Heller, H. 61, 64, 105
help motivation 49
Hirsch, F. 13
Hobbes, T. 163
Horkheimer, M. 12, 14
household: adaptation 126–35;
   goods and services 129;
   income 203, 246;
   industrialized 140, 141; and
   labor market 121–4;
   modernization 122, 124,
   125–6; networking 141–2;
   nonmarital 125; self-
   provision 124, 126, 127, 139;
   single-person 124–5; size
   124–5, 141; structure 122
human rights 169
Hungary 249 (n5)

inclusion, and differentiation
   8–9
income: distribution 139, 229;
   entitlement 210–12;
   household/individual 203,
   246; inequality 229, 246; loss
   245; self-provision 127–8

individualization 96
individuals: biography/social
    situation 114–15; and
    collective interests 214–15;
    concurrence with oneself 101
    (n2); income 203; moral
    capacity 49, 50
industrial relations 50–2
industrial revolution 231–2
inequality 229, 246
inflation 247
inflexibility 7–8, 15–16
institutions 51–2; as collective
    identity 110; deregulation 86,
    87; as filters 45–9; formation
    of 229–30; moral problems
    33, 49–54; obligations 117;
    political 5–6, 13–14, 95, 96–8;
    postcommunist countries
    244–5; societal 65; welfare-
    maximizing 110–11
insurance 164–5, 166, 178, 185–6
interdependence 26–7, 77–8
interest communities 173–4
International Labor Office 129

Jessen, J. 131
job creation 206–7
justice 50–1; distributive 178,
    195–6; procedural 37; social
    233

Kaufmann, F. X. 118
Kirsch, G. 86
Klaus, V. 249–50 (n12)
Kornai, J. 247
Krieger, J. 170

labor: black economy 128–31;
    and capital 55 (n13);
    commodified 121–2;
    deregulated 204;
    domesticated 140; foreign

129; formal/informal 127,
    131, 140; independent 127,
    214, 216–17; inequalities
    173–4; *see also* employment;
    wage labor
labor market: crisis 206–7, 208;
    debates 139–44; gendered
    215; household 121–4;
    transition costs 227–8;
    unemployment 189–90
law 50, 65–6, 83–4, 151
leadership 258
left, political: exhausted 108;
    ideological shifts 158–9;
    postindustrial 16, 19–21,
    36–7; strong public policy 67;
    see also socialism
legislative representative bodies
    94
legitimacy 111–13, 162–3, 195
liberal democracy: citizenship
    90–1, 260; divisiveness 260–1;
    failings 95, 171–2; institutions
    95–6; legitimacy 162–3; as
    norm 89–90, 254; political
    resources 96–7; procedures
    43–4, 94, 255, 257; public
    discourse 97–8; rationality
    154–5; representative bodies
    94–5, 98–101; values 164; will
    of the people 14, 89–93, 101
liberalism 149–53
life chances, disparities 173–4
lifestyle issues 119
lifeworld 14, 31–2, 42, 152
limit values 80
local authorities 219
Luhmann, N. 62, 67, 188

March, J. G. 117
marginalization 33, 34, 192, 196
market principle 6, 11–12, 73–4,
    78, 137, 149, 150

Marshall, T. H. 147, 171, 232, 249 (n9)
Marxism: alienation 14; income entitlement 212; revolution 41; state 62, 107
Mayntz, R. 84
Mead, L. M. 152
middle class, new 176–7
minimum wage 190, 194
modern society 7–8, 10–12, 14–15, 22–5
modern state 147–8; *see also* nation-state; state
modernity ix–x, 3–5; functional differentiation 8–9; options 8, 9, 10; regressive potential 21–2; self-destruction 14; specialization 9; values 16–17, 21
modernization ix–x, 3–5, 6; households 122, 124, 125–6; limitation 10; political 249 (n9); problems 22–3
Mommsen, T. 17
moral philosophy 32–3, 36
morality 18, 169; capacity for 49, 50; consciousness 32; infrastructure 259; insights 31; and institutions 33, 49–54; norms 44–5; and politics 119; obligation 136–7; universality 46; welfare state 150, 153, 178
motivation, effectiveness 49–50

nation-state 61–2, 64–5, 105–7, 111, 231
national barriers viii, 73
nationhood 168, 257–9
need principle 135–9, 211–12
negative freedom 75, 82
negative income tax 202, 220 (n2)
neighborhood assistance 131–5, 141

neoconservatism 16–19, 72, 149, 150, 179
neo-utilitarian state theory 109, 111–12
networking 141–2
New Political Economy 109–11
non-cooperation 162–3, 173
norms: ad hoc 87; addressees 85; authority 137; binding 72–3; cultural 7; fixed 82; moral 44–5; politics 169; rational 35–6; regulative policy 80–1, 82, 84; social policy reform 210–14; socioethical 18–19; validity 160; violation of 83–4

obligations 117, 136–7, 155–6, 165–6
Olsen, J. P. 117
Olson, Mancur 78, 161–4
opinion polls 93–4
optimization problems 29–30, 38–9
options: and capacities 29–30; expanding 8, 12–13, 16; modernity 8, 9, 10; and regulation 10–11; use value 13; zero 25–7
order 10–15, 17–19, 34
organizations 87–8, 95–6, 240; *see also* social movements, new

Pahl, R. E. 129
parliaments 94
Parsons, T. 163
part-time work 121, 205–6
paternalism 101, 152, 192–3, 236, 250 (n21)
pensions 218
plebiscites 95, 100
pluralism, state theory 62
Polanyi, M. 244

political elites 94, 99–100, 152, 156, 169, 233
political organizations 95–6
political parties 95–6, 98–9, 199 (n3)
political rights 231
political will formation 112, 113, 147
politics 116–17, 256; and citizens 95; conflicts 7, 76–8; and economy 11–12; institutions 5–6, 13–14, 95, 96–8; legitimacy 111–13; modernization 119; morality 119; norms 169; opinion polls 93–4; participation 13–14; reorientation 67
poor 153, 192; *see also* poverty
postcommunist countries: agency and social policy 239–44; associative relations 241–2; economic problems 225–6; ethnic factors 234, 247, 258, 260; health system 248; illegal substitutes 234; inequality 234; information and evaluation 259–60; institutions 244–5; leadership 258; moral infrastructure 259; nationhood 257–8; privatization 225, 231, 233–4; revenue decline 247–8; social justice 233; social policy 225–30, 235–9, 244–8; social security 226, 232–3, 246; subsidiarity 241; transition costs 227; unemployment 228, 251 (n26)
postindustrial left 16, 19–21, 36–7
postmodernism viii, 4, 37
Potucek, M. 237
poverty: institutionalized

213–14; new 205; transition countries 231, 247; welfare state 151; women 206
Preuss, U. K. 50, 83–4
price liberalization 225, 226
privatization 195, 196, 225, 231, 233–4, 247
procedural justice 37
procedural rules 43
production: in household 122–4, 125; material 6; socialist societies 235, 238, 250 (n19)
progress 4, 41–2, 254–5
Przeworski, A. 158, 255, 257
public choice 111
public discourse 97
public good 73, 155, 161–4, 167–8; *see also* collective good
public policy 7; individuals 118; interdependence 111–12; left wing 37; limits of 107–8; policy takers ix
public spirit 44–5, 46

quality-of-life issues 119

rational choice 111, 181 (n40)
rationality 5–6; collective action 154–5; contribution 164; decision-making 62–3; democracy 154–5; indirect 38–9; natural/educated 86; and norms 35–6; self-limitation 26, 27–9, 87–8; trust and welfare 161–70
Rawls, J. 195
reactionary elites 169–70
reciprocity 129, 132, 135–6, 138, 141
referendums 93
regulative policy 50, 64, 68, 70, 79–80, 81–5

relatives, help from 132
responsibility: ethics 17, 23, 44;
for self 191; and sovereignty
68–9; state 68–9, 107, 111
revolution 41
rights 169, 231
risk society 19, 33, 34–5
Risk Society (Beck) 33
risks 100, 184–5, 186, 187
Rosanvallon, P. 87
Rose, R. 234
Rousseau, J. J. 86, 136, 160, 260
rule of law 50, 83–4, 151
rules 43, 48–9, 86–7

sacrifices 76–7
sanctions 83, 84
Scharpf, F. W. 64
Schumpeter, J. 39, 40, 178
security: *see* social security
self-binding: action 41–2;
capacity 45; industrial
relations 52; moral capacity
33, 34, 50; Ulysses model
38–9
self-control 35–7
self-employment 241
self-help 131–5, 241
self-injury 25, 33–4, 35
self-limitation: citizens 85;
functionalist view 40; logic of
192; as method and result
33–7; mistrust of 39;
optimization 38–9; rational
26, 27–9, 87–8; social systems
44
self-paternalism 166–7
self-provision: domestic 124,
126, 127, 139; handicraft work
127; limitations 127–8, 131,
140–1; skills 128
self-service economy 122–3
service exchange 142

service vouchers 142–3
shop opening hours 81
Skolka, J. 123
social assistance 194, 205, 218
social change 168–9
Social Democrats 66–7, 69, 80
social insurance 185–7, 195, 218
social movements, new 19–20,
65–7, 194
social policy: agency 239–44;
agenda 244–8; basic income
197–8, 201–3, 214–19; debates
139–44; game theory 183–4;
legitimacy 195; models
227–30; postcommunist
societies 225–30, 235–9,
244–8; reform 210–14;
reoriented 203–10; socialist
societies 235–9; welfare state
151
social science 4, 78–85
social security: beneficiaries
185; collective 238; derived
206–7; expansionist nature
192; financing 192, 211, 212,
218–19; guarantees/
restrictions 188;
overprovision of entitlements
191–2; postcommunist
countries 226, 232–3, 246;
redistribution 190–1;
unemployment 190; and
wage labor 187; *see also*
welfare benefits
social structure 114–15
socialism 36, 54 (n9), 140, 157,
237–8
socialist societies 207–8, 235–9,
250 (n19)
socialization 46, 64
societal constitutionalism 42–9
sociology, systems-theoretical
108

sociopolitical movements 19–20
solidarity 44, 47, 50–1, 136, 155
sovereignty: lacking viii–ix, 34;
    nation-state 61, 63–5, 105–7;
    and responsibility 68–9
Späth, L. 191
specialization 7–8, 9, 143, 226
Spieker, M. 152
state: authority/functions 107,
    147–8; competencies 65;
    conflicts 112–13; coordination
    64; cultural/national 17, 64;
    etatism 66, 105–9;
    governability 62–3; and
    individual freedom 138;
    inefficiencies 40; need
    satisfaction 137–8; and order
    11–12; political legitimation
    111–13; power 61, 63–4;
    regulatory activities 64, 68,
    70; responsibilities 68–9, 107,
    111; roles 65–6; sovereignty
    68–9; steering capacity
    117–18; strong ix, 69–70, 113;
    utilitarianism 109–11; *see also*
    nation-state; state theory
state benefits: *see* welfare
    benefits
state intervention 68, 74, 75–6,
    117–19
state theory 62, 109, 111–12, 155
steering capacity 14–15, 16–17,
    24, 25, 117–18
steering principles 24, 235–9
Streeck, W. 80, 115
subsidiarity 133, 241
subsidies 245
subsystems, societal 67
Sunday working 79–80
supplier and consumer 73
Sweden 51, 68, 171

taxation 202, 211, 212, 218–19

Taylor-Gooby, P. 170
Therborn, G. 155
time, as resource 122–3, 126
Titmuss, R. 154
trade unions 47, 50–1, 52, 76,
    213, 214–15, 218
traditionalism 17–18
transformation: *see*
    postcommunist countries
transport, public/private 85
trust 131, 143–4, 160, 161–70,
    248

Ulysses model 38, 39
Ulysses and the Sirens (Elster) 38
unemployment: and employed
    203–5; growing 126, 193;
    labor market 189–90;
    payments 178;
    postcommunist countries
    228, 251 (n26); self-provision
    141; welfare state 158
unemployment benefit 204–5,
    218
universalism 138
USA 17–18, 67, 152
utilitarianism 109–11

validity 44, 160–1
values: binding 17, 72–3, 167,
    217; changing 98; legitimized
    164; limit values 80
van Parijs, P. 220 (n2)
voluntary associations 112,
    150–1
voluntary work 132–4
voting 163

wage, minimum 190, 194
wage bargaining 245–6
wage labor: commodified 121;
    diminishing 203; exclusion

wage labour – *cont.*
212–13; illegal 129, 131;
income entitlement 210–11;
part-time 121, 205–6; social
state 207; time spent in 215;
see also employment; labor
Wallace, C. 129
Wallerstein, M. 158
Weber, M. 8, 14, 16–17, 22–3, 26,
86
Wehler, H. U. 4
welfare benefits 158, 186, 188–9,
198–9, 215
welfare production: bottlenecks
121–6; collective
arrangements 109, 135;
domestic self-provision 124;
institutions 110–11; losses 26;
steering principles combined
139–44; temporal dimension
175; trust 161–70
welfare state 63–4, 105–6, 155;
anonymity 150–1;
antagonistic views 157;
citizens 148; continuation
156; democracy 153–9;
destructuration 172; elitism
156; expenditures 157–8;
frustration 151–2;
interventionist 148;
Keynesian 19–20; legitimacy

184; and liberalism 149–53;
macro-sociology 159–61;
means of implementation
175–6; moral element 150,
153, 178; politics/economics
175; poverty 151; private
alternatives 176–7; rights
231; status guarantee 151;
threatened 183;
unemployment 158
Westernization 3–4, 230–2
Wilensky, H. L. 177
will: of the people 89–93, 101;
political 112, 113, 147;
weakness of 166–7
women: basic income 219;
earning ability 206–7;
employment 210; labor
205–6; poverty 206;
unemployment 251 (n29)
women's movement 97, 194
work: *see* employment; labor;
wage labor
work collective 235
workers 155, 197, 199 (n3), 235–7
workers' movement 19
working-class politics 158
working hours 140, 207, 213,
214–17

zero options 25–7

Studies in Contemporary German Social Thought
Thomas McCarthy, General Editor

Theodor W. Adorno, *Against Epistemology: A Metacritique*

Theodor W. Adorno, *Hegel: Three Studies*

Theodor W. Adorno, *Prisms*

Karl-Otto Apel, *Understanding and Explanation: A Transcendental-Pragmatic Perspective*

Seyla Benhabib, Wolfgang Bonß, and John McCole, editors, *On Max Horkheimer: New Perspectives*

Seyla Benhabib and Fred Dallmayr, editors, *The Communicative Ethics Controversy*

Richard J. Bernstein, editor, *Habermas and Modernity*

Ernst Bloch, *Natural Law and Human Dignity*

Ernst Bloch, *The Principle of Hope*

Ernst Bloch, *The Utopian Function of Art and Literature: Selected Essays*

Hans Blumenberg, *The Genesis of the Copernican World*

Hans Blumenberg, *The Legitimacy of the Modern Age*

Hans Blumenberg, *Shipwreck with Spectator: Paradigm of a Metaphor for Existence*

Hans Blumenberg, *Work on Myth*

James Bohman, *Public Deliberation: Pluralism, Complexity, and Democracy*

Susan Buck-Morss, *The Dialectics of Seeing: Walter Benjamin and the Arcades Project*

Craig Calhoun, editor, *Habermas and the Public Sphere*

Jean Cohen and Andrew Arato, *Civil Society and Political Theory*

Maeve Cooke, *Language and Reason: A Study of Habermas's Pragmatics*

Helmut Dubiel, *Theory and Politics: Studies in the Development of Critical Theory*

John Forester, editor, *Critical Theory and Public Life*

David Frisby, *Fragments of Modernity: Theories of Modernity in the Work of Simmel, Kracauer and Benjamin*

Hans-Georg Gadamer, *Philosophical Apprenticeships*

Hans-Georg Gadamer, *Reason in the Age of Science*

Jürgen Habermas, *Between Facts and Norms: Contributions to a Discourse Theory of Law and Democracy*

Jürgen Habermas, *Justification and Application: Remarks on Discourse Ethics*

Jürgen Habermas, *On the Logic of the Social Sciences*

Jürgen Habermas, *Moral Consciousness and Communicative Action*

Jürgen Habermas, *The New Conservatism: Cultural Criticism and the Historians' Debate*

Jürgen Habermas, *The Philosophical Discourse of Modernity: Twelve Lectures*

Jürgen Habermas, *Philosophical-Political Profiles*

Jürgen Habermas, *Postmetaphysical Thinking: Philosophical Essays*

Jürgen Habermas, *The Structural Transformation of the Public Sphere: An Inquiry into a Category of Bourgeois Society*

Jürgen Habermas, editor, *Observations on "The Spiritual Situation of the Age"*

Axel Honneth, *The Critique of Power: Reflective Stages in a Critical Social Theory*

Axel Honneth, *The Struggle for Recognition: The Moral Grammar of Social Conflicts*

Axel Honneth and Hans Joas, editors, *Communicative Action: Essays on Jürgen Habermas's* The Theory of Communicative Action

Axel Honneth, Thomas McCarthy, Claus Offe, and Albrecht Wellmer, editors, *Cultural-Political Interventions in the Unfinished Project of Enlightenment*

Axel Honneth, Thomas McCarthy, Claus Offe, and Albrecht Wellmer, editors, *Philosophical Interventions in the Unfinished Project of Enlightenment*

Max Horkheimer, *Between Philosophy and Social Science: Selected Early Writings*

Hans Joas, *G. H. Mead: A Contemporary Re-examination of His Thought*

Michael Kelly, editor, *Critique and Power: Recasting the Foucault/Habermas Debate*

Hans Herbert Kögler, *The Power of Dialogue: Critical Hermeneutics after Gadamer and Foucault*

Reinhart Koselleck, *Critique and Crisis: Enlightenment and the Pathogenesis of Modern Society*

Reinhart Koselleck, *Futures Past: On the Semantics of Historical Time*

Harry Liebersohn, *Fate and Utopia in German Sociology, 1887-1923*

Herbert Marcuse, *Hegel's Ontology and the Theory of Historicity*

Larry May and Jerome Kohn, editors, *Hannah Arendt: Twenty Years Later*

Pierre Missac, *Walter Benjamin's Passages*

Gil G. Noam and Thomas E. Wren, editors, *The Moral Self*

Guy Oakes, *Weber and Rickert: Concept Formation in the Cultural Sciences*

Claus Offe, *Contradictions of the Welfare State*

Claus Offe, *Disorganized Capitalism: Contemporary Transformations of Work and Politics*

Claus Offe, *Modernity and the State: East, West*

Claus Offe, *Varieties of Transition: The East European and East German Experience*

Helmut Peukert, *Science, Action, and Fundamental Theology: Toward a Theology of Communicative Action*

Joachim Ritter, *Hegel and the French Revolution: Essays on the* Philosophy of Right

William E. Scheuerman, *Between the Norm and the Exception: The Frankfurt School and the Rule of Law*

Alfred Schmidt, *History and Structure: An Essay on Hegelian-Marxist and Structuralist Theories of History*

Dennis Schmidt, *The Ubiquity of the Finite: Hegel, Heidegger, and the Entitlements of Philosophy*

Carl Schmitt, *The Crisis of Parliamentary Democracy*

Carl Schmitt, *Political Romanticism*

Carl Schmitt, *Political Theology: Four Chapters on the Concept of Sovereignty*

Gary Smith, editor, *On Walter Benjamin: Critical Essays and Recollections*

Michael Theunissen, *The Other: Studies in the Social Ontology of Husserl, Heidegger, Sartre, and Buber*

Ernst Tugendhat, *Self-Consciousness and Self-Determination*

Georgia Warnke, *Justice and Interpretation*

Mark Warren, *Nietzsche and Political Thought*

Albrecht Wellmer, *The Persistence of Modernity: Essays on Aesthetics, Ethics and Postmodernism*

Joel Whitebook, *Perversion and Utopia: A Study in Psychoanalysis and Critical Theory*

Rolf Wiggershaus, *The Frankfurt School: Its History, Theories, and Political Significance*

Thomas E. Wren, editor, *The Moral Domain: Essays in the Ongoing Discussion between Philosophy and the Social Sciences*

Lambert Zuidervaart, *Adorno's Aesthetic Theory: The Redemption of Illusion*